Palgrave Politics of Identity
and Citizenship Series

The politics of identity and citizenship has assumed increasing importance as our polities have become significantly more culturally, ethnically and religiously diverse. Different types of scholars, including philosophers, sociologists, political scientists and historians make contributions to this field and this series showcases a variety of innovative contributions to it. Focusing on a range of different countries, and utilizing the insights of different disciplines, the series helps to illuminate an increasingly controversial area of research and titles in it will be of interest to a number of audiences including scholars, students and other interested individuals.

More information about this series at
http://www.springer.com/series/14670

Mario Peucker

Muslim Citizenship in Liberal Democracies

Civic and Political Participation in the West

Mario Peucker
Victoria University
Centre for Cultural Diversity and Wellbeing
Melbourne, Australia

Palgrave Politics of Identity and Citizenship Series
ISBN 978-3-319-81032-4   ISBN 978-3-319-31403-7   (eBook)
DOI 10.1007/978-3-319-31403-7

© The Editor(s) (if applicable) and The Author(s) 2016
Softcover reprint of the hardcover 1st edition 2016
This work is subject to copyright. All rights are solely and exclusively licensed by the Publisher, whether the whole or part of the material is concerned, specifically the rights of translation, reprinting, reuse of illustrations, recitation, broadcasting, reproduction on microfilms or in any other physical way, and transmission or information storage and retrieval, electronic adaptation, computer software, or by similar or dissimilar methodology now known or hereafter developed.
The use of general descriptive names, registered names, trademarks, service marks, etc. in this publication does not imply, even in the absence of a specific statement, that such names are exempt from the relevant protective laws and regulations and therefore free for general use.
The publisher, the authors and the editors are safe to assume that the advice and information in this book are believed to be true and accurate at the date of publication. Neither the publisher nor the authors or the editors give a warranty, express or implied, with respect to the material contained herein or for any errors or omissions that may have been made.

Cover illustration: © icollection / Alamy Stock Photo

Printed on acid-free paper

This Palgrave Macmillan imprint is published by Springer Nature
The registered company is Springer International Publishing AG Switzerland

Acknowledgements

This research study gave me the opportunity to meet 30 people—all self-declared Muslims—in Australia and Germany who willingly told me their life stories as committed citizens, sharing with me their personal experiences and beliefs, their passion, hopes and joys as well as their concerns, anger and frustration. I owe these people my deepest gratitude. This study would not have been possible without their contributions. I also feel humbled by the conversations with these 30 people, who are dedicated to 'be good human beings' for the benefit of others. Thanks to these conversations, this study has become much more than an academic exercise, and I sincerely hope that my participants' compassion and optimism will stay with me as a reminder of how one's personal resilience and commitment to a peaceful diverse society can overcome ignorance and hostility, and eventually lead to recognition and appreciation of all people regardless of their background or religion.

I also feel indebted to all those who offered their invaluable support, encouragement and critical comments during this research. My thanks go in particular to Shahram Akbarzadeh, Helen Sullivan and Michael Herbert. And there is of course my family—Erika and my son Basti, who was born just months after the project started and who is now old enough to ask me all these questions about why Muslim women "don't want others to see their hair". My answer is: "You have to ask them, I'm sure they are happy to tell you."

Contents

1	Introduction	1
2	What Is Active Citizenship?	9
3	Methodology: Exploring Muslims' Civic and Political Participation	43
4	Muslims in Australia and Germany: Demographics, Resources, Citizenship	59
5	The Muslim Community and Political Context in Australia and Germany	115
6	Types and Trajectories of Muslims' Activism	143
7	Goals, Motives and Driving Forces	201
8	Empowering and Discouraging Factors	237
9	Personal Implications of Civic Activism	267
10	Conclusion	287
Index		303

List of Figures

Fig. 2.1	Two axis of civic engagement (Adapted from Adler and Goggin 2005)	22
Fig. 4.1	Top ten countries of birth of Muslims (2001, 2006 and 2011)	61
Fig. 4.2	Age profile of Muslims and total population in Australia (2011)	61
Fig. 4.3	Highest educational attainment of Muslims and total population, Australia (2011)	67
Fig. 4.4	Educational attainment of Muslims in Germany	69
Fig. 4.5	Labour force status of Muslims by country/region of origin, Germany (2008)	73
Fig. 4.6	Non-electoral political participation: First/second generation migrants, Germany	97
Fig. 4.7	Unconventional participation of migrants in Germany	98
Fig. 4.8	Active participation of Muslims in selected organisational settings, Australia	101
Fig. 4.9	Thematic context of organisation-based volunteering (people of Turkish origin)	104
Fig. 6.1	Illustration of three overlapping types of activity focus	169
Fig. 6.2	Initiation and recruitment of volunteering (Turkish background migrants) in Germany	188
Fig. 7.1	Overlapping types of civic goals as identified in the interview data	202

List of Tables

Table 2.1	Two-dimensional classification: Basis for selection of interview partners	46
Table 2.2	Key characteristics of Australian sample	52
Table 2.3	Key characteristics of German sample	53
Table 4.1	Main countries and regions of origin of Muslims in Germany	63
Table 4.2	Secondary school degree by sex, 2013	71
Table 4.3	Selected occupational/tertiary education qualifications by sex, 2013	72
Table 4.4	Employment status and inactivity rate of selected groups in Germany, 2011	74
Table 4.5	Occupational status of selected groups in Germany, 2010	74
Table 4.6	Monthly household net income of selected groups in Germany, 2011	76
Table 4.7	Muslims' involvement in informal political activities	93

1

Introduction

We are part of the community. We are not going to sit on the periphery. We are not non-Australians! We are just as Australian as everyone else! We have a faith that will enhance our citizenship, our participation as Australians.
  (Maha Abdo, Muslim community activist from Sydney)

'Democracy depends on all of us: the price of liberty is not just eternal vigilance, but eternal activity', said Abraham Lincoln. This is how British political theorist Sir Bernard Crick (2008: 18) underscored the vital importance of citizens' active participation in liberal democratic societies.[1]

While this view is widely shared by scholars and policymakers in the West, there is also a broad consensus about the general decline of citizens' interest in politics and the 'disinclination on the part of growing sectors of the citizenry to become involved in political and civic life' (Kivisto and Faist 2007: 136). A seemingly increasing proportion of the population in Western societies are neither vigilant nor active in the political sphere, and their willingness to commit and contribute to their community and become actively engaged in the

---

[1] The term *citizen* is used throughout this study, unless indicated otherwise, to refer to any member of society, and not in a legal sense to describe those who formally hold full citizenship rights.

© The Author(s) 2016
M. Peucker, *Muslim Citizenship in Liberal Democracies*,
DOI 10.1007/978-3-319-31403-7_1

public space has been dwindling. The 'bowling alone' diagnosis of Robert Putnam (2000) illustratively captures this alleged civic passivity, which, as he claims, weakens collective solidarity and mutual trust, and aggravates processes of social isolation and fragmentation.

This book on active citizenship of Muslims in Australia and Germany is situated within this broad thematic context. It takes as its starting point the tenet that citizens' engagement in civil society and political life plays a key role in building and sustaining a vibrant, cohesive society (Forrest and Kearns 2001) and in maintaining the legitimacy of the democratic system (Hoskins and Mascherini 2009). If it is true, however, that the democratic project 'depends on all of us', as Sir Bernard Crick argues, why does this study then chose to explore active citizenship of one particular group—Muslims? Do Muslims in Western countries differ from others in the way they participate? Is there a certain Muslim quality to their citizenship, which requires specific analytical attention?

Within the scholarly context of citizenship—by definition, an egalitarian space—singling out one group of citizens based on their faith needs legitimate reasons. This is particularly true when this group has a collective history of being stigmatised as the 'Other', whose equal citizenship and loyalty to society have been called into doubt in many Western societies, including Australia and Germany, the two countries under investigation in this study. Ironically, the main reason why this research explores Muslims' civic and political participation is attributed to precisely these experiences of marginalisation: Why would someone who consistently faces external questioning of their loyalty and belonging invest time and effort to contribute to the very society that treats them as strangers, second-class citizens or even as a potential threat to society?

Academic interest in how civically and politically active Muslims position themselves against this exclusionary discourse gives legitimacy to the research focus on Muslims as a particular group of citizens. This climate of scrutiny and marginalisation may also contribute to the emergence of Muslim-specific manifestations of active citizenship, which have thus far been under-researched. Does this discourse, for example, provide Muslims with a cause for collective mobilisation to make claims of equal recognition and to express dissent with the current political rhetoric and decisions (O'Loughlin and Gillespie 2012; Maira

2009)? Or, alternatively, does it paralyse some forms of civic and political commitment to a seemingly hostile or sceptical societal environment, and reinforce active Muslims' proneness to community-internal engagement?

A second key factor that may affect the specific nature of Muslims' active citizenship is the role their religious beliefs possibly play for their civic performance. This has been an underexplored theme of active citizenships of Muslims. A considerable proportion of the mainstream population in Australia and Germany consider Islam to be incompatible with liberal democratic value systems (Peucker and Akbarzadeh 2012: 92–96). This view resonates oddly with the claims of a very small minority of (typically Salafi) Muslims at the community fringes that argue along similar lines of incompatibility, prohibiting any Muslim participation in a Western non-Muslim society and polity (March 2007: 408). If such views were accurate, Islam would be a major barrier to active citizenship in the West. This minority position, however, is not supported by the realities of Muslims' every-day lives in Germany and Australia—and it is also rejected by dominant interpretations of Islamic jurisprudence that strongly argue against the alleged contradiction between Islamic and liberal democratic principles (Ramadan 1999; March 2009).

While this research study explores potential particularities of Muslims' active citizenship, such as the possible impact of the exclusionary climate and their Islamic faith, it fundamentally views Muslims as 'ordinary' citizens of Islamic faith. Muslims' active citizenship is regarded as being performed not at the margins, but as an inherent component of an ethnically, religiously, linguistically and (in the broadest sense) culturally diverse polity and civil society. Framed by this fundamental tenet, this research deploys a qualitative methodology to examine manifold issues revolving around civic and political participation experiences of Muslims in Australia and Germany. This includes the goals and driving forces behind their activism, their views on empowering factors or discouraging barriers and personal implications of their active involvement. The explorative, interview-based methodology is complemented with a cross-national comparison between interviewed Muslims in Australia and Germany. These two countries were selected as case studies based on a combination of, on the one hand, cross-national similarities in terms of Muslims' socioeconomic situation and experiences of exclusion and, on the other hand, differences regarding the policy framework and civic recognition of Muslim communities as civil society stakeholders. Such a comparative approach has been very effective in facilitating a deeper level of analysis of the qualitative interview data.

This research is not only innovative in addressing major gaps in social and political science—it is also highly relevant and timely in its endeavour to shed light on Muslims' civic and political contributions to liberal democratic societies. This *Muslims as citizens* prism provides a much needed alternative to the prevalent political and academic discourse on Muslims as either victims of Islamophobia, as the deviant or dangerous Other (Poynting et al. 2004) or as the subject of governance strategies of domestication and securitisation (Humphrey 2009). These dominant lines of discourse have largely ignored that Muslims in Western countries like Australia and Germany are also—at least in many or most ways—ordinary members of these secular democratic societies. Current scholarship has been remarkably silent on this egalitarian membership perspective on Muslims in the West. This research seeks to address this underexplored area, generating evidence-based insights into how Muslims enact their citizenship. This is not solely an academic exercise, but it is also of vital importance for policymakers to have a more accurate and realistic understanding of how and why Muslims participate in civil society and the polity, contributing to the strengthening of social cohesion in Australia's and Germany's pluralistic societies and the legitimacy of their democratic political system.

Chapter 2 outlines the key concept of this study—citizenship—and elaborates more precisely what is meant by *active* citizenship, combining republican, communitarian and more pluralistic perspectives. This conceptual chapter situates the theme of the book in the contemporary discourse around citizenship as a social process, emphasising the performative nature of citizenship, enacted through various forms of civic and political participation. It also presents a theoretical framework outlining key factors, identified in previous theoretical and empirical research, that encourage or discourage civic and political participation of citizens in general and of ethno-religious minorities in particular. Chapter 3 elaborates on the methodology, based on in-depth biographical interviews with a sample of 30 systematically selected active and self-declared Muslims in Australia and Germany, analysed through a cross-national comparative lens. The realised interview sample is briefly described as well as the limitations of the research design.

The next two chapters contextualise the research. Chapter 4 presents a succinct overview on the demographic and socioeconomic situation of Muslims in Australia and Germany. It also provides insights into Muslims' legal citizenship, the contestation of their equal citizenship and what is known about their civic and political participation. Chapter 5 discusses key dimensions of Muslim community structures in both countries and the national policy frameworks that may influence Muslims' citizenship. Here particular attention is paid to those factors that have been identified by previous research and theoretical accounts as being potentially influential for the emergence of civic and political engagement.

Chapters 6, 7, 8 and 9 present the empirical findings from the research study on Muslims' civic and political participation in Australia and Germany. These results are discussed from a comparative perspective and in reference to existing scholarship in the pertinent areas. Chapter 6 explores the various ways in which the interviewed Muslims have enacted their citizenship over the course of their often longstanding civic biographies, and examines the shifts and transition processes within these individual citizenship careers. Muslims' goals, motives and fundamental driving forces behind their active citizenship are explored in Chap. 7. Chapter 8 focuses on Muslims' views on empowering or discouraging factors that have affected their own willingness to participate and those that may—in their personal views—have had an impact on other Muslims' proneness to civic or political engagement. The final empirical chapter examines interviewed Muslims' views on the various implications that their active engagement has had for them personally, especially with regards to their expanded social networks and skills.

The concluding Chap. 10 summaries the key research findings and draws a complex and multifaceted picture of Muslim active citizenship in the West beyond the prevalent discourse on misrepresentation and victimhood, on the one hand, and securitisation and counter-terrorism, on the other hand. While these results are all explorative and thus not representative of all Muslims in Australia and Germany, they tell a story about Muslims' place in liberal democratic societies that radically differs from widespread stereotypes of politically disloyal and socially self-isolating Muslims whose faith is at odds with liberal principles. In addition to these innovative empirical insights into Muslim citizenship, this final chapter also draws tentative conclusions on the impact of national political opportunity structures on their engagement and civic trajectories, and suggests a thematic area that deserves more empirical attention in the future.

References

Crick, B. (2008). Democracy. In J. Arthur, I. Davis, & C. Hahn (Eds.), *SAGE handbook of education for citizenship and democracy* (pp. 13–19). London: Sage.

Forrest, R., & Kearns, A. (2001). Social cohesion, social capital and the neighbourhood. *Urban Studies, 38*(12), 2125–2143.

Hoskins, B. L., & Mascherini, M. (2009). Measuring active citizenship through the development of a composite indicator. *Social Indicators Research, 90*(3), 459–488.

Humphrey, M. (2009). Securitisation and domestication of Diaspora Muslims and Islam: Turkish immigrants in Germany and Australia. *International Journal on Multicultural Societies, 11*(2), 136–154.

Kivisto, P., & Faist, T. (2007). *Citizenship. Discourse, theory, and transnational prospects*. Malden: Blackwell Publishing.

Maira, S. (2009). Citizenship and dissent: South Asian Muslim youth in the US after 9/11. *South Asian Popular Cultures, 8*(1), 31–45.

March, A. F. (2007). Reading Tariq Ramadan: Political liberalism, Islam, and "overlapping consensus". *Ethics & International Affairs, 21*(4), 399–413.

March, A. F. (2009). *Islam and liberal citizenship. The search for an overlapping consensus*. Oxford: Oxford University Press.

O'Loughlin, B., & Gillespie, M. (2012). Dissenting citizenship? Young people and political participation in the media-security nexus. *Parliamentary Affairs, 65*(1), 115–137.

Peucker, M., & Akbarzadeh, S. (2012). The vicious cycle of stereotyping: Muslims in Europe and Australia. In F. Mansouri & V. Marotta (Eds.), *Muslims in the West and the challenges of belonging* (pp. 171–197). Carlton: Melbourne University Press.

Poynting, S., Noble, G., Tabar, P., & Collins, J. (2004). *Bin Laden in the suburbs: Criminalising the Arab other*. Sydney: Sydney Institute of Criminology.

Putnam, R. D. (2000). *Bowling alone: The collapse and revival of American community*. New York: Simon and Schuster.

Ramadan, T. (1999). *To be a European Muslim*. Leicester: Islamic Foundation.

2

What Is Active Citizenship?

Despite its frequent use in everyday discussions and political debates, citizenship is an elusive concept. While a general consensus prevails on the abstract understanding of citizenship as one's full membership of a society, it has remained a complex and contested challenge to specify the substance, prerequisites and manifestations of this membership status. This complexity derives from the myriad of responses that have been given to two key questions concerning the 'relevant determinants of membership' and the 'indicia of fullness' (Schuck 2002: 131).

Since the proliferation of citizenship studies as a *'de facto* field in the humanities and social sciences' (Isin and Turner 2002: 1, emphasis in original) in the 1990s, a seemingly infinite array of ambitious attempts to define and (re-)frame citizenship have been made. 'The boundaries and the meaning of modern citizenship are currently being challenged', Engin Isin and Patricia Wood (1999: 6) maintained in the late 1990s. This has not changed since. Thousands of academic articles and books have been published on citizenship in different disciplines and from a variety of empirical and theoretical angles (Isin and Turner 2002: 9–10), 'widening its scope and deepening its meaning', as Isin and Bryan Turner (2007: 16) concluded a few years later. This prolific work of political theorists, philosophers, historians and sociologists—not to mention the attempts of policymakers and educationalists to revitalise citizenship in practice—has transformed citizenship into a conceptually rich but murky field of scholarly and political debates, laden with different ideological, political and social ideals (Schuck 2002: 131; Isin and Wood 1999: 6). For any empirical investigation of (active) citizenship it is instrumental to position one's study within this diverse landscape of traditions and approaches. None of these theoretical concepts are true or false. Thus, every researcher needs to pragmatically choose those that appear most fruitful for the specific empirical interests at hand, without ignoring the prevalent theoretical discourses of contemporary political and social sciences. Making this pragmatic selection process transparent is the purpose of this chapter.

Despite the multitude of conceptions and the growing number of hyphenated citizenships, some general tenets of modern citizenship in the twenty-first century have become widely accepted across various schools of thoughts and scholarly traditions. This consensus shall serve as a foundation for this study. Three basic and intertwined principles are rendered particularly relevant for the investigation of active citizenship of Muslims: first, citizenship as the foundation of equal rights; second citizenship as an equal membership status[1] and third, citizenship as a social process of engagement and activism in civil society, community life or the political arena, which calls for an active participatory citizenry. 'So membership, rights and participation go together', as Richard Bellamy (2010: xix) summaries the three defining components of citizenship.

Equal Legal Rights, Liberties and Membership

If there has been one unchallenged cornerstone in every conceptualisation of modern citizenship, it is that this membership status in a political community rests on the basic principle of equal legal rights of all citizens. 'Indeed,

---

[1] Isin (2009: 371) recently expressed a rare alternative view on this broad consensus claiming that 'Citizenship is not membership'. He conceptualises it as 'a relation that governs the conduct of (subject) positions that constitute it. The essential difference between citizenship and membership is that while the latter governs conduct within social groups, citizenship is about conduct across social groups all of which constitute a body politic' (2009: 371).

the principle of equality is historically inherent in the concept of citizenship itself' (Conover et al. 2004: 1037). Wherever the external boundaries of citizenship are drawn—and they might be drawn very restrictively to exclude segments of the population—those who are admitted into the circle of the citizenry have by definition the same legal rights. Accordingly, citizenship can be 'most adequately defined in terms of both rights and duties' and as a 'social status that confers membership of a political community that in turn determines an individual's share' (Turner 2013: 231).

The most prominent account of citizenship as an ensemble of rights can be found in the seminal work of the British sociologist Thomas H. Marshall, *Citizenship and Social Class* (1950). Marshall's elaborations on the historic evolution of civil, political and social rights as key dimensions of citizenship in post-war Britain have become the most common (and often critically referred to) point of departure in theorising citizenship during the second half of the twentieth century. Strongly influenced by Keynesian economic models in Britain of the 1940s and 1950s, Marshall's class-focussed work was ground-breaking in recognising that individuals may face high hurdles in *practicing* their citizenship status despite holding formally equal political rights. To realise the 'claim to be accepted as full member of society' (1950: 5), Marshall emphasises the importance of social rights as an additional vital component of citizenship. To safeguard social rights, he called for effective redistribution policies and the establishment of welfare institutions (Isin and Turner 2007: 7).

While Marshall's attention to welfare policies as a facilitator of citizenship in practice was innovative and progressive at the time, his focus on individuals' equal rights and freedoms positions him in a long tradition of liberalism that reaches back to classical theorists like John Locke. This liberal tradition of democracy and citizenship has many different facets and does not constitute a coherent political or philosophical theory. What all these theorists have in common, however, is their emphasis on the primacy of the individual's rights and liberties. Liberal thinking always 'begins with the individual' (Schuck 2002: 132). Citizenship in liberal conceptions does not depend on individuals' active civil-political engagement to make society 'a better place'. Political and civic participation is seen as a right that needs to be granted to all citizens, who then have to decide whether they make use of it or not. 'Their status of citizen is not derogated or jeopardized if they choose not to be so active' (Isin and Wood 1999: 7). What Peter Kivisto and Thomas Faist write about Marshall's view of citizens applies to some degree also to other rights-based concepts of citizenship: The 'citizen in modern welfare states [is regarded] as essentially passive—a recipient of rights ..., but not an active participant in democratic decision making' (2007: 3).

> Liberal citizens are thus left to their own devices without much guidance from the state. They must decide for themselves how to use their constitutionally secured freedoms ... they must decide what kind of citizen to be—including the possibility that they forswear any political activity, preferring into ... a world largely indifferent to any public goods (Schuck 2002: 137).

Since the 1990s increasing unease with such a rights-centred understanding of citizenship has been voiced in the political arena and within academic circles (Crowley 1998, 167; Kymlicka 2002; Isin and Turner 2002: 4). Instead of promoting solidarity and advancing a common democratic project, the liberal emphasis on individual rights has been accused of contributing to a continuous rise of individualism, social isolation and fragmentation (Berry et al. 1993: 2–4). Putnam's (2000) *Bowling Alone* portrays this popular lament of 'an appreciable disinclination on the part of growing sectors of the citizenry to become involved in political and civic life' (Kivisto and Faist 2007: 136)—despite the fact that most people in Western societies enjoy the rights to do so. Moreover, social inequalities have not disappeared, although the legal scope of citizenship has continuously expanded to include previously excluded groups. This persistent lack of substantive equality illuminates the 'incomplete and contradictory nature of inclusion' (Kivisto and Faist 2007: 132) and the problem of *de jure* equal but *de facto* second-class citizens.

Citizenship as a Social Process of Civic Engagement: Active Citizenship

The widespread unease with individualistic rights-centred models of citizenship has gradually led to a paradigm shift in citizenship studies. Without abandoning the fundamental notion of equal rights and liberties, citizenship has been conceptualised as a social practice and active process rather than merely a legal status. This double agenda is reflected in the definition of citizenship, proposed by Isin and Wood, as '*both* a set of practices … and a bundle of rights and duties … that define an individual's membership in a polity' (1999: 4, emphasis in original). Only three years later, Isin and Turner (2002) proposed in the introduction to their edited *Handbook of Citizenship Studies* that these broadened perspectives on citizenship have come to prevail in pertinent scholarly discourses. The notion of citizenship as a 'status held under the authority of a state' has been expanded to 'include various political and social struggles of recognition and redistribution as instances of claim-making' (Isin and Turner 2002: 2).

Citizenship is not ultimately defined by someone's legal status, and it may be performed without equal rights (Isin 2008), struggling for full membership of society. The assumption of a quasi-evolutionary expansion of citizenship towards the recognition of hitherto excluded groups (e.g., women, racial minorities) is deliberately rejected. Instead, this line of argument stresses that the incorporation of new groups into the citizenry have been achieved precisely through successful mobilisation against the existing political and societal order. Social movements are typical examples for this, ranging from the struggle for redistribution since the nineteenth century (e.g., workers' rights) to the Civil Rights Movement in the 1960s and from early women's rights movements to more contemporary gay mobilisation for recognition. These dissenting claims against the political status quo and collective struggles for legal rights, recognition and 'equal standing in civil society' (Conover et al. 2004: 1037; Crowley 1998: 167) are part and parcel of all modern democratic societies—and they are also reminders that the performance of citizenship may be closely tied to the individuals' identity and belonging to a particular social group.

The procedural and performative conceptualisation of citizenship has been further emphasised by the recently introduced concept of 'acts of citizenship' (Isin and Nielsen 2008), which has given the academic debate around citizenship new momentum and broadened its scope by including the creation of new 'scripts' and 'scenes' of enacted citizenship (Isin 2008: 38). Isin defines acts of citizenship in a broad and somewhat blurry way as 'those acts that transform forms (orientations, strategies, technologies) and modes (citizens, strangers, outsiders, aliens) of being political by bringing into being new actors as activist citizens (claimants of rights and responsibilities) through creating new sites and scales of struggle' (2008: 39).

The emphasis on *citizenship as practice* has stimulated greater sociological interest in citizenship studies. This has generated an array of new analytical tools and flexible approaches to examine social phenomena of active participation that were previously difficult to address in the thematic realm of citizenship, such as social movements, the role of agency and identity politics. Theorising citizenship as a political and social struggle transcends the 'non-participatory, interest-based politics of *homo economicus*, which traditionally served both as an empirical generalization and as an implicit norm of citizenship' (Crowley 1998: 167). Since the 1990s the buzzwords in citizenship studies as well as in the political discourse in many Western societies have shifted from legal status and equal rights to active participation, performance and civic engagement, from passive entitlement to active citizenship and from an elitist, vote-centric to a participatory deliberative democracy with a strong civil society (Kymlicka 2002: 292; Head 2007: 442; Chambers 2002).

Citizens' participation in civil society and their commitment to a joint democratic project has come to be regarded as a fundamental cornerstone of citizenship and essential for the promotion of a cohesive and vibrant democratic society. 'Contemporary theorists are expansive in their claims for citizenship participation', as Berry et al. (1993: 6) posited. In a similar vein, Bellamy emphasises that 'participation in the community's political, economic and social processes' (2010: xvi) is a key component of citizenship. This is also the context in which the concept of *active* citizenship has gained further prominence (Bee and Pachi 2014). Hoskins and Mascherini (2009: 459–460), for example, argue in the European context that active citizenship refers to 'particular forms of participation which should be promoted within Europe in order to ensure the continuation of participatory and representative democracy, to reduce the gap between citizens and governing institutions and to enhance social cohesion'. Notwithstanding the broad consensus on the procedural nature of citizenship, on closer inspection, adherents of different political theories and philosophical schools of thought have advocated quite different avenues to put active citizenship into practice.

It is not the aim of this chapter to elaborate in detail on the various facets of republican, communitarian and more pluralistic models of democracy and citizenship, which all reach beyond the narrow focus of classical liberalism on individual legal status. However, a brief discussion of two interwoven aspects of active citizenship from different theoretical perspectives is fruitful for the conceptual framing of this study: first, the different notions of the individual, community and identity as a basis for active engagement and second, the general objects and goals of citizens' active engagement.

Republican Models of Citizenship

While republican theories on citizenship do not constitute a consistent and homogeneous paradigm, all its proponents, from classical accounts like Rousseau's Social Contract (1794), Tocqueville's Democracy in America (1835) or Hannah Arendt's The Human Condition (1958), to more contemporary models of republican citizenship in the twenty-first century have one basic tenet in common: They all place a paramount emphasis on citizens' becoming active stakeholders in negotiating the shape and future of society and the polity in deliberative democracies. Some go as far as to advocate 'unmediated self-government' (Barber 1984: 261) as the ultimate ideal. Republican citizens participate in the public domain seeking to advance the wellbeing of the society at large. In doing so, they are 'prepared to overcome their personal inclinations and set aside their private interest when necessary to do what is best for the public as a whole' (Dagger 2002: 147). Republican citizenship is based on a normative concept of what constitutes 'good citizens'—citizens who should not only have the capacity (civic skills) but also the ethical predisposition (civic virtues) to participate in the public domain for the bettering of the political community and society (Dahlgren 2006: 269). Delanty describes the core notion of republicanism provocatively and somewhat paradoxically as 'a radical form of liberal individualism … [that] reaches its highest expression in commitment to public life, as opposed to the liberal emphasis on the private pursuit of interest or personal autonomy' (2002: 165).

Proponents of republican citizenship highlight that this public commitment is driven by citizens' 'public ethos' (Slaughter 2007: 91), which is anchored in 'a strong attachment to their polity' (Dagger 2002: 148). Without such a positive identification with the political community citizens are unlikely to enact their commitment to public life. In Stuart Mill's words: 'Let a person have nothing to do for his country, and he will not care for it' (cited in Berry et al. 1993: 6). Thus, republican citizens, irrespective of their other layers of identity, can share a common civic identity. Given such a sense of civic belonging to the overarching 'imagined community' of the nation-state (Andersen 1991), the pursuit of the common good would either coincide with personal goals of public-spirited members of the polity (Isin and Wood 1999: 9) or, in case of conflicts between private and public interest, trump individual urges. The republican model has a lot to offer for the analysis of Muslim active citizenship. It provides the framework for the analysis of Muslims' active civic engagement as ordinary citizens in public life, driven by their sense of civic belonging. It falls short, however, when applied to more particularistic and group-specific struggles and claim-making. Even if there were a collectively shared civic identity among all citizens, other group affiliations and layers of identity would not vanish and may become salient in certain situations. This is where communitarian models of citizenship offer a valuable theoretical corrective.

Communitarian Models of Citizenship

Communitarian citizenship is based on the conviction that the self is shaped by its social embedding in a particular cultural community context, which profoundly affects one's identity, emotional attachments and moral viewpoints (Etzioni 1996: 127) and, as a consequence, the performance of citizenship. Sandel (1982: 150) maintains that 'members of a society are bound by a sense of community', which entails that they 'profess communitarian sentiments and pursue communitarian aims' and 'conceive their identity ... as defined to some extent by the community of which they are a part'.

Such a perspective challenges the republican claim of an overriding civic identity and renders the assumption that all citizens would always pursue a clearly definable common good as simplistic, naïve and unrealistic. 'For communitarians, citizenship is about participation in the political community but it is also about the preservation of identity, and therefore citizenship is always specific to a particular community' (Delanty 2002: 163). In this communitarian logic, civic partaking through community groups constitutes a typical manifestation of active citizenship, regardless of whether this engagement strives for the bettering of society or for the advancement of a particular community—and regardless of how community is defined (Kivisto 2003), be it in terms of spatial proximity (e.g., 'local community') or based on members' relationship and choice (Brint 2001; Dandy and Pe-Pua 2013). Political and social scientists have emphasised the vital role of community agency and collective identity for political and civic engagement especially of migrants and minorities. 'To ignore the ethnic community blinds us to a key mechanism facilitating immigrants' incorporation into the political system' , Bloemraad maintains (2007: 323). She concludes that '"groupedness"… may be a prerequisite for political incorporation' (Bloemraad 2007: 328). These considerations illustrate that communitarian approaches are indispensable elements of the theoretical foundation for the study of Muslim active citizenship.

Communitarian citizenship are often 'on the whole more concerned with protecting the majority culture' (Delanty 2002: 164) and tend to display a restrictive undercurrent when it comes to minority communities. Berry and his research team point out that 'strong community bonds can lead to efforts to exclude those who do not fit the community's image of itself' (1993: 3). In the same vein, Bendor and Mookherjee (2008: 3) found that the often deliberately anti-universalistic norms in communitarianism 'hurt minorities the most: the smaller the minority, the greater the harm caused by these norms'. There is often the implicit assumption of a hegemonic cultural mainstream which defines the expectations and boundaries of desirable expressions of citizenship.

Multicultural Citizenship and Radical Democracy Models

Similar to communitarian models, pluralistic citizenship theorists, like Gutmann (1980), Young (1989), Mouffe (1995) and Kymlicka (1995), to name only a few particularly influential academic figures, recognise the salience of collective identities in the manifestation of citizenship. While rejecting the liberal image of self-regarding individuals, they also question the simplistic republican notion of a unitary common good that all citizens pursue. However, they disagree with those communitarian models that suggest cultural hegemony. While pluralistic models of (multicultural) citizenship are anything but a coherent field, and scholars are located in sometimes quite different theoretical traditions (Joppke 2002), they are all concerned with issues of recognition and accommodation of difference in pluralistic societies, calling for some form of 'differentiated citizenship' (Young 1989: 251). What they have in common is the viewpoint that 'a "difference-blind" strategy does not work ... because it is not neutral but instead biased in favor of privileged groups, whose identities, values, and ways of life tend to define the "common", cultural character of citizenship' (Conover et al. 2004: 1039).

The common denominator of most of these pluralistic strategies is to establish a set of specific group-affirmative rights for minorities, aimed at redressing their lack of equal civic standing in negotiating or representing their views in the public competition of ideas and claims. Without affirmative rights, support and accommodation of minority groups, they would not get a fair chance to make their voices heard, neither in vote-centric, elitist nor in 'talk-centric' participatory democracies (Kymlicka 2002: 290–293). The tyranny of the majority would effectively mean a domination of minorities, regardless of how legitimate the demands of the latter are. Thus, Will Kymlicka (2002: 261) advocates 'greater deliberation as one of the key priorities for modern democracies', in which special group rights assist ethno-religious minorities and immigrants to participate on equal footing. More radically, Iris M. Young (1989: 261) identifies the need of a pluralistic democracy to 'provide mechanisms for the effective representation and recognition of the distinct voices and perspectives of those of its constituent groups that are oppressed and disadvantaged within it'. Taking on board this emphasis on enabling and empowering minority communities as an inherent part of society and political community, citizenship studies in theory and practice need to pay attention to forms of civic engagement and collective mobilisation processes of minorities, which pursue particularistic civic agendas of group recognition.

What some of these pluralistic models of citizenship tend to do, however, is to implicitly essentialise individuals' affiliation with a certain minority community as if this group membership ultimately determined their collective identity. In so doing, they underestimate the fluid nature of identities as key drivers for active participation in various forms of civic engagement. Chantal Mouffe (1995), also a supporter of pluralistic conceptions of citizenship and of radical democracy, advocates a less rigid notion of identity or, using her terminology, of individuals' identifications and subject positions. For Mouffe, the individual 'social agent [is] not … a unitary subject', but rather a bundle of shifting, context-specific identifications, 'always contingent and precarious, temporarily fixed at the intersection of those subject positions' (1995: 33). Equipped with this non-essentialist conception of volatile identities, she develops a model of democracy that pays attention to the reality of 'new movements' as legitimate manifestations of citizens' active engagement. New and multiple group allegiances and identifications continue to unfold, without erasing individual differences and without questioning their fundamental belonging to the political community at large. Accordingly, the individuals' citizenship agenda and the way they enact them are constantly shifting.

'[R]adical democratic citizens depend on a collective form of identification among the democratic demands found in a variety of movements: women, workers, black, gay and ecological as well as other oppositional movements' (Isin and Wood 1999: 11) within a 'political community whose rules we have to accept' (Mouffe 1995: 34). This corresponds with the elaborations of de Koning et al. (2015: 123) on multiple citizenships, which may 'emerge in the centre of the nation-state, at its margins and beyond,… often competing, contradictory, and ambiguous', but not 'mutually exclusive'. Such an understanding of citizenship addresses the weaknesses of republican and communitarian models of citizenship, making a vital contribution to the conceptual framework for the empirical examination of Muslims' active citizenship in liberal democracies. It offers an analytical foundation that reflects the shifting, context-specific nature of multiple identities and their implications for civic engagement. These multiple identifications need to be constantly negotiated in a way 'to make our belonging to different communities of values, language, culture and others compatible with our common belonging to a political community' (Mouffe 1995: 34). Mouffe's theoretical considerations of complex, volatile identifications and of social movement as a form of citizens' collective mobilisation and political participation outside the often rather rigid community boundaries are promising perspectives for the analysis of Muslims' public and political engagement for group-specific—but not necessarily Islam-related—goals.

Eclectic Theoretical Framework: A Summary

Active citizenship, like citizenship in general, relies on the core principle of equal rights and liberty of all citizens and their recognition as full member of society and the political community. This liberal principle of citizenship is instrumental also for this study. (Neo-)liberal conceptions of citizenship, which regard citizens mainly as passive bearers of rights, however, neither reflect the dominant understanding of citizenship in the twenty-first century nor does it provide the analytical tools to examine phenomena of *active* citizenship. To address this shortcoming, citizenship in this study is conceptualised as social practice involving processes of mobilisation, performance and active engagement. Republican citizenship offers a strong emphasis on citizens' active involvement in society and polity, which is crucial for this study. Where republican citizenship fares rather poorly is the complex realm of identity politics, for it prioritises a general and commonly shared civic identity as the predominant (or only) driver of active citizenship. This leaves little room for the acknowledgement and empirical investigation of collective forms of civic engagement and struggles as common manifestations of active citizenship. Communitarian, pluralistic and radical democratic theories of citizenship offer conceptual tools that address the narrow republican view on identity politics and its blindness to group-specific engagement, often channelled through collective agencies. This is indispensable for the framing of this study on Muslims' active citizenship. Communitarian concepts of citizenship are particularly useful for analysing Muslims' community activism, pursuing community-specific objectives and mobilising for recognition. However, Muslims do not only enter the stage of engagement as either representatives of the Muslim community or as republican citizens. Mouffe's elaborations are a stark reminder that identities are volatile and that numerous identity layers—not only the civic or the religious one—can become salient, triggering certain forms of civic and political participation in different situations.

Towards a Definition of Civic and Political Participation

Applying this understanding of citizenship, a vibrant and healthy democratic society requires an active citizenry, that is, citizens who participate and engage in public and political affairs and civil society. This resonates with one of the very few concrete definitions of active citizenship as 'participation in civil society, community and/or political life, characterised by mutual respect and non-violence and in accordance with human rights and democracy' (Hoskins and Mascherini 2009: 462). But what forms of participatory activities and public engagement constitute relevant manifestations of active citizenship? Drawing on a systematic examination of various definitions of civic engagement, Adler and Goggin (2005: 241) conclude that '[c]ivic engagement describes how an active citizen participates in the life of a community in order to improve conditions for others or to help shape the community's future'. This definition is specified with a two-dimensional model (Fig. 2.1), which illustrates the broad spectrum of activities that may fall under civic and political participation.

The horizontal axis of this model refers to individual or collective agency and the degree of institutionalisation of civic engagement, 'between individual or informal activities and more formal, collective actions that involve participation in organizations'. The vertical dimension focusses on the site or addressee, locating engagement 'between involvement in community activities … and involvement in political activities' (Adler and Goggin 2005: 240; see also Hoskins and Mascherini 2009: 462). The latter axis can be regarded as oscillating between civic and political participation, without drawing a clear-cut line between both. Conceptualising this dimension as a continuum acknowledges the interconnectedness of

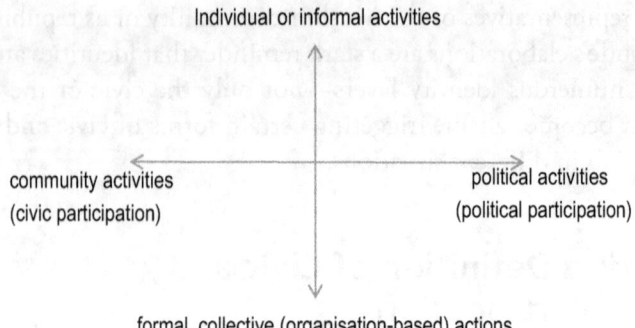

Fig. 2.1 Two axis of civic engagement (Adapted from Adler and Goggin 2005)

the political arena and civil society as sites of active citizenship (Weissberg 2005: 23–24).

The array of definitions of civic participation and, even more so of political participation, is vast. Systematic examinations of various approaches to conceptualise these two areas of activism confirm the blurry boundaries between civic and political participation, but they also suggest nuanced differences between both. The prominent United States study *Voice and Equality* by Verba et al. (1995) deploys a widely accepted definition of political participation: 'Political participation affords citizens in a democracy an opportunity to communicate information to government officials about their concerns and preference and to put pressure on them to respond' (1995: 37). The three scholars continue to elaborate that this refers to any 'activity that has the intent or effect of influencing government action' (1995: 38). Such an explicit reference to political decision-making processes as the target of political participation is dominant also in the academic discourse in other national context, including Germany. The prominent German political scientist, Max Kaase conceptualises political participation as 'those activities of citizens, which they carry out voluntarily either alone or together with others with the intent of influencing political decisions' (1995: 462; own translation).

The meaning of civic as opposed to political participation is often 'hidden' in general definitions of civic engagement; it becomes clearer when leaving the politics-directed and government-oriented components aside.

Civic participation can then be described as any activities that take place in a public or community environment aimed at solving problems and seeking to 'improve conditions for others or to help the community's future' (Adler and Goggin 2005: 241). It is about citizens' endeavours to make their community, local neighbourhood, the society at large or even the world 'a better place' through often small but immediate actions that tend to avoid the detour via political decisions and government actions. As the scope and repertoires of civic engagement have expanded enormously (Bellamy 2010), the boundaries between civic and political participation have become increasingly blurry over time. In the first half of the twentieth century, performing citizenship was primarily seen (and researched) as a matter of conventional political participation, mostly associated with general elections. This changed fundamentally with the shift towards more unconventional forms of non-electoral political activism (e.g., civil disobedience, protests) in the 1960s and 1970s, and it further expanded 'to include "civil" activities such as volunteering and social engagement' (van Deth 2013: 12) in the 1990s (also Keeter et al. 2002).

In recent years, the scope of civic and political participation has continued to broaden with the proliferation of increasingly individualised, less institutionalised and often informal and temporary forms of activism, especially among young people (Vromen 2003). The activity focus, followed by empirical research attention, moved into areas hitherto not associated with active citizenship, such as consumption (e.g., product boycott; Clarke et al. 2007), arts projects or comedy performance (Bilici 2012; Spielhaus 2013). Moreover, the internet and, more specifically, social media (Johns 2014) has generated new ways of participation and claim-making (e.g., political blogging), facilitating new (e.g., flash mobs) as well as rather traditional forms of political participation (e.g., online petitions). Conceptualising civic engagement as the 'product of individual agency' (Vromen 2003: 95) has opened up, in principle, an unlimited range of avenues to perform one's citizenship. Similarly, James Sloam (2012: 4) asserts in the context of youth participation in Britain that 'if we want to understand political participation at all, we must explore how each new generation comes to develop its own conception of citizenship and expresses itself through civic and political engagement'. These elaborations call for openness and flexibility in defining what types of activities are to be regarded and empirically investigated as manifestations of active citizenship or 'acts of citizenship' (Isin and Nielsen 2008). With the latter concept, Isin and Nielsen advocate an alternative paradigm in contemporary citizenship studies, criticising the previously (too) narrow emphasis on status and habitus in the performance of citizenship (Isin 2008). Isin argues that any investigation of citizenship needs to focus on 'subjects becoming activist citizens through scenes created' (2008: 38). Instead of (only) analysing existing scripts and scenes of active citizens' participation, researchers need to take into account that 'activist citizens' constantly reinvent their performance of citizenship and 'engage in writing scripts and creating the scene' (2008: 38).

Isin and Nielsen's proposed paradigm has prominently drawn attention to less conventional and more individualised forms of enacted citizenship (which research has had difficulties keeping up with) and called for a more flexible approach in investigating the ever evolving realms of civic performance. For many scholars, Isin and Nielsen's proposed paradigm offered a conceptual basis to examine a very broad range of social interactions in everyday life under the banner of citizenship (see, for example, Mansouri and Mikola 2014). Anita Harris and Joshua Roose (2014: 801), for example, in their work on 'do-it-yourself' citizenship among young Muslims in Australia, classify 'informal civic network-building in everyday space', including interactions at the workplace and in the neighbourhoods and talking to friends and family about social issues, forms of civic engagement and citizenship. Participating in the workforce and interacting with neighbours may have implications for people's sense of belonging and recognition (see also Roose and Harris 2015), which is relevant to their citizenship. However, notwithstanding that such interactions are important subjects of research and meaningful contextual factors in investigating active citizenship, they are of an entirely different quality than people's commitment and deliberate decision to become politically and civically active. Thus, while advocating a broad understanding of citizenship, Bellamy (2010) warns against casting the net of citizenship studies too wide when he argues that 'citizenship is different… to other kinds of social relationship, such as being a parent, a friend, a partner, a neighbour, a colleague or a customer' (xi).

The operational understanding of active citizenship, as espoused in this study, follows Bellamy's argument, considering processes of negotiating ones' belonging or every-day social interactions without a civic agenda to be beyond the scope of civic engagement as enacted citizenship. At the same time, it does recognise the in principle infinite possibilities of active citizenship. Performing citizenship is often a highly individualised and creative process of claim-making, advocacy and engagement in the public sphere. This includes political and civic participation within community groups as well as unaffiliated and/or ad-hoc forms of engagement, pursuing a range of agendas on the local level of the neighbourhood, in a nation-state context or beyond (de Koning et al. 2015). While a basic acceptance of the political system, norms and codes (e.g., human rights, democratic fairness) is necessary (Bellamy 2010: xvii; Mouffe 1995: 34), active citizenship shall encompass—in addition to conventional forms of political participation—a wide range of unconventional and constantly evolving ways of actively engaging in the public-political sphere, including critical or oppositional agendas of 'dissenting citizenship' (O'Loughlin and Gillespie 2012; Maira 2009).

Taking into consideration the various attempts to capture the nature and multiple facets of active citizenship, this study deploys an understanding of civic engagement that seeks to be as broad as possible to include a maximum range of civic and political activism. However, it does operate—in contrast to Isin and Nielsen (2008)—within a framework of existing 'scripts' and 'scenes' of enacting citizenship. In line with operationalisations of civic and political participation in contemporary political science, active citizenship shall be defined for this study as a*ny conduct of individual citizens, independently or as members of an organisation or group, which is located outside the purely private context and which is directly or indirectly aimed at making a contribution to the wellbeing of others, be it a certain community, social group, the neighbourhood or the society at large.*

Theoretical Framework: Determinants of Participation

What factors and conditions encourage or hamper civic and political participation of citizens in general and ethno-religious minorities in particular? How do certain—possibly country-specific—circumstances and conditions affect the emergence of typical forms of civic engagement?

These questions are at the centre of the following elaborations, which outline the theoretical framework for this study.

There are a range of theoretical and empirical models to explain (political) participation of citizens in general and of minorities and immigrant groups in particular. While some scholars locate the key determinants primarily on the macro level of institutional structures and policies, others identify personal predispositions and resources as primary factors in citizens' disposition to actively participate. Some analysts have stressed the impact of collective agency, highlighting the importance of taking into consideration the 'internal differentiation' of minority communities (Bousetta 2000: 238) and the 'interaction effects between individual determinants … and the structure of the ethnic civic community' (Tillie 2004: 529).

Although many of these empirically tested approaches propose sound arguments for their particular way of explaining political activity and commitment, most of them tend to prioritise one or two of these three dimensions—individual, organisational or structural factors—and underestimate the effects of the respective other(s). The explanatory model in this study takes into account all three levels, pragmatically drawing on a combination of several established concepts and theories. This offers the most fruitful basis for the investigation of Muslim active citizenship. Such an eclectic approach follows the argument of the Scandinavian anthropologist Barth (1994), who stressed in his thematically broader analysis of the negotiation of ethnicity in pluralistic societies that the investigation of these complex processes need to consider 'three penetrating levels': identity and the 'lived context' on the micro level, agency and ethnic movement on the intermediary level and, lastly, the macro level of state policies (1994: 20–21).

The Civic Voluntarism Model is central for this study, emphasising individual resources as the key explanatory factor of political participation (Verba et al. 1995). This model is complemented by the institutional channelling theory, which focusses on opportunity structures and institutional policy factors (Ireland 1994). Combining these two analytical frameworks ensures a robust coverage of micro and macro level determinants of political participation, and it allows for a thematic extension to include varied manifestations of civic participation. However, neither of the two models pays sufficient tribute to the prominence of community organisations as platform of collective political involvement as well as site of individuals' civic engagement. To address these weaknesses, other theoretical accounts will be drawn on that deal more explicitly with the potentials of community agency for active citizenship.

Civic Voluntarism Model

The Civic Voluntarism Model was developed by Sidney Verba, Kay L. Schlozman and Henry E. Brady (1995) and was empirically tested within the large-scale study *Voice and Equality* on political participation in the United States. The research seeks to explain and investigates citizens' engagement in (voluntary) activities targeting the political decision-making process. Verba and his colleagues begin their theoretical discussion by asking the inverted question: Why do citizens *refrain* from becoming politically active? The answer they offer is simple yet illuminating: People do not participate 'because they can't; because they don't want to; or because nobody asked' (1995: 269). These three reasons for non-involvement constitute the point of departure for the development of their Civic Voluntarism Model, a widely recognised 'sound theoretical and substantive account of the relationship between people's personal traits and their political participation' (Diehl and Blohm 2001: 404).

This explanatory model identifies three key determinants of political participation: resources, psychological predispositions (which they refer to as 'political engagement') and political recruitment (Verba et al. 1995: 269–273). These three factors are put in a hierarchical order:

> All three components of the model are important. However, we place greater emphasis on the resources that facilitate participation and on the variety of psychological predispositions towards politics that we label "political engagement" than on political recruitment … With respect to resources and engagement … we place greater stress on the former (Verba et al. 1995: 270).

The first and most essential factor for the explanation of political activism refers to individual resources, which encompasses three aspects: time, money and civic skills, the latter being described as a person's organisational and communication capacity (271). Time and money are regarded as 'the resources expended most directly in political activity' (289), although their usefulness differs, depending on the specific type of political activity. Time and money can usually be invested more effectively in political activities by those who know how to 'communicate effectively' (306) and to organise their political involvement. These civic skills are regarded as being acquired in the family and at school, but also later at the workplace and through one's involvement in church groups and other voluntary organisations. A higher level of civic skills does not only lower the access threshold to political participation, but, as Verba and colleagues argue, makes the involvement also more effective (304).

The second factor to explain political participation can be described in general terms as personal interests in politics and a basic motivation to become politically active. These internal psychological stimuli are labelled 'political engagement' (344).[2] '[I]t is hard to image that at least some psychological engagement with politics is not required for almost all forms of political participation' (345). This component is then broken down into four interrelated aspects: political interest, a sense of political efficacy (i.e., belief in being able to contribute to changes), political information and political party identification. Verba et al. are aware of the 'ambiguity of causal direction' between this motivational dimension of engagement and the participation itself, for the former is not only an explanatory factor for the latter, but 'reciprocally, being more active may [also] increase engagement as participants become more interested, informed, and efficacious' (344).

Verba and colleagues' empirical analysis indicates that 'resources and political engagement jointly matter for political participation' (351). Both factors together provide the basis for active involvement of citizens in the political process by giving citizens a motive as well as the ability to become active. In addition, the US research team introduced a third determinant of political activity: citizens' personal involvement in (non-political) institutions of adult life—'the workplace, voluntary association, or church' (369). They describe three ways in which these institutions may 'operate to

---

[2] This refers to *mental* engagement and must not be confused with *enacted* engagement as used throughout this study.

enhance political participation' (369). Firstly, they function as a 'training ground' for organisational and communication (civic) skills, transferable to political activities. Secondly, they might be sites where people are directly requested to become politically active. Thirdly, many of these organisations offer political stimuli (e.g., as sites of political discussions), which may encourage people to get involved in political participation (369).

The involvement of African-Americans in church groups is presented as an illustrative example in their study *Voice and Equality*. The researchers empirically demonstrate that African-Americans more often 'belong to churches whose internal structure nurtures opportunities to exercise politically relevant skills' (383). In addition, these church groups tend to be 'more *politicized*' (384, emphasis in the original); that is, their members are exposed to political stimuli, requests for political participation, and messages from the pulpit about political matters. Such stimulating effects of churches as a recruiting agency on African-Americans' proneness to become politically active may also be found within Muslim communities, although Verba and colleagues' examination does not pay attention to Muslim citizens in particular. Scholars including Jamal (2005), Foley and Hoge (2007) and most recently Read (2015) and Fleischmann et al. (2015) have argued that mosques may also serve as sites of political mobilisation of Muslims.

The Civic Voluntarism Model constitutes a multi-dimensional microlevel approach focussing chiefly on factors that lie within the individual person. Although Verba and colleagues admit that '[n]o explanation of political activity will ever be complete' (1995: 273) due to the complexity of individual (internal) and social (external) influences, their general model claims that researchers can gain a deep understanding of citizens' political involvement by solely looking at the individuals. Through their empirical research they were able to demonstrate that insights into political participation can be achieved by examining citizens' time and monetary resources, their communication and organisational skills, motivations, interest and political passions, and their participation in the workforce, non-political non-governmental organisations (NGOs) and certain religious groups.

Against this backdrop, this general model appears to be an appropriate foundation for the analysis of Muslims' political participation. More specifically, it is compatible with the above outline conceptual understanding of performed citizenship. The model has, however, several shortcomings as an analytical basis for an investigation of Muslim active citizenship. The most obvious drawback of the Civic Voluntarism Model as an explanatory model for this study on Muslims' active citizenship is its focus on political participation, that is on 'activity that has the intent or effect of influencing government action—either directly … or indirectly' (Verba et al. 1995: 38); citizens' non-political (voluntary) civic engagement and community work as members of civil society organisations are treated as an independent variable to explain political participation, but not as a manifestation of civic engagement itself. However, arguing along the lines of van Deth (2013) and other scholars (Weissberg 2005; Keeter et al. 2002), who reject the clear-cut distinction between civic and political participation, Verba et al. (1995) analytical focus on political participation does not render their model useless for explaining civic engagement more broadly.

Another caveat of the Civic Voluntarism Model is that it largely neglects factors that lie outside the individual citizen's resources and disposition, not taking into account the effects of potentially influential factors on the macro level, such as access to political rights and opportunity structures for civic engagement, and the intermediary level, such as the role of community agency. Another related weakness—one that may constitute a particularly problematic limitation for an investigation of Muslim active citizenship—is linked to its ambitious attempt to explain political participation *in general*. It appears too broad to sufficiently consider possible differences in the way certain minority groups enact their citizenship. The particularities of political participation of groups like women, Hispanics (ethnic minorities), African-Americans (racial minority) and Protestants and Catholics are explained on the basis of the same model, instead of delving into a close-up analysis of group-specific manifestations of collective mobilisation as a form of social movement. Verba and colleagues argue that the empirical testing of group consciousness of Blacks, Hispanic and women as an additional determinant of political activity did not generate any statistically significant results and was thus not further considered in the analysis and the explanatory model (1995: 355–356). The authors themselves describe these findings as 'puzzling' as they contradict previous research from the 1960s and 1970s, where collective identity was often a crucial factor for political participation. One possible reason the authors mention is that 'the nature of group politics in America' may have changed since the era of the civil right movement (356). However, the continuous prevalence of Muslims' collective mobilisation for equality and recognition in many Western societies (Meer and Modood 2009; Modood 2010) suggest that ignoring identity politics and collective agency would entail severe limitation for the analysis of Muslims' political mobilisation and participation (Fetzer and Soper 2005: 8).These conceptual shortcomings are located on the intermediary and macro levels. They can be overcome by adding explanatory dimensions borrowed from other analytical models of immigrants' and minorities' participation.

Political Opportunity Structures

Political opportunity structure models, like the institutional channeling theory of Patrick Ireland (1994), appear useful to address these caveats on the structural level and to consider the effects of country-specific policies and institutional arrangements. Ireland underscores 'the influence of host-society institutional structures on immigrant political mobilization' (1994: 8). National policies, laws and institutional and administrative practices, Ireland argues, 'seem particularly likely to spark certain kinds of ethnic and immigrant group activity' (1994: 9). These policy frameworks create opportunity structures for the emergence of specific types of ethnic or religious agencies and for their collective forms of claims-making (Diehl and Blohm 2001: 403) as well as for individuals' active engagement, be it as representative of the particular group or as non-affiliated citizens (Kortmann 2011: 59–60). National political opportunity structures impact on immigrants' access to equal rights—a defining element of citizenship and an instrumental factor for certain forms of active participation. According to Ireland, 'immigrants' legal situation; their social and political rights; and host-society citizenship laws, naturalization procedure, and policies (and nonpolicies) in such areas as education, housing, the labour market, and social assistance … shape conditions and immigrants' responses' (1994: 10). Moreover, Ireland's theoretical model takes into account the role and impact of mainstream 'institutional gatekeepers', like welfare agencies, trade unions and political parties, 'controlling access to the avenues of political participation available to immigrants' (ibid.).

The institutional channeling theory and other models of political opportunity structure became very popular in social and political sciences during the 1990s (Boussetta 2000: 230) and have been applied and tested in empirical research on ethnic politics, political participation and claim-making of immigrants and ethnic/ethno-religious minority. Besides Ireland's own study on immigrant politics in France and Switzerland, Ruud Koopmans (2004: 451), for example, uses 'aspects of the political opportunity structure relevant to the field of immigration and ethnic relations politics, and for the mobilisation of migrants in particular'. Karen Bird and her colleagues (2011a: 13) also 'draw strongly on the concept of political opportunity structures' in their theoretical framework on political participation and representation of ethnic minorities. Fetzer and Soper (2005: 10–12) referred to political opportunity structure models and country-specific inherited church-state relations in their investigation of policy responses to Muslims' struggle for accommodation in Germany, France and the United Kingdom. In a similar vein, Matthias König (2007: 912) argues in his cross-national comparative analysis of Muslims' integration that country-specific 'Church–State relations, national identities, political opportunity structures and deliberate policy initiatives ... have led to distinctive patterns of Muslim incorporation'.

Adding these macro-level perspectives to the theoretical basis for the cross-national analysis of Muslim active citizenship addresses one of the key weaknesses of the Civic Voluntarism Model. It broadens the analytical horizon towards the impact of citizenship regimes, state-church regulations and other administrative practices and national policies (Kortmann 2011: 59). This is vital given the implications of such macro-level factors on both individual Muslims' legal status and access to socio-economic resources, civic skills and social networks, as well as on Muslim agencies and their role in political mobilisation and civic participation within civil society.

Community Structures and Collective Social Capital

Ireland's institutional channeling theory and the Civic Voluntarism Model make some references to the role of community or voluntary organisations for the emergence of political participation. While Ireland (1994: 24) stresses that immigrant participation has taken place 'quite extensively' within the context of 'collective immigrant political activities', his analysis is less concerned with the specific mechanisms of these group-based processes of claim-making. Verba et al. (1995: 369) do specify the way in which non-political voluntary organisations may promote citizens' political participation, but they elaborate primarily on the *indirect* role of these organisations as learning grounds for civic skills and as sites of political stimuli for individual citizens (Putnam 2000: 338–339; Bloemraad 2006). The recognition of a more immediate role as enabling and facilitating platforms of collective political lobbying or, more broadly, for civic engagement is, however, largely absent in the Civic Voluntarism Model.

Since the 1960s and 1970s, social and political scientists have repeatedly emphasised that community organisations are crucial for political mobilisation and civic participation of their members. In an early study, Verba et al. (1978: 15) described organisations generally as the 'weapons of the weak' in their struggle for equity and recognition. 'Lower-status groups … need a group-based process of political mobilization if they are to catch up to the upper-status groups in terms of political activity. They need a self-conscious ideology as motivation and … organization as a resource' (Verba et al. 1978: 14).

This appears particularly relevant to communities of immigrant and ethnic, racial and religious minority groups. The German social scientist Dirk Halm (2011), for example, argues that 'there are strong indicators that collective orientations … are permanently of greater importance [for the engagement of immigrants, M.P.] than they are within non-migrant population groups' (2011: 21, own translation). More specifically, the US researcher Jamal maintains that religious institutions, including mosques, 'can also serve as conduits for direct political mobilisation' (2005: 522). Jamal found in her empirical investigation that Arab Muslims' participation in mosques is positively 'linked to political activity, civic participation and group consciousness' (2005: 537). These findings were confirmed by Read (2015: 43) who concluded that Arab Muslim men who regularly attend a mosque and those who are very actively involved in mosque activities are more likely to be involved in civic participation outside the Muslim community context. Research in the Netherlands (Fleischmann et al. 2015) and the UK (McAndrew and Voas 2014) have recently come to similar conclusions.

The relevance of community organisations for the political participation of immigrant and ethno-religious minorities (Herman and Jacobs 2015) is attributed to general socioeconomic and specific ethnicity-related reasons. Firstly, many of these minorities groups are overrepresented in what Verba et al. (1978) refer to as lower-status groups. They disproportionately face socioeconomic disadvantages and have often less resources and social capital. This makes collective forms of claim-making particularly important. The second reason is linked more directly to their ethnic or ethno-religious minority status. Tariq Modood asserts in the British context that second and third generation migrants 'may continue to mobilise around identities of cultural difference and demand equality of respect, especially when those identities are the basis of discrimination and structural inequalities' (2012: 46). This argument is not new. Already in the 1960s, analysts like Parenti (1967, in Bloemraad 2007: 328) assumed that ethnic politics, channelled through community agency, can persist over generations simply because minority group-based interests and claims of equity and cultural maintenance persist. The descendants of immigrants may have expanded their human capital, social networks and economic resources, but continue to feel they lack full recognition and equal civic standing. 'According to Parenti, economic mobility provides greater resources to sustain ethnic organizations, greater confidence in the group's ability to organize, and concrete grievance when economically mobile individuals face continued prejudice because of their ethnicity' (Bloemraad 2007: 328). This seems highly relevant also for Muslim communities in Australia and Germany.

Several scholars have argued that not all ethnic or religious community organisations have the same capacity to facilitate and foster their members' political engagement. Bowler et al. (2003), for example, demonstrate in their studies on the mobilisation effects of group membership across Europe that certain types of (non-political) organisations are more likely to encourage their members to become politically engaged than others (see also Togeby 1999; Fennema and Tillie 1999). The Dutch scholar Jean Tillie (2004) offers a sophisticated empirical analysis of why in a given national context some ethnic community organisations are more effective than other in mobilising their members into political participation. Tillie found that it is the *collective* social capital of immigrant community organisations and its interrelation with *individual* social capital of immigrants that play a key role. Drawing on empirical work carried out in the Netherlands during the late 1990s, Tillie argues that individual resources, social networks and membership in ethnic, cross-ethnic and mainstream organisations have positive effects on the political participation of ethnic minorities, but these three factors cannot fully explain the level of participation. He proposes that the 'amount of social capital generated by the membership of an organisation is dependent upon the position of the organisation in the organisational network' (Tillie 2004: 532) and its horizontal connectedness with other ethnic organisations—what he tags 'civic community'. The more connected an organisation is the better it fares at mobilising its community members, because its members benefit from the collective resources and assets of other organisations within this ethnic network. Tillie explains this also with the example of immigrant community elites: 'Political trust of the ethnic elite can 'travel' through the networks of the community, thus increasing the political trust of the community', but it 'can only travel through a community if the organisations of that community are connected to each other' (2004: 534).

Fetzer and Soper (2005: 7) make a similar argument, referring to resource mobilisation theories which 'stress the organizational structure [of Muslim communities] that link individuals into a social movement'. Accordingly, community-internal networks are deemed instrumental for the effective mobilisation of community members and thus influence the power of the social movement. Like Tillie's explanatory model of political participation, Fetzer and Soper also point to two influential factors:

> The key features of an effective social movement are, first, a skilled cadre of leaders who can translate the amorphously held values of the group into political capital, and second, a well-established institutional structure from which group leaders can draw resources … and recruit members for social movement organizations (2005: 8).

Accordingly, models to explain Muslim political participation gain depths when taking into account the nature of Muslim community organisations, more specifically their internal collective assets of social capital, connectedness and the capacity of their leadership. Civil society organisations in general and Muslim community groups in particular are not only platforms of political mobilisation, but they are also the place where many citizens become actively engaged in the most common type of civic engagement, which is an essential dimension of active citizenship: volunteering and community work. This holds true for most mainstream civil society organisations as well as for minority community organisations, regardless of their ethnic or religious composition. There is no reason to assume Islamic organisations, including mosque associations, are an exception.

Volunteering for community organisations represents not only a direct manifestation of civic engagement. It often has also a more far-reaching indirect impact on their active citizenship. In his general elaboration on social capital Kenneth Newton describes this as the internal and external effects of voluntary organisations on their members. 'Internally, organisations ... socialise them into a democratic culture and teach them the subtleties of trust and cooperation' (Newton 1999: 10). As part of their community work volunteers often take responsibility, and at times represent the organisation vis-à-vis third parties, which requires and enhances their communication, organisational and conflict resolution skills (Foner and Alba 2008: 364–365). These indirect effects of volunteering are complemented, according to Newton, by external effects: 'Externally, organisations link citizens with the political system and its institutions, aggregate and articulate interests and provide the range and variety of competing and cooperating groups which constitute the pluralistic polity' (Newton 1999: 10–11). These external effects may not be equally manifest in all types of volunteering in civil society organisations, as it depends on the type of community work (e.g., leadership role) and the specific character and profile of the respective organisation. The latter has been a key argument in many social capital models, proposing a differentiation between bridging capital of broadly connected organisations and bonding capital of rather inward-looking community groups (Briggs 2003; Putnam 2000). Applying this differentiation to Newton's argument about the external effects of organisational membership suggests that those community organisations with intensive connections and relationship to other social actors outside their own community circles are better suited to link their members to the wider community and political arena. This resonates with the findings of an empirical study by the US researcher Pamela Paxton (2002) who argues that 'connected associations had a strong *positive* influence on democracy, while isolated associations had a strong *negative* impact on democracy' (2002: 272; emphasis in original).

Drawing on these theoretical considerations on collective agency and individuals' affiliations with community organisations, this study on Muslims' active citizenship pays attention to the multiple ways in which voluntary community groups, including Islamic organisations, may affect Muslims' civic and political participation. Combining these analytical perspectives with the micro and macro level determinants, proposed by the Civic Voluntarism Model and Ireland's institutional channeling theory, provides a guiding framework for investigating Muslims' civic and political participation in Australia and Germany.

References

Adler, R., & Goggin, J. (2005). What do we mean by "civic engagement". *Journal of Transformative Education, 3*(3), 236–253.

Andersen, B. (1991). *Imagined communities: Reflections on the origin and spread of nationalism*. London: Verso.

Barber, B. (1984). *Stronger democracy: Participatory politics for a new age*. Berkley: University of California Press.

Barth, F. (1994). Enduring and emerging issues in the analysis of ethnicity. In H. Vermeulen & C. Govers (Eds.), *The anthropology of ethnicity: Beyond 'ethnic groups and boundaries'* (pp. 11–32). Amsterdam: Het Spinhuis.

Bee, C., & Pachi, D. (2014). Active citizenship in the UK: Assessing institutional political strategies and mechanisms of civic engagement. *Journal of Civil Society, 10*(1), 100–117.

Bellamy, R. (2010). Introduction. In R. Bellamy & A. Palumbo (Eds.), *Citizenship* (pp. xi–xxv). Farnham: Ashgate.

Bendor, J., & Mookherjee, D. (2008). Communitarian versus universalistic norms. *Quarterly Journal of Political Science, 3*(1), 1–29.

Berry, J. M., Portney, K. E., & Thomas, K. (1993). *The rebirth of urban democracy*. Washington, DC: The Brookings Institution.

Bilici, M. (2012). *Finding Mecca in America: How Islam is becoming an American religion*. Chicago: University of Chicago Press.

Bird, K., Saalfeld, T., & Wüst, A. M. (2011a). Ethnic diversity, political participation and representation: A theoretical framework. In K. Bird, T. Saalfeld, & A. M. Wüst (Eds.), *The political representation of immigrants and minorities. Voters, parties and parliaments in liberal democracies* (pp. 1–21). London: Routledge.

Bloemraad, I. (2006). Becoming a citizen in the United States and Canada: Structured mobilization and immigrant political incorporation. *Social Forces, 85*(2), 667–695.

Bloemraad, I. (2007). Unity in diversity. Bridging models of multiculturalism and immigrant integration. *Du Bois Review, 4*(2), 317–336.

Bousetta, H. (2000). Institutional theories of immigrant ethnic mobilisation: Relevance and limitations. *Journal of Ethnic and Migration Studies, 26*(2), 229–245.

Bowler, S., Donovan, T., & Hanneman, R. (2003). Art for democracy's sake? Group membership and political engagement in Europe. *Journal of Politics, 65*(4), 1111–1129.

Briggs, de Souza X. (2003). *Bridging networks, social capital, and racial segregation in America* (John F. Kennedy School of Government Harvard University Faculty Research Working Papers Series). Cambridge: Harvard University.

Brint, S. (2001). *Gemeinschaft* revisited: A critique and reconstruction of the community concept. *Sociological Theory, 19*(1), 1–23.

Chambers, S. (2002). A critical theory of civil society. In S. Chambers & W. Kymlicka (Eds.), *Alternative conceptions of civil society* (pp. 90–110). Princeton: Princeton University Press.

Clarke, N., Barnett, C., Cloke, P., & Malpass, A. (2007). Globalising the consumer: Doing politics in an ethical register. *Political Geography, 26*(3), 231–249.

Conover, P. J., Searing, D. D., & Crewe, I. (2004). The elusive ideal of equal citizenship: Political theory and political psychology in the United States and Great Britain. *The Journal of Politics, 66*(4), 1036–1068.

Crowley, J. (1998). The national dimension of citizenship in T.H. Marshall. *Citizenship Studies, 2*(2), 165–178.

Dagger, R. (2002). Republican citizenship. In B. S. Turner & E. F. Isin (Eds.), *Handbook of citizenship studies* (pp. 145–157). London: Sage.

Dahlgren, P. (2006). Doing citizenship. The cultural origins of civic agency in the public sphere. *European Journal for Cultural Studies, 9*(3), 267–286.

Dandy, J., & Pe-Pua, R. (2013). *Research into the current and emerging drivers for social cohesion, social division and conflict in multicultural Australia*. Online document viewed 25 December 2015: https://www.dss.gov.au/our-responsibilities/settlement-and-multicultural-affairs/publications/current-and-emerging-drivers-for-social-cohesion-social-division-and-conflict-in-multicultural-australia

de Koning, A., Jaff, R., & Koster, M. (2015). Citizenship agendas in and beyond the nation-state: (En)countering framings of the good citizen. *Citizenship Studies, 19*(2), 121–127.

Delanty, G. (2002). Communitarianism and citizenship. In B. S. Turner & E. F. Isin (Eds.), *Handbook of citizenship studies* (pp. 159–174). London: Sage.

Diehl, C., & Blohm, M. (2001). Apathy, adaptation or ethnic mobilisation? On the attitudes of a politically excluded group. *Journal of Ethnic and Migration Studies, 27*(3), 401–420.

Etzioni, A. (1996). *The new golden rule*. New York: Basic Books.

Fennema, M., & Tillie, J. (1999). Political participation and political trust in Amsterdam: Civic communities and ethnic networks. *Journal of Ethnic and Migration Studies, 25*(4), 703–726.

Fetzer, J., & Soper, J. C. (2005). *Muslims and the state in Britain, France, and Germany*. New York: Cambridge University Press.

Fleischmann, F., Martinovic, B., & Böhm, M. (2015). Mobilising mosques? The role of service attendance for political participation of Turkish and Moroccan minorities in the Netherlands. *Ethnic and Racial Studies, 39*(5), 746–763.

Foley, M. W., & Hoge, D. R. (2007). *Religion and the new immigrants: How faith communities form our newest citizens*. Oxford: Oxford University Press.

Foner, N., & Alba, R. (2008). Immigrant religion in the U.S. and Western Europe: Bridge or barrier to inclusion? *International Migration Review, 42*(2), 360–392.

Gutmann, A. (1980). *Liberal equality*. Cambridge: Cambridge University Press.

Halm, D. (2011). Bürgerschaftliches Engagement in der Einwanderungsgesellschaft. Bedeutung, Situation und Förderstrategien. *Forschungsjournal Soziale Bewegungen, 24*(2), 14–24.

Harris, A., & Roose, J. (2014). DIY citizenship amongst young Muslims: Experiences of the "ordinary". *Journal of Youth Studies, 17*(6), 794–813.

Head, B. W. (2007). Community engagement: Participation on whose terms? *Australian Journal of Political Science, 42*(3), 441–454.

Herman, B., & Jacobs, D. (2015). Ethnic social capital and political participation of immigrants. In L. Ryan, U. Erel, & A. D'Angelo (Eds.), *Migrant capi-*

tal: *Networks, identities and strategies* (pp. 117–132). Basingstoke: Palgrave Macmillan.

Hoskins, B. L., & Mascherini, M. (2009). Measuring active citizenship through the development of a composite indicator. *Social Indicators Research, 90*(3), 459–488.

Ireland, P. (1994). *The policy challenge of ethnic diversity. Immigrant politics in France and Switzerland.* Cambridge: Harvard University Press.

Isin, E. F. (2008). Theorising acts of citizenship. In E. F. Isin & G. M. Nielsen (Eds.), *Acts of citizenship* (pp. 15–43). London: Zed Books.

Isin, E. F. (2009). Citizenship in flux: The figure of the activist citizen. *Subjectivity, 29*, 367–388.

Isin, E. F., & Nielsen, G. M. (Eds.). (2008). *Acts of citizenship.* London: Zed Books.

Isin, E., & Turner, B. (2002). Citizenship studies: An introduction. In B. Turner & E. Isin (Eds.), *Handbook of citizenship studies* (pp. 1–10). London: Sage.

Isin, E. F., & Turner, B. (2007). Investigating citizenship: An agenda for citizenship studies. In E. F. Isin, P. Nyers, & B. Turner (Eds.), *Citizenship between past and future* (pp. 5–17). London: Routledge.

Isin, E. F., & Wood, P. K. (1999). *Citizenship and identity.* London: Sage.

Jamal, A. (2005). The political participation and engagement of Muslim Americans: Mosque involvement and group consciousness. *American Politics Research, 33*(4), 521–544.

Johns, A. (2014). Muslim young people online: "Acts of citizenship" in socially networked spaces. *Social Inclusion, 2*(2), 71–82.

Joppke, C. (2002). Multicultural citizenship. In B. S. Turner & E. F. Isin (Eds.), *Handbook of citizenship studies* (pp. 245–258). London: Sage.

Kaase, M. (1995). Politische Beteiligung/politische Partizipation. In U. Andersen, & W. Woyke (Eds.), *Handwörterbuch des politischen Systems der Bundesrepublik Deutschland* (pp. 462–466). Bonn: BpB.

Keeter, S., Zukin, C., Andolina, M., & Jenkins, K. (2002). *Civic and political health of the nation: A generational portrait.* Medford: CIRCLE.

Kivisto, P. (2003). Social spaces, transnational immigrant communities, and the politics of incorporation. *Ethnicities, 3*(1), 5–28.

Kivisto, P., & Faist, T. (2007). *Citizenship. Discourse, theory, and transnational prospects.* Malden: Blackwell Publishing.

König, M. (2007). Europeanising the governance of religious diversity: An institutionalist account of muslim struggles for public recognition. *Journal of Ethnic and Migration Studies, 33*(6), 911–932.

Koopmans, R. (2004). Migrant mobilisation and political opportunities: Variation among German cities and a comparison with the United Kingdom and the Netherlands. *Journal of Ethnic and Migration Studies, 30*(3), 449–470.

Kortmann, M. (2011). Wie definieren islamische Dachverbände Integration? Ein deutsch-niederländischer Vergleich. *Forschungsjournal Soziale Bewegungen, 24*(2), 59–67.

Kymlicka, W. (1995). *Multicultural citizenship: A liberal theory of minority rights*. Oxford: Clarendon Press.

Kymlicka, W. (2002). *Contemporary political philosophy. An introduction*. Oxford: University Press Oxford.

Maira, S. (2009). Citizenship and dissent: South Asian Muslim youth in the US after 9/11. *South Asian Popular Cultures, 8*(1), 31–45.

Mansouri, F., & Mikola, M. (2014). Crossing boundaries: Acts of citizenship among migrant youth in Melbourne. *Social Inclusion, 2*(2), 28–37.

Marshall, T. H. (1950). *Citizenship and social class*. Cambridge: Cambridge University Press.

McAndrew, S., & Voas, D. (2014). Immigrant generation, religiosity and civic engagement in Britain. *Ethnic and Racial Studies, 37*(1), 99–119.

Meer, N., & Modood, T. (2009). The multicultural state we're in: Muslims, "multiculture" and the "civic re-balancing" of British multiculturalism. *Political Studies, 57*(3), 473–497.

Modood, T. (2010). Multicultural citizenship and Muslim identity politics. *Interventions: International Journal of Postcolonial Studies, 12*(2), 157–170.

Modood, T. (2012). *Post-immigration 'difference' and integration. The case of Muslims in Western Europe*. London: The British Academy.

Mouffe, C. (1995). Democratic politics and the question of identity. In J. Rajchman (Ed.), *The identity in question* (pp. 33–45). London/New York: Routledge.

Newton, K. (1999). Social capital and democracy in modern Europe. In J. van Deth, M. Maraffi, K. Newton, & P. Whitely (Eds.), *Social capital and European democracy* (pp. 3–24). London: Routledge.

O'Loughlin, B., & Gillespie, M. (2012). Dissenting citizenship? Young people and political participation in the media-security nexus. *Parliamentary Affairs, 65*(1), 115–137.

Paxton, P. (2002). Social capital and democracy: An interdependent relationship. *American Sociological Review, 67*(2), 254–277.

Putnam, R. D. (2000). *Bowling alone: The collapse and revival of American community*. New York: Simon and Schuster.

Read, J. G. (2015). Gender, religious identity, and civic engagement among Arab Muslims in the United States. *Sociology of Religion, 76*(1), 30–48.

Roose, J. M., & Harris, A. (2015). Muslim citizenship in everyday Australian civic spaces. *Journal of Intercultural Studies, 36*(4), 468–486.

Sandel, M. J. (1982). *Liberalism and the limits of justice*. Cambridge: Cambridge University Press.

Schuck, P. H. (2002). Liberal citizenship. In B. S. Turner & E. F. Isin (Eds.), *Handbook of citizenship studies* (pp. 131–144). London: Sage.

Slaughter, S. (2007). Cosmopolitanism and republican citizenship. In W. Hudson & S. Slaughter (Eds.), *Globalisation and citizenship: The transnational challenge* (pp. 85–99). London: Routledge.

Sloam, J. (2012). Introduction: Youth, citizenship and politics. *Parliamentary Affairs, 65*, 4–12.

Spielhaus, R. (2013). Clichés are funny as long as they happen on stage: Comedy as political criticism. In J. S. Nielsen (Ed.), *Muslim political participation in Europe* (pp. 322–338). Edinburgh: Edinburgh University Press.

Tillie, J. (2004). Social capital of organisations and their members: Explaining the political integration of immigrants in Amsterdam. *Journal of Ethnic and Migration Studies, 30*(3), 529–541.

Togeby, L. (1999). Migrants at the polls: An analysis of immigrant and refugee participation in Danish local elections. *Journal of Ethnic and Migration Studies, 25*(4), 665–684.

Turner, B. (2013). Contemporary citizenship: Four types. In S. A. Arjomand & E. Reis (Eds.), *Worlds of difference* (pp. 230–251). London: Sage.

van Deth, J. (2013). Citizenship and the civic realities of everyday life. In M. Print & D. Lange (Eds.), *Civic education and competences for engaging citizens in democracies* (pp. 9–21). Rotterdam: Sense Publishers.

Verba, S., Nie, N. W., & Kim, J. (1978). *Participation and political equality: A seven-nation comparison*. New York: Cambridge University Press.

Verba, S., Schlozman, K. L., & Brady, H. (1995). *Voice and equality. Civic voluntarism in American politics*. Cambridge: Harvard University Press.

Vromen, A. (2003). "People try to put us down …": Participatory citizenship of "Generation X". *Australian Journal of Political Science, 38*(1), 79–99.

Weissberg, R. (2005). *The limits of civic activism: Cautionary tales on the use of politics*. New Brunswick: Transaction Publishers.

Young, M. I. (1989). Polity and group difference: A critique of the ideal of universal citizenship. *Ethics, 99*(2), 250–274.

3

Methodology: Exploring Muslims' Civic and Political Participation

This study examines the ways in which Muslims engage as active citizens in different forms of civic and political participation in Australia and Germany, exploring their civic trajectories, motives and reasons for their commitment, and the implications this engagement has had for them personally. The above outlined theoretical-conceptual framework highlights the multi-dimensional character of these participatory processes, influenced by a complex interplay of factors on the individual, the community and the policy level. This study has been designed to investigate these processes with a qualitative methodology, combined with a cross-national comparative perspective. The following sections briefly outline the methodological rationales as well as the sampling strategy, data collection and analysis. In the second part of this chapter the realised sample of civically and politically active Muslims who participated in this study will be briefly described.

Outlining the Methodology

The research study pursues an explorative methodological approach. The fieldwork consisted of a series of 30 semi-structured interviews with active citizens of Islamic faith, designed to investigate their subjective views on

© The Author(s) 2016
M. Peucker, *Muslim Citizenship in Liberal Democracies*,
DOI 10.1007/978-3-319-31403-7_3

their personal activism. This empirical component is complemented by an analytical cross-national comparison, examining the explorative findings, where relevant, against the backdrop of country-specific conditions and opportunity structures. This section first locates the study in epistemological terms and then elaborates on the qualitative data collection and analysis and on the cross-national comparison of Muslims' active citizenship in Australia and Germany.

Epistemological Location and Methodological Rationale

Given the complex, highly subjective and under-researched nature of Muslims' active citizenship, a qualitative explorative methodology was chosen as the most suitable way to empirically investigate these issues. The aim of the qualitative fieldwork is not to ultimately *explain* civic engagement and active citizenship in a positivistic or statistically representative manner. Instead, the study seeks to better *understand* Muslims' personal experiences revolving around their active commitment. Such a deeper understanding relies on a highly context-specific analysis and has the potential to unveil patterns and mechanisms of Muslims' performed citizenship, based on an interpretation of the individuals' experiences and context factors.

This subjectivistic, hermeneutic approach underscores the location of this study within the interpretivist paradigm. Loosely drawing on the classical Thomas Theorem 'If men [*sic*] define situations as real, they are real in their consequences' (Thomas and Thomas 1928: 571–572), pivotal weight was given to the subjective views of Muslim citizens who actively engage in different forms of civic and political participation. Accordingly, in-depth, semi-structured face-to-face interviews were deployed as the primary data collection method.

The analysis of these data was carried out in a multi-stage process. It began with the hermeneutic exercise of uncovering Muslims' subjective views, motives and experiences of active citizenship in each national sample. Close attention was paid to the differences between the manifestations of Muslims active citizenship in both national contexts. These explorative findings were then analysed and interpreted against the backdrop of, on the one hand, country-specific conditions and opportunity structures and, on the other hand, a cross-national comparison. While the primary aim of this study is to better understand the nature of active citizenship of the interviewed Muslim citizens, these additional comparative, analytical steps helped identify—on a more abstract level—indicators for general mechanisms and patterns of Muslims' activism.

Qualitative Fieldwork: Interviews with Active Muslim Citizens

Interviews with active Muslims were the key method of data collection. The following section outlines the process of selecting participants, the interview guidelines and core aspects of the data analysis process.

The selection of Muslim citizens as interview partners was based, as a first step, on their self-identification as Muslims. This self-identification was not validated or questioned as part of the sampling process, which circumvented the pitfalls of externally defining what it means to be Muslim. The process of identifying *active* citizens was guided by the proposed scope of civic engagement and conceptual framework of active citizenship as outlined in Chap. 2. The general sampling rational behind the selection process was to ensure a diverse sample in terms of participants' demographics and types of civic as well as political participation. In order to ensure a maximum variety of manifestations of active citizenship, the selection of interview partners systematically sought to cover civic and political participation along two axes: the goals of the activity and the organisational setting or agency of the engagement (Table 2.1).

Potential interview partners were identified through a combination of the researcher's personal networks and acquaintances within Muslim communities, and an intensive and systematic internet and media search. Seeking to establish a similar composition of both national sub-samples, the aim was to include active Muslims without any organisational affiliations (e.g., media activists) as well as Muslim representatives, activists or volunteers from similar types of Muslim organisations (e.g., mosques,

Table 2.1 Two-dimensional classification: Basis for selection of interview partners

Goal	Agency	
	Independent engagement without organisational affiliation	Collective engagement within an organisational setting
Communitarian goals (Muslims)	*Media activism against misrepresentation of Islam*	*Lobbying of Muslim organisations for recognition of Islam* *Volunteering at a mosque*
Other (non-Muslim) group-based goals	*Public protest or signing petitions for environmental issues, women's rights*	*Trade union activism* *Engagement in students' union*
Republican goals ('greater good')	*Public protest, signing petitions, letter to local MP, lobbying for general improvements*	*Political mandate* *Environmentalist activism*

women's, student and youth organisations) as well as non-Muslim organisations (e.g., trade unions, political parties). Most people invited to participate in this study agreed to be interviewed.

A total of 30 interviews were conducted in a semi-structured way. Interview guidelines (see Appendix) were deployed to ensure a basic thematic coverage, but applied flexibly and in a non-directive, open fashion in order to give the interview partners maximum freedom to express their views and what they consider to be important for their engagement. This openness led, in some cases, to interviews that can be described as partially bibliographical as some participants spoke in depth about their childhood and shared life stories they deemed relevant to the emergence of their civic commitment. Overall, the guidelines were designed to elicit the subjective perspectives of interviewed Muslims on their specific experiences with civic engagement, their reasons and driving forces and on the perceived implications of their activism. Questions about what encouraged and empowered, or discouraged and hampered, their decisions to become actively engaged were also included. In addition, most interview partners were asked to share their views on the extent of other Muslims' civic and political commitment and factors that hamper or encourage their activism. This set of questions sought to gain additional insights by tapping into the personal experiences and views of active Muslim citizens about the active (or lack of) engagement of fellow Muslims. These elaborations helped shed some light, from the interview partners' perspective, on the broader picture of Muslims' active citizenship and identify obstacles of engagement.

The analysis of the fieldwork data began with the transcript of the audio-recorded interview material. The transcripts of the German and the Australian fieldwork were examined, first separately and then in a cross-national comparative way. The analysis technique was inspired by Glaser and Strauss' grounded theory (1967) and Strauss and Corbin's (1998) method of open codification.[1] As a first step, preliminary thematic codes were ascribed to the transcribed material. As the data analysis and the coding process continues, the coding labels change and the data were re-coded accordingly until the developed categories reached a level of theoretical saturation. This is when the codes did not require any substantial adjustment to accurately capture all discovered dimensions of Muslims' active citizenship.

After all 30 interviews were coded according to this analysis method, using the same coding system for both national data sets, the coded data were categorised under more general thematic headings with the aim of 'integrating the data around a central theme, hypothesis, or story' (Walker and Myrick 2006: 556); these thematic headings correspond roughly with the structure of the empirical chapters in this study. NVivo 10 data analysis software was used for the examination of the interview material. The final step in the data analysis focussed on the cross-national comparison, which constituted, next to the qualitative fieldwork, the second main methodological pillar of this study. This facilitated the interpretation of the empirical findings on a more general level and helped gain a more comprehensive understanding of Muslims' active citizenship in both countries.

---

[1] However, the fieldwork and data analysis for this study does not strictly adhere to grounded theory principles, which emphasise that the researcher needs to approach the topic under investigation without any preconceptions or theoretical assumptions. This is not the case here given the broader conceptual and analytical framework of this study.

Cross-National Comparison and Selection of National Cases Studies

Previous research suggests that active citizenship of Muslims has unfolded in partially divergent ways in different national settings, which makes a cross-national comparative analysis appear particularly fruitful. Comparing the country-specifics of these phenomena assisted in identifying national factors and conditions that affect Muslims' ability and motivations to become actively engaged and the way in which they participate. Arguing that national policies, laws and administrative practices have implications for the emergence of political participation, political opportunity structure models have particularly high explanatory potential when deployed in a cross-national research designs. Fetzer and Soper, for example, describe it as '[o]ne of the chief advantages of a political opportunity structure theory … that it is inherently comparative' (2005: 12).

Pragmatic and analytical considerations have informed the selection of Australia and Germany as the two case studies for this cross-national comparison of Muslim active citizenship. The author had established personal links with Muslim communities in both countries and speaks both English and German. Having previously conducted research on social and civic incorporation of minorities in both countries, he has been very familiar with the national research situation, public debates and policy frameworks relevant to citizenship and civic and political integration. The analytical reasons for the selection of Germany and Australia for a comparative study draw from a combination of, on the one hand, cross-national similarities in terms of Muslims' socioeconomic situation and experiences of exclusion and, on the other hand, of differences regarding the policy framework and the civic recognition of Muslim community agencies as civil society stakeholders (see Chap. 5). Against this backdrop of similar experiences of exclusion and public stigmatisation in quite divergent national policy settings, a cross-national comparison of Muslim active citizenship in Germany and Australia seems particularly promising for the exploration of various factors that may affect Muslims' civic and political engagement and the process of becoming active citizens.

Limitations of This Research

The explorative nature of this qualitative research proved indispensable for generating innovative insights into various interconnected facets of Muslims' active citizenship and their complexly evolving civic trajectories in Australia and Germany. Instead of providing positivistic explanations, these findings explore the subjective experiences and perspectives of 30 civically or politically active Muslims. Hence, given its interpretivist and subjectivistic paradigm, this study cannot draw any representative conclusions on the nature of Muslims' civic and political participation in the two national settings. Future research is necessary to build on the findings of this study by pursuing a more quantitative approach, producing data suitable for statistical analysis and, ideally, representative findings about various aspects of Muslims' performed citizenship. Such empirical data could then also provide the platform for closer examination of the impact of political opportunity structures and other explanatory factors.

Linked to the lack of representativeness is another methodological limitation: the problem of selection bias. The overall picture of Muslim active citizenship, painted on the basis of the empirical evidence of this study, relies heavily on who is being selected as participants. It needs to be acknowledged that, while it is impossible to accurately quantify, some Muslim individuals and fringe organisations (e.g., certain Salafi groups) in Australia and Germany do advocate or pursue a deliberately exclusivist, self-segregationist or even (violently or not) anti-democratic agenda. These individuals and groups were not included in the sample. However, it is important to note that the sample was covering a broad range of Muslim community views, and it did not only encompass Muslim groups known for their integrationist dialogue agenda (e.g., groups associated with the Gülen movement), but also a number of Islamic organisations with a rather orthodox reading of Islam and those with a strong intra-community focus on catering for Muslim communities. These include, for example, certain Muslim student associations, traditional mosque associations and Muslim umbrella organisations, and, in Germany, community organisations that have been under surveillance by the intelligence agencies due to suspected anti-constitutional tendencies or affiliations.

Another limitation of this study is attributed to its deliberate attempt to ensure a maximum diversity in terms of both the demographics of interviewed Muslims as well as their specific manifestations of active citizenship. This approach helped identify convergences between various types of civic and political participation, enacted by a range of Muslims—man and women, young and old, first and second generation—from various ethnic backgrounds and Islamic denominations. Thus, the study shed light on what can be described as the unspecific essence of Muslims' activism—their personal goals and motives, empowering factors and implications—across a range of manifestations of activism. While such a thematically broad approach has its merits, it also comes with limitations. The study cannot delve into the depths of analysing the specifics of certain types of civic and political participation, although this would generate a more detailed understanding of how Muslims' citizenship evolves in particular civic and political areas. For example, formal political participation, especially within political party contexts, deserves greater research attention. The theoretical model of minority representation in the electoral political arena, proposed by Bird et al. (2011a), and the various empirical studies in their edited volume (e.g., Wüst 2011) illustrate the need for more specific research in this particular area of active citizenship. The same applies to many other locations of Muslims' active involvement, be it in trade unions, student associations, Muslim and non-Muslim civil society groups or even in more informal forms of political activism (e.g., public protests) to name but a few. Active engagement of (young) Muslims through and within social media has also been insufficiently examined in this and previous studies.

Interview Sample

The fieldwork and data collection for this study took place between May and December 2013. Sixteen in-depth interviews were carried out with active self-identifying Muslims across Germany (May—July 2013, all conducted in German) in the states of North Rhine-Westphalia (NRW), Berlin, Lower Saxony, Baden-Wuertemberg and Bavaria, mostly in larger and medium size cities. The Australian fieldwork encompassed 14 interviews, conducted between August and December 2013 (all in English) in Melbourne and Sydney. The majority of interviews took approximately one hour; the shortest one was completed within around 30 minutes and others went for more than one and a half hours. There were no significant length differences between the interviews conducted in Germany and those carried out in Australia.

Seven interview partners in the German and two in the Australian sample chose to participate in this study anonymously; pseudonyms (spelt in *italics* throughout this study) were used when referring to them. All other 21 interview partners agreed to be named by their real name. As outlined in the methodology section, the selection process sought to obtain a diverse interview sample both in terms of the participants' demographics and their type of civic and/or political participation. This aim has been achieved (see Tables 2.2 and 2.3).

Age and Gender

In Australia, seven of the total 14 interview partners were conducted with women. The age of interview partners generally ranged between the early 20s to around 60 years of age, with one interviewed person being approximately 80 years old. The German sub-sample comprised of eight women and eight men aged between the early 20s and mid-50s.

Nationality and Origin

All interview partners in Australia hold Australian (legal) citizenship, but only four of them were actually born in Australia; six were born overseas but grew up (i.e., went to school) in Australia.[2] The remaining four were born and raised outside of Australia and immigrated as adults. Six of the 14 interviewed Australian Muslims were of Lebanese background, with most having been born overseas but raised in Australia. Two interview

---

[2] One moved to Australia when she was 11 or 12 years old, and then attended primary school.

Table 2.2 Key characteristics of Australian sample

				Australian sample		
ID	Name	Age[a]	Sex	Country born (background)	Country raised	Primary reason(s) for selection
AUS1	Omar Merhi	39	m	AUS (Lebanese)	AUS	Trade union representative
AUS2	Joumanah El Matrah	ca. 45	f	Lebanon	AUS	Community worker
AUS3	Berhan Ahmed	ca. 50	m	Eritrea	Sudan	African community activist, politician
AUS4	Hass Dellal	62	m	AUS (Turkish)	Turkey/ AUS	Executive Director of Australian Multicultural Foundation, SBS chair
AUS5	Saara Sabbagh	41	f	Lebanon	AUS	Muslim community worker
AUS6	*Serap* (anonymous)	35	f	AUS (Turkey)	AUS	Volunteer at a young Muslim women's group
AUS7	Abdul Kamareddine	27	m	Lebanon	Lebanon	Candidate in local council election
AUS8	Ferroz Sattar	28	m	AUS (Fiji)	AUS	Volunteer at Mission of Hope
AUS9	Maha Abdo	ca. 55	f	Lebanon	Lebanon/AUS	Muslim community worker, director of Muslim Women's organisation
AUS10	Sara Saleh	25	f	Egypt	AUS	Media and Public Affairs Coordinator at Amnesty International Australia
AUS11	Riad Galil	ca. 80	m	Egypt	Egypt	Representative of interfaith forum
AUS12	Mohamad Tabbaa	28	m	Lebanon	AUS	Board member of Islamic Council of Victoria
AUS13	Mehreen Faruqi	45–50	f	Pakistan	Pakistan	Politician (MP in NSW Upper House)
AUS14	*Ashtar* (anonymous)	ca. 24	f	Saudi Arabia (Iraqi)	AUS	Representative of Community Relations Commission NSW

[a]Age at the time of the interview; f, female; m, male; AUS, Australia; MP, member of parliament; NSW, News South Wales; Special Broadcasting Services (public radio and TV broadcaster)

Table 2.3 Key characteristics of German sample

				German sample		
ID	Name (ID)	Age[a]	sex	Country born (background)	Country raised	Primary reason(s) for selection
DE1	*Burak* (anonymous)	ca. 45	m	Germany (Turkish)	Germany	Local councillor
DE2	Nadia Al-Ammarine	44	f	Germany (Syrian)	Germany	Community worker at Muslim women's organisation
DE3	Erika Theißen	ca. 55	f	German (convert)	Germany	Community worker and director of Muslim women's organisation
DE4	Samir Fetić	40	m	Bosnia-Herzegovina	Germany$	Representative of Grüne Muslime (sub-group within political party The Greens)
DE5	Houaida Taraji	47	f	Syria	Germany	Representative of Central Council of Muslims
DE6	Ekrem Şenol	38	m	Germany (Turkish)	Germany	Media activist
DE7	*Esra* (anonymous)	27	f	Germany (Turkish)	Germany	Representative of Muslim youth network and of a socialist youth organisation
DE8	Hülya Dogan	38	f	Germany (Turkish)	Germany	Local councillor for alternative political initiative
DE9	Fatih Cicek	21	m	Germany (Turkish)	Germany	Representative of Muslim youth network

(*continued*)

Table 2.3 (continued)

				German sample		
ID	Name (ID)	Age[a]	sex	Country born (background)	Country raised	Primary reason(s) for selection
DE10	Erdin Aydin	40–45	m	Turkey	Turkey/ Germany	Engagement in local cross-community network, representative of local Migration Council
DE11	*Alev* (anonymous)	38	f	Germany (Turkish)	Germany	Representative and founder of Muslim organisation for dialogue and education
DE12	*Miran* (anonymous)	23	f	Germany (Turkish)	Germany	Representative of Turkish-German sub-group of the Social Democratic Party
DE13	*Leyla* (anonymous)	22	f	Germany (Turkish)	Germany	Chair of Muslim student association
DE14	Bayram Yerli	43	m	Turkey	Turkey/ Germany	Chairman of mosque association
DE15	*Asim* (anonymous)	24	m	Pakistan	Germany	Representative of Muslim youth organisation
DE16	*Onur* (anonymous)	29	m	Germany (Turkish)	Germany	Trade union activist

[a]Age at the time of the interview; f, female; m, male

partners were of Egyptian heritage, further two were of Turkish origin (both born in Australia) and the other participants were of Iraqi, Fiji, Pakistani and Eritrean background (the latter two were not raised in Australia).

While the interview sampling process did not deliberately seek to mirror the overall demographics of the Muslim community in Australia, the composition of the interview partners does reflect in some ways the national-cultural diversity of the Muslim community in Australia. According to the 2011 census, Lebanese are the largest ancestry group of Muslims in Australia, and all the other countries of origin represented in this interview sample are among the top ten countries of Muslim heritage in Australia (Peucker et al. 2014: 287). Moreover, the sample encompasses a relatively large proportion of overseas-born Muslims, similar to the general demographics of Muslims in Australia. It is also indicative of the high citizenship rate that all interview partners hold Australian citizenship.

In the German sample, at least four (possibly up to six) Muslims did not have German citizenship at the time of the interview, although none of the 16 interview partners immigrated to Germany as an adult. Ten were born in Germany and the other six came at a young age and were raised and schooled in Germany. Thus, in contrast to the Australian sample, not a single interview partner in Germany can be described as a first generation immigrant. Eleven participants were of Turkish background and the others were of Syrian (two), Bosnian (one) and Pakistani (one) origin, and one interviewed woman was a German convert. This high proportion of people with Turkish heritage among Muslims in Germany reflects the general demographics of Muslims in Germany (Chap. 4). The fact that at least four interview partners did not have full citizenship rights is indicative of the generally lower citizenship rate among (Muslim) immigrants and minorities in Germany compared with their Australian counterparts.

Religiosity

All 30 interview partners described themselves as Muslims. They differed greatly, however, with regards to their religiosity, ranging from non-practicing to highly devout, and their personal religious convictions, which sometimes aligned with rather traditional orthodox views and in other instances represented highly individualised interpretation of their

Islamic faith. This diversity could be found in both sub-samples. Although the selection process did not deliberately try to ensure religious diversity among the Muslim interview partners, various denominational groups ended up in the sample, such as Alevi (of Turkish background, in the German sub-sample), Shia (in the Australian sub-sample) and, of course, Sunnis. A substantial number of interview partners in both countries can be broadly described as followers of a spiritual Islam (Sufism), and some of those of Turkish background have expressed personal affiliation with, or inspiration by, the global Hizmet or Gülen movement, both in the German and the Australian sample.[3] Most interview partners did not explicitly state their Islamic denomination, and it was outside the scope of the interview guidelines to identify their specific Islamic orientation or religious practices.

Education and Occupational Background

The German and the Australian samples comprised primarily well-educated Muslims, with many of them holding a university degree. This large proportion of highly educated Muslims does not represent the on average lower level of educational qualifications and attainments of all Muslims in Australia and Germany.

Of the 14 interviewed Australian Muslims, 11 have a university degree, including two who were currently enrolled in a Master's (AUS8) and a PhD program (AUS12). Four interview partners have obtained their doctorate (all from an Australian university), including one interview partner with an Honorary Doctorate in social sciences (AUS4) with the

---

[3] The Hizmet or Gülen movement is a growing global movement of contemporary Islam, led or inspired by the Islamic preacher Fethullah Gülen, who was born in Anatolia, Turkey, and currently lives in exile in the US. Supporters and adherents of Gülen's religious and social views both within Muslim majority as well as in other Western countries, including Germany and Australia, have been very active in promoting education (e.g., from tutoring centres to university chairs and private schools) and interfaith dialogue. The Gülen movement can be described as being inspired by Sufi Islam, with the leader Said Nursi being particularly influential; Yavuz (2013), an expert on the Gülen movement, describes the movement as both communitarian as well as liberal and tolerant to other groups.

other three obtaining a PhD in technical academic fields of engineering (AUS7, AUS13) and forest science (AUS3). Three of those four with a doctorate are first generation immigrants who came to Australia as adults and undertook their entire secondary education overseas (AUS3, AUS7, AUS13).

The occupations of the Australian interview partners at the time of the interview included teacher, community worker, university lecturer, trade union employee, radio presenter at a public broadcaster, public relations officer at amnesty international and one full-time politician. One person was retired and one was unemployed and looking for part-time employment after completing his PhD.[4] Altogether five interviewed Muslims in Australia used to work, or are still working, within the secondary or tertiary education system.

The German sub-sample was also characterised by participants' above average educational and occupational status, although it seems to be on average slightly lower than the Australian sample. Twelve of the total of 16 interview partners in Germany attained the highest secondary school degree (*Abitur*), which is a precondition for studying at a university in Germany.[5] Six of them subsequently completed their university degree; four are currently studying at university and the other two studied at tertiary level (medicine and law) but did not finish their degree. At least two interview partners worked as blue collar workers (printing machinist and metal worker), while the others were in white collar jobs, working as a self-employed medical doctor, medical therapist, financial expert (within a large corporation), trade union employee, freelance graphic designer, community worker and administration office employee.

---

[4] The only unemployed person in the Australian sample stated that his family in Lebanon is 'well-off' and financially supports him (AUS7). He made it clear that without this support he would not have been able to volunteer to that extent.

[5] In addition, one interviewee (DE16) obtained *Fachabitur*, which entitles him to tertiary studies at only certain types of universities (e.g. universities for applied science).

References

Bird, K., Saalfeld, T., & Wüst, A. M. (2011a). Ethnic diversity, political participation and representation: A theoretical framework. In K. Bird, T. Saalfeld, & A. M. Wüst (Eds.), *The political representation of immigrants and minorities. Voters, parties and parliaments in liberal democracies* (pp. 1–21). London: Routledge.

Fetzer, J., & Soper, J. C. (2005). *Muslims and the state in Britain, France, and Germany*. New York: Cambridge University Press.

Glaser, B. G., & Strauss, A. L. (1967). *Discovery of grounded theory: Strategies for qualitative research*. Chicago: Aldine.

Peucker, M., & Akbarzadeh, S. (2014). *Muslim active citizenship in the West*. London/New York: Routledge.

Peucker, M., Roose, J. M., & Akbarzadeh, S. (2014). Muslim active citizenship in Australia: Socioeconomic challenges and the emergence of a Muslim elite. *Australian Journal of Political Science, 49*(2), 282–299.

Strauss, A., & Corbin, J. (1998). *Basics of qualitative research: Techniques and procedures for developing grounded theory*. Thousand Oaks: Sage.

Thomas, W. I., & Thomas, D. S. (1928). *The child in America: Behavior problems and programs*. New York: Alfred A. Knopf.

Walker, D., & Myrick, F. (2006). Grounded theory: An exploration of process and procedure. *Qualitative Health Research, 16*(4), 547–559.

Wüst, A. M. (2011). Migrants as parliamentary actors in Germany. In K. Bird, T. Saalfeld, & A. M. Wüst (Eds.), *The political representation of immigrants and minorities. Voters, parties and parliaments in liberal democracies* (pp. 250–265). London: Routledge.

Yavuz, M. H. (2013). *Toward an Islamic enlightenment: The Gülen movement*. Oxford: Oxford University Press.

4

Muslims in Australia and Germany: Demographics, Resources, Citizenship

This chapter contextualises the empirical study on Muslims' civic and political engagement in Australia and Germany by providing an overview on the demographic and socioeconomic situation of Muslims in both countries. According to the Civic Voluntarism Model (Verba et al. 1995), resources and skills enable citizens to become politically active, and there is evidence that these facilitating factors apply to both political and civic participation. This chapter also elaborates on various dimensions of Muslim citizenship, based on existing research, namely their legal status, sense of belonging, recognition (or lack thereof) and participation.

Demographics of Muslims

Although there was a very modest Muslim presence in Australia and Germany already in the nineteenth and early twentieth century (Abdullah 1981; Cleland 2001), today's communities in both countries have emerged and consolidated almost entirely as a result of post-World War II immigration processes, especially since the 1960s and 1970s (Peucker and Akbarzadeh 2014).

© The Author(s) 2016
M. Peucker, *Muslim Citizenship in Liberal Democracies*,
DOI 10.1007/978-3-319-31403-7_4

Australia

In Australia, the 1971 census counted only 22,000 Muslims, less than 0.2 % of the total population. The size of their communities increased to around 200,000 people in 1996 and 340,000 in 2006 (1.7 %). Since then the number of people who identify as Muslims has continued to grow by almost 40 % to 476,292 people in 2011, according to the latest census figures. This constitutes 2.2 % of the Australian population and makes Islam the second largest minority religion after Buddhism (Peucker et al. 2014).

This proportion of just over 2 % stands in contrast to the high concentration of Muslims in certain urban localities. An analysis of the 2011 Census data shows that the vast majority of Muslims live in New South Wales (NWS; 46 %) and Victoria (32 %), with almost all of them (around 95 %) residing in the metropolitan areas of Sydney and Melbourne. Within these large cities, Muslims tend to gravitate towards certain urban pockets, where they constitute an often large proportion of the local population. In some neighbourhoods in Sydney, for example, Lakemba-Wiley Park and Punchbowl, one in two or one in three residents are of Islamic faith. In Melbourne, the spatial concentration of Muslims is only slightly lower (e.g., 42 % in Meadow Heights and around 25 % in Broadmeadows or Fawkner) (ABS 2012).

Thirty eight percent of all Muslims were born in Australia; hence, the majority of Muslims are first generation immigrants. The ratio of Australian-born Muslims has not changed much over the past decade (36.4 % in 2001 and 37.9 % in 2006), which indicates—given the general growth of the Muslim population—ongoing immigration and new settlement processes of Muslims. Census figures show that one in five Muslims who lived in Australia in August 2011 had arrived within the previous five years, and just under one third had lived in Australia for no more than 10 years. Despite this young immigration history almost three quarters of Muslims hold Australian citizenship (74.1 %). A special analysis found that naturalisation rates are particularly high among immigrants from many of those countries where Muslims predominantly come from (Smith et al. 2011).

Overseas-born Muslims have come from across the world, the main countries of birth being Lebanon, Pakistan, Afghanistan, Turkey and Bangladesh (Fig. 4.1). The relative majority of Muslims in Australia con-

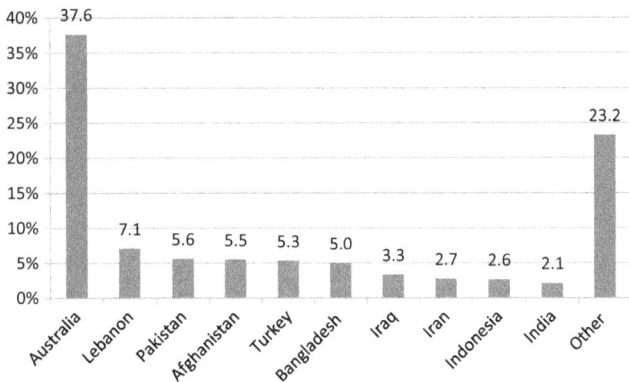

Fig. 4.1 Top ten countries of birth of Muslims (2001, 2006 and 2011)
Source: ABS 2012 (Table Builder; own tabulation)

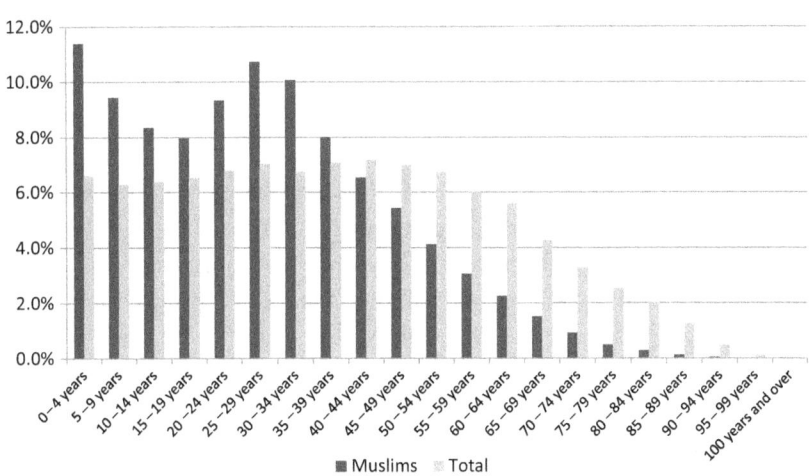

Fig. 4.2 Age profile of Muslims and total population in Australia (2011)
Source: ABS 2012

sider their ancestry to be Lebanese (16 %), Turkish (11 %) and 6 % each as Pakistani, Afghan and Australian respectively (ABS 2012).

Muslims in Australia are on average much younger than the population as a whole. The 2011 census data showed that they are overrepresented in all age brackets up to 40 years and underrepresented in all other age groups (Fig. 4.2). In 2011, 29 % of Muslims were younger than 15 years of age (total population, 19 %), 17 % were 15–24 years of age (total population, 13 %), 29 % were 25–40 years of age (total population, 21 %) and only 3 % of Muslims were 65 years of age or older, in contrast to 14 % of the total population (ABS 2012).

Germany

Although official population statistics on Muslims in Germany do not exist, there is no doubt that Islam has been for many years the largest minority religion in Germany. The representative study Muslim Life in Germany (MLG)[1], which has provided a previously unknown degree of statistical insights into the demographics of the Muslim population, concluded that an estimated four million (self-declared) Muslims were living in Germany (Haug et al. 2009). This number only refers to Muslims with a personal or family migration history ('migration background') and does not include German converts or Muslims whose parents were both born in Germany. These four million Muslims constitute about 5 % of the total population and approximately 25 % of all first and second generation migrants in Germany. While Muslims in Germany have come from every corner of the world, the largest group in terms of national origin is, and has been, of Turkish descent. They make up more than 60 % of all Muslims in Germany. Other major national ancestry groups are Muslims from Southeast Europe (14 %), the Middle East (8 %), North Africa (7 %) and Southeast Asia (5 %) (Haug et al. 2009: 81; Table 4.1). Latest immigration statistics indicate that the national composition of Muslim communities is diversifying to an unprecedented degree, as the net immigration from Turkey has dropped and influx from other Muslim-majority countries has gained more momentum (BAMF 2015: 182–186).

Like other immigrant communities the Muslim population is predominantly urban. There are no specific empirical data on the spatial con-

---

[1] The MLG study was based on a survey among 6000 (Muslim and non-Muslim) migrants and their descendants from around 50 Muslim-majority countries. The survey was carried out in eight different community languages so that the respondents' German proficiency would not affect their participation in the survey. This survey became and remains the key resource for statistical examinations of Muslims in Germany, despite its methodological limitations deriving from its focus on first and second generation immigrants only.

Table 4.1 Main countries and regions of origin of Muslims in Germany

Country of origin	Number (mean value)	Percentage
Turkey	2 561 028	63.2 %
South East Europe	549 658	13.6 %
among those: former Yugoslavia	536 740	
Albania	11 585	
Middle East	329 652	8.1 %
among those: Lebanon	127 804	
Iraq	97 978	
Egypt	37 863	
Syria	35 271	
Yemen/Jordan	25 509	
Iran	70 096	1.7 %
North Africa	279 720	6.9 %
among those: Morocco	163 666	
Africa (without North Africa)	61 426	1.5 %
South/Southeast Asia	186 332	4.6 %
among those: Afghanistan	89 248	
Pakistan	67 992	
Bangladesh	13 545	
Central Asia/CIS	17 222	0.4 %
Total (all countries and regions)	4 055 129	100 %

Source: Haug et al. (2009: 81)

centration of Muslims, but an analysis of over 1800 spatial clusters in 33 western German cities found a relatively low level of spatial segregation among selected nationality groups. In only very few of these urban clusters, the Turkish population added up to more than 10 % of all local residents (Schönwälder and Söhn 2009). Although these findings referred to national instead of religious immigrant groups, they do suggest that Muslims in Germany tend to live less concentrated and spatially more dispersed across urban neighbourhoods than their Australian counterparts.

Robust data are also lacking on the proportion of Muslims born in Germany. The large-scale MLG study surveyed only first and second generation immigrants and so drew a skewed picture in this regard with a bias towards those born abroad. The survey found that about 70 % of all Muslim respondents with a personal or family migration history immigrated to Germany; just under one-third were born in Germany (Haug et al. 2009: 116). This average share of German-born Muslims was found to differ substantially depending on the national background.

For example, the survey found that the proportion of second generation Muslims of Turkish and North African origin were clearly above the average 30 % mark. Official statistics broken down by national origin show that around half of all three million people of Turkish origin in Germany did not migrate themselves, while almost 80 % of people from the Middle East are first generation immigrants (DESTATIS 2012: 56–62). Thus, one can conclude that there are large and well-established Muslim communities primarily of Turkish immigrants and their descendants, born in Germany, as well as communities of more recent arrivals from various other countries of origin (e.g., Afghanistan, Arabic countries).

Muslims continue to immigrate to Germany, but the scope of their influx has been fairly moderate in recent years compared with previous immigration periods.[2] This is another interesting difference to Muslims in Australia. The predominant immigration channel through which Muslims enter Germany is family reunification, especially from Turkey, and humanitarian immigration, especially from Afghanistan, Iraq, Iran, Pakistan and more recently, Syria. The number of recent arrivals of immigrants from Muslim majority countries who come to Germany through other schemes, for example as students or highly qualified workers, has remained negligible.

Similar to Australia, Muslim communities in Germany are characterised by their very young age profile. Muslims are on average much younger than the general population and also non-Muslim (first or second generation) migrants. Haug et al. (2009: 104) found that one in four Muslims was younger than 15 years of age, while this applied to less than 15 % of the population as a whole and to 23 % of all people with a personal or family migration history. Moreover, Muslims were slightly overrepresented in the working age bracket, while being extremely underrepresented among those of retirement age (65 years of age and older).

The representative MLG study of Haug et al. (2009: 125) reported that Muslims had lived in Germany for an average of 23.5 years. There were substantial differences between the various nationality groups.

---

[2] *This book was completed before the arrival of large numbers of predominantly Muslim refugees from Syria and other Muslim majority countries in 2015 and 2016. The Muslim population in Germany is assumed to have changed significantly as a result of these developments, but the extent of these change has not been accurately investigated yet.*

Muslims of Turkish origin, for example, had lived in Germany for a particularly long time (27 years), while Muslims from other regions predominately settled in Germany in more recent times. In stark contrast to the situation in Australia and despite the average very long residence in Germany, the majority of Muslims in Germany do not have equal political rights. While official statistics on Muslims' legal citizenship are lacking, the representative MLG study (Haug et al. 2009) found not even 40 % of self-declared Muslims enjoy full political rights as German citizens. This is the same ratio that Brettfeld and Wetzels (2007: 85) discovered a few years earlier in their representative survey among Muslims in Germany. Further statistical analysis suggests that the low citizenship rate can be attributed to a combination of legal barriers in the access to citizenship (see Chap. 5), and a generally low personal inclination among foreign residents to apply for citizenship, especially among Turkish nationals, among whom a vast majority would formally qualify for naturalisation (DESTATIS 2013: 127–140; Sauer 2014: 109).

***

The Muslim population in Australia and Germany are both characterised by their very young age profile and more specifically by the high proportion of under-aged children. This is an important factor in explaining lower volunteering and political participation rate of Muslims in Germany and Australia. The majority of Muslims in both countries are first generation immigrants. These recent immigration processes have resulted in ethno-religious pluralisation of the society at large, and has also led to an unprecedented degree of diversity within Muslim communities themselves. Settlement processes of these recent arrivals are likely to affect their readiness to actively engage in civic and political participation.

Muslims in Australia and Germany differ enormously in terms of their legal status. While around 75 % of Muslims in Australia enjoy full political rights as (formally) equal citizens, around 60 % of Muslims in Germany do not have citizenship rights and are consequently excluded from voting in general elections or running for a political office. On a more general note, holding citizenship rights may have broader implications for the tendency for public engagement. Ruud Koopmans (2004), for example, discovered in the late 1990s a statistically significant positive correlation between migrants' naturalisation rate and the level of migrants' active participation in the public debate in Germany. He concluded that through naturalisation many migrants 'obtain the right to vote and thereby gain a political leverage that makes them more relevant as speakers in the public discourse' (2004: 461).

Socioeconomic Status and Education of Muslims

Community work and political participation are more common among people with a higher degree of educational resources and socioeconomic status. This has been confirmed by various empirical studies on political participation and civic volunteering. Although the causal relationship between education and socioeconomic status, on the one hand, and civic engagement, on the other hand, is a matter of ongoing scholarly discussions (Berinsky and Lenz 2011; Cohen et al. 2001), Muslims' educational attainments, labour market position and their financial situation are important factors to consider when analysing their civic and political participation.

Australia

In Australia[3], Muslims are in some ways educational overachievers, as they are significantly overrepresented among those with a university degree (Bachelor, graduate and post-graduate level). Muslims are, however, also less likely to hold a post-secondary educational degree at the certificate or Diploma level, obtained usually outside the university sector, and they are overrepresented among those who have no educational degree beyond a completed high school Year 12. The 2011 census data painted an ambiguous picture of Muslims' educational situation. While a substantial and growing number of Muslims held a university degree, 53 % reportedly had no post-secondary education, compared with 46 % of the total population, with 28 % of Muslims

---

[3] The 2011 census statistics presented in this section on Australia have been included in a previous article by the author; they all refer to Peucker et al. (2014) unless indicated otherwise.

leaving high school without finishing their final year (total population, 29 %) (Fig. 4.3).

Being able to speak the language of the country of residence is vital for many forms of civic engagement, especially those that involve cross-community interaction in the political arena or civil society. The vast majority of Muslims in Australia consider their English proficiency to be very high or fairly high. According to the 2011 census data, 82 % Muslims speak either only English (13.0 %) or they speak English as a second language very well (46.5 %) or well (22.9 %). Around 16 % of all Muslims in Australia had poor ('speak not well', 11.4 %) or no English language skills at all (4.2 %). Not surprisingly, recent immigrants were overrepresented in this low English proficiency group, while around 86 % of Australian-born Muslims professed no difficulties communicating in English (ABS 2012). However, more than one in 10 Muslims born in Australia could speak English either 'not well' (5.6 %) or not at all (5.3 %). Interestingly, the latter proportion was slightly higher than among Muslims who were born overseas.

Muslims in Australia continue to occupy a disadvantaged socio-economic position. In 2011 their unemployment rate was at 12.6 %,

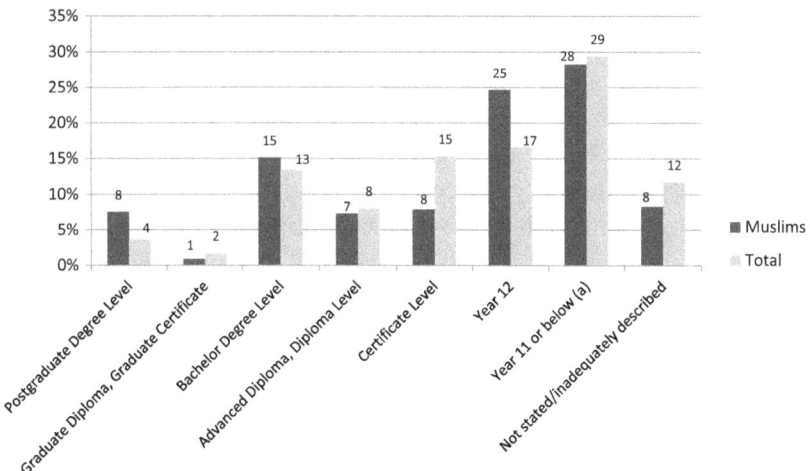

Fig. 4.3 Highest educational attainment of Muslims and total population, Australia (2011)
Source: ABS 2012 (customised unpublished data packet) (a) Includes 'no educational attainment'

compared to 5.6 % in the total population. The disparities have decreased—albeit rather slowly—over the past decade. In 2001, almost one in five Muslims was unemployed, while the national average was at 7.4 %. Muslims' high unemployment rates appear not predominantly attributed to recent immigration and subsequent adjustment processes during early stages of settlement. An analysis of the 2011 census data reveals that Australian-born Muslims are only slightly less often unemployed (11.8 %) than Muslims in general.

The educational divide between highly educated Muslims with a university degree and those with no post-secondary education is in some ways reflected in the occupational status of Muslims. Around 30 % of all employed Muslims in Australia work as managers (9.2 %) or professionals (20.3 %), which is almost five percentage points below the national average (12.9 % and 21.3 %, respectively). Muslims are less likely to work in clerical jobs or as administration workers (11.4 %, compared to an average of 14.8 %) and they are overrepresented in low-skill occupations, often characterised by strenuous working conditions and bad working hours, such as drivers, machinery operators and labourers (22.0 %, compared to 16.0 %).

This disadvantaged labour market position has implications for Muslims' financial situation. The 2011 census data highlighted that Muslims have substantially less income than the general population. For example, 43 % of all Muslims aged 15 years or older reported having a personal annual income of less than AU$ 16,000, while this applied to only 26 % of the population as a whole in this age bracket (the younger age profile of Muslims may also contribute to these disparities). Overseas-born Muslims from Afghanistan or Lebanon were even more likely to have less than these AU$16,000 per year (53.4 % and 47.5 %, respectively). In all higher income brackets Muslims were underrepresented. Consistent with this lower personal income level, Muslims' households also had significantly less financial means than the national average. One in 10 Muslim households reported earnings of less than AU$ 200 per week (including negative and no income), compared with 4 % of all Australian households. Furthermore, 24 % of Muslim households had no more than AU$ 400 (compared to 16.5 % of all households). In all weekly income groups above AU$ 600, Muslims were underrepresented.

Germany

In Germany, Muslims consistently reach lower secondary school attainments than the general population and compared with many other migrant and minority groups. The MLG survey (Haug et al. 2009) of first and second generation immigrants from Muslim majority countries (16 years of age and older) found that 15 % of Muslim and 7 % of non-Muslim respondents had no formal school qualifications (Fig. 4.4). As a point of reference, according to official statistics, about 3 % of the total population do not have any formal school qualification (DESTATIS 2012: 150–151).

The MLG survey by Haug et al. (2009) revealed major differences in the educational attainment of Muslims from different national origins. Muslims of Turkish background and from the Middle East, for example, more often had no formal qualifications (16.5 % and 17.1 %, respectively), while the figure for Muslims from Southeast Europe in the survey was 6.3 %. Muslims in Germany were also on average less likely to hold an upper secondary school degree, which is a formal requirement to studying at a university. Just over one-third of all surveyed Muslims had attained the higher school degree, compared to 42 % of the non-Muslim survey sample. Again, Muslims of Turkish origin were underrepresented

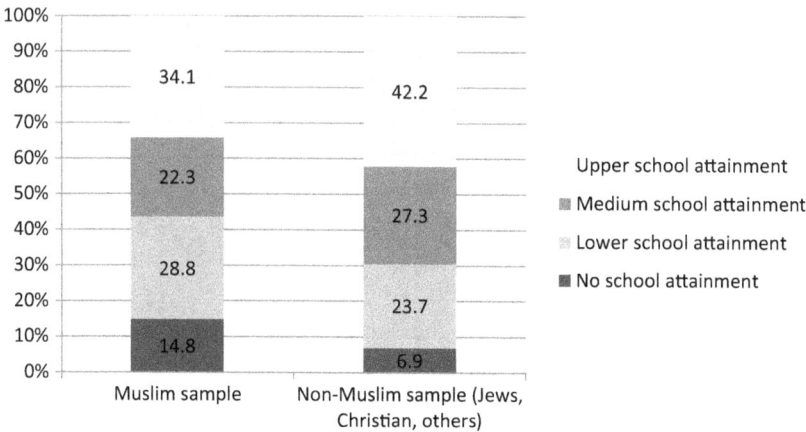

Fig. 4.4 Educational attainment of Muslims in Germany
Source: Haug, Müssig and Stichs 2009: 211

among those with a higher secondary education degree (27.5 %), while more than eight in 10 Muslims of Iranian background had attained an upper secondary school degree. These patterns of educational underachievement among Muslims, especially those of Turkish origin, applies in principle to those who have undergone schooling in Germany as well as those who went to school in their country of origin (Haug et al. 2009: 212).

The official population statistics in Germany, the Micro-Census, does not differentiate by religion but by national origin. This census has confirmed the educational underachievement of Turkish immigrants, and paints a bleaker picture in comparison to the total population. First and second generation immigrants of Turkish origin have been extremely underrepresented among those with an upper secondary degree and overrepresented among those without any secondary school degree (Table 4.2). Moreover, they are much more likely to have no occupational qualifications and are particularly underrepresented among those with a university degree (Table 4.3). Given the large number of Muslims of Turkish background, their educational underperformance skews the general statistical picture of Muslims' educational performance. This 'Turkish bias' conceals major disparities between Muslim groups from different national backgrounds and, more specifically, the higher performance of some Muslim subgroups.

Haug et al. (2009: 243–244) found that around 60 % of their respondents considered their German language skills to be very good or good. Most others described their language proficiency as 'average' (28 %); only a small minority stated that their German was poor (8 %), very poor (1 %) or that they did not speak any German (2 %). Muslims of Turkish and of African (other than North Africa) origin were slightly overrepresented among those with lower German proficiency, but even among those only a minority of 15 % and 13 %, respectively, spoke German poorly or not at all.

While the data situation on the socioeconomic status of Muslims is poor in Germany, statistics generally indicate that Muslims are socioeconomically disadvantaged. Haug et al. (2009: 223) found that 5.6 % of all Muslim respondents 16 years of age and older were unemployed and currently looking for work, 51.2 % were employed and 21.4 % were

Table 4.2 Secondary school degree by sex, 2013

	Still/not yet in education system		Lower secondary school degree		Intermediary secondary school degree		Upper secondary school degree (Fachabitur)		Upper secondary school degree (Abitur)		No secondary school degree
	m	f	m	f	m	f	m	f	m	f	All
Total Population	17.0	15.5	29.8	30.4	17.3	21.3	7.2	4.7	18.8	17.9	3.2
All first/second generation migrants	27.2	25.9	25.5	21.4	15.4	17.2	4.8	4.4	16.7	19.3	9.8
					Among those						
Of Turkish background	30.4	31.0	28.3	23.3	12.6	12.4	3.2	2.7	8.1	6.7	19.8
Of Middle Eastern background[a]	25.2	25.4	23.3	18.3	22.0	25.6	4.5	5.4	13.9	15.3	9.1

Source: DESTATIS (2014: 248–249)

[a] Includes Iran, Iraq, Uzbekistan, Turkmenistan, Tadzhikistan, Kirgizstan, Georgia, Azerbaijan, Armenia, Kazakhstan and 'other countries' in the region (e.g. Jordan, Israel, Lebanon and Syria) f, female; m, male

Table 4.3 Selected occupational/tertiary education qualifications by sex, 2013

	Apprenticeship		Higher tertiary degree (university for applied science)		Higher tertiary degree (university)		No occupational qualification[a]	
	m	f	m	f	m	F	m	f
Total population	41.7	39.8	6.0	3.3	8.8	7.5	10.6	18.8
All first/second generation migrants	26.8	22.1	3.2	2.5	7.3	8.6	22.7	28.5
Among those								
Of Turkish background	21.3	13.9	1.1	0.7	2.4	1.5	34.4	43.6
Of Middle Eastern background[b]	27.9	26.1	3.3	3.1	5.8	7.0	24.1	26.1

Source: DESTATIS (2014: 282–284)
[a] Excluding those still in secondary or tertiary education or apprenticeship
[b] Includes Iran, Iraq, Uzbekistan, Turkmenistan, Tadzhikistan, Kirgizstan, Georgia, Azerbaijan, Armenia, Kazakhstan and 'other countries' in the region (e.g. Jordan, Israel, Lebanon and Syria). f, female; m, male

undertaking vocational training or other (mostly post-secondary) education. The rest were either retired, on parental leave or stated they were doing unpaid house/family work. Marked disparities occur across different countries of origin (Fig. 4.5) and between male and female respondents. Employment rates of men are generally fairly high, and hardly any of the male respondents stated that they stayed home to do house/family work. Muslim men from the Middle East (15.9 %), from North Africa (9.3 %) and the rest of Africa (13.6 %) were particularly often unemployed. Between 14 and 21 % of all working-aged Muslim women stated that they were neither employed nor in any educational or training courses, but were looking after the home and the family. Only among non-Muslim women from Turkey and Muslim women from African countries (other than North Africa), this proportion was much higher (36.4 % and 33.3 %, respectively).

4 Muslims in Australia and Germany 73

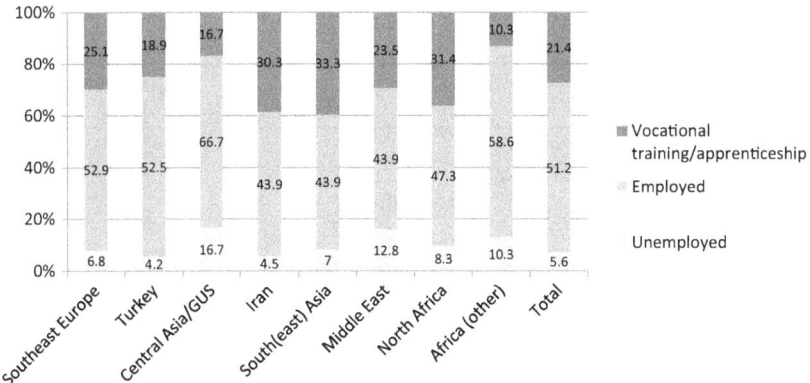

Fig. 4.5 Labour force status of Muslims by country/region of origin, Germany (2008)
Source: Haug, Müssig and Stichs 2009: 223

How do Muslims compare to the general population? The Micro-Census offers some proxy data on first and second generation immigrants from Muslim majority countries and regions, such as Turkey or the Middle East. Especially, statistics on the almost three million people with Turkish background provide quantitatively relevant (although skewed 'due to the 'Turkish bias') hints to the situation of Muslims. These official population data suggest major labour market disadvantages. People of Turkish origin are, for example, much more likely to be unemployed than the general population (13.3 % compared to 5.9 %). First and second generation immigrants from the Middle East also occupy a disadvantaged labour market position, although their unemployment rate is lower than among their Turkish counterparts and their labour market availability is particularly high (Table 4.4).

Muslims in Germany do not only resemble their Australian counterparts in terms of their higher unemployment rate; they also work more often in blue collar jobs, characterised by lower social prestige, than the population as a whole. This is evident in the Micro-Census statistics presented in Table 4.5. More than one in two economically active first or second generation immigrants from Turkey and the Middle East, for example, are employed as blue collar workers, while this applies only to one quarter of the total working population and to 41 % of all people with a migration background.

Table 4.4 Employment status and inactivity rate of selected groups in Germany, 2011

	Not in the work force	Unemployment rate[a]
Total Population	48.2	5.9
All first/second generation migrants	51.2	9.5
Among those		
Of Turkish background	54.2	13.3
Of Middle Eastern background[b]	47.0	12.2

Calculation on the basis of total numbers provided by Destatis (2012: 290, 300)
[a] *Proportion of those unemployed in relation to all persons available to the labour market*
[b] *Includes Iran, Iraq, Uzbekistan, Turkmenistan, Tadzhikistan, Kirgizstan, Georgia, Azerbaijan, Armenia, Kazakhstan and 'other countries' in the region (e.g. Jordan, Israel, Lebanon and Syria)*

Table 4.5 Occupational status of selected groups in Germany, 2010

	Blue collar workers	White collar workers	Self-employed	Civil servant
Total population	26.2	56.9	11.0	5.2
All first/second generation migrants	41.1	47.0	10.2	1.1
Among those				
Of Turkish background	52.6	38.7	8.3	0.5
Of Middle Eastern background[a]	50.6	40.6	7.68	0.8

Source: Destatis (2012: 280–281)
[a] *includes Iran, Iraq, Uzbekistan, Turkmenistan, Tadzhikistan, Kirgizstan, Georgia, Azerbaijan, Armenia, Kazakhstan and 'other countries' in the region (e.g. Jordan, Israel, Lebanon, Syria)*

These findings by national origin, as proxy for the situation of Muslims, were generally confirmed by Haug et al. (2009), who found that Muslims were more likely to work in blue-collar jobs than non-Muslims of the respective national background. This pattern, which applies to most nationality groups under analysis, was particularly dominant among Muslims from former 'guest worker' recruitment countries, like (ex-)Yugoslavia and Turkey. Muslims from Iran, Southeast Asia and the Middle East had higher rates for white-collar and self-employment (Haug et al. 2009: 131). The researchers posited that these disparities appear partially attributed to factors related to Germany's history of 'guest worker' immigration and structural changes of the German economy, but they also pinpoint a persistently lower level of socioeconomic mobility among many (Muslim) immigrant groups (2009: 229).

The disadvantaged labour market position has implications for Muslims' financial situation. Data on the income of Muslim households is not available in Germany, but Micro-Census data offer insights into the financial situation of first and second generation immigrants' households. The net income of households whose primary earner is of Turkish descent is significantly below the general household average, and households with a national background from the Middle East have even less financial resources at their disposal (Table 4.6). Comparing these data with those from previous years indicate an upwards development. It is worth highlighting, however, that 'Turkish' households are on average much larger than households of the general population (e.g., less one-person households). Thus, on an individual level, the disparities in terms of available financial resources and poverty levels of people of Turkish background and the general population is much larger than these household income statistics suggest.

***

What Muslim communities in Australia and Germany have in common is their on average lower socioeconomic status and disadvantaged financial situation, which might contribute to making Muslims on average less likely to be involved in political activism and civic volunteering. Muslims in both countries more often than the total average population struggle financially, which may hamper their time and monetary resources that could be put into voluntary (and unpaid) forms of civic and political participation. The other factor that supposedly affects the likelihood of civic engagement is higher education and, related to that, civic skills and language proficiency. For the vast majority of Muslims in both Australia and Germany, there are no significant language barriers; most of them have a good command of English or German, respectively. However, a small group of Muslims—and they are not all first generation immigrants—lack basic (English or German) language skills. That is not to say that these Muslims cannot become active citizens and, for example, engage in community work, but the spectrum of their potential civic engagement is limited.

Table 4.6 Monthly household net income of selected groups in Germany, 2011

	<500	500–900	900–1300	1300–1500	1500–2000	2000–2600	2600–3200	3200–4500	>4500
Total population	2.3	10.0	13.8	7.4	15.5	14.6	10.1	12.1	8.1
				Head of household: first or second generation migrant					
Of Turkish background	2.4	10.9	14.1	7.1	17.5	17.5	11.1	9.4	3.2
Of Middle Eastern background[a]	3.5	15.8	15.7	7.1	15.2	16.1	9.8	8.1	3.0

Source: Destatis (2012: 204–205) (own calculations)
[a] includes Iran, Iraq, Uzbekistan, Turkmenistan, Tadzhikistan, Kirgizstan, Georgia, Azerbaijan, Armenia, Kazakhstan and 'other countries' in the region (e.g. Jordan, Israel, Lebanon, Syria)

In terms of their formal education degree, Muslim communities in Australia and Germany differ with regards to their higher tertiary education attainments. Australian Muslims are overrepresented among those Australians with a university degree, with around one in four Muslims holding a Bachelor, graduate or post-graduate degree. This continuously increasing proportion of highly educated Muslims illustrates the rapid accumulation of human capital among communities and suggests an evolvement of an articulate civic Muslim elite in Australia, as Peucker et al. (2014) argue. Such a development is not entirely absent but it is less advanced among Muslims in Germany, who on average appear to be less successful in the education system. This is likely to affect Muslims' inclination to actively engage in various forms of civic and political participation (see also Pędziwiatr 2010).

Sense of Belonging

Beyond the dimension of holding full political rights and having 'time, money, and civic skills' (Verba et al. 1995: 271) to become civically and politically engaged, active citizenship is often tied to the individuals' self-identification as a member of society or a community. 'Any discussion of citizenship … remains inconclusive without reference to the need for belongingness', as the Australian scholar Samina Yasmeen put it (2007: 43). This emotional dimension resonates with the elaborations of the Syrian-born German scholar Bassam Tibi (2007) on European Muslims' path from being immigrants to becoming 'citizens of the heart'.

What Muslims in both countries have in common is that most of them regard their Islamic faith as a highly important dimension of their identity. This has been consistently demonstrated by representative studies on self-defined religiosity in Germany and by explorative surveys among Muslims in Australia. The MLG study, for example, reported that around 86 % of (self-identifying) Muslims described themselves as either very devout (36 %) or rather devout (50 %), with Muslims of Turkish and African origin showing particularly high rates of religiosity (Haug et al. 2009: 141; see also Bertelsmann Foundation 2008; Thielmann 2008: 15).

In Australia, studies on the situation of Muslims tend to have a 'bias towards those who self-identify as practicing Muslims', as Rachel Woodlock (2011: 397) critically maintains (also) about her own study. Against this backdrop, it may not be surprising that Woodlock's research and other surveys among Muslims in Australia have discovered a degree of subjective importance of Islamic belief among Australian Muslims that is even higher than among Muslims in Germany. In Woodlock's questionnaire-based survey of 200 Australian-born Muslims 72.5 % stated that preserving their Muslim identity was 'extremely important' and a further 24.5 % described it as 'very important' (12.5 %) or 'important' (12 %). Similarly, Shahram Akbarzadeh and his colleagues (Monash University 2009a: 24) found in their (non-representative) survey of 500 Muslims in Greater Melbourne that for 67 % of respondents their religion was 'completely important' in their personal life and for further 27 % it was 'important'. A recent survey among almost 600 Muslims from Sydney, based on face-to-face and telephone interviews, found that almost eight out of ten consider their religion to be very important and further 15 % describe it as important (Dunn et al. 2015: 24).

Differences between Muslims in Australia and Germany become more pronounced when examining their emotional attachment to, and self-identification with, the country they live in. Within the study *Voices Shaping the Perspective of Young Muslim Australians* a research team at the University of Technology Sydney conducted a survey among more than 300 young Muslims (Jakubowicz et al. 2012). The researchers found that more than nine out of 10 young Muslims regarded themselves as Australians, often without renouncing their ethnic or religious identity.

> In reality, young Muslim Australians overwhelmingly identify as Australian, *and* as Muslims, *and* as coming from a particular ethnic background. They do not see this as contradictory nor do they view these aspects of their identity as mutually exclusive (Jakubowicz et al. 2012: 43, emphasis in original).

This is consistent with other Australian survey results. In the above-mentioned study among Muslims in Sydney, 84 % agreed (or strongly agreed) with the statement 'I feel I am Australian', and only 6 % disagreed

(Dunn et al. 2015: 30). Similarly, in Woodlock's (2011) study, 84 % of Muslim respondents stated that preserving their Australian identity was extremely important (36 %), very important (27.5 %) or important (20.5 %), and was 'not at all important' for only 6 %.[4] In combination with the respondents' emphasis on also preserving their Islamic identity, these findings suggest that most Muslims in Australia do not seem to have a problem reconciling their civic and religious identity. This is confirmed by other survey findings, in which the vast majority of Muslims in Australia stated they 'can be a good Muslim and a good Australian': 85 % of the respondents in Woodlock's (2011) study expressed such an inclusive sense of multiple belonging. Similarly, the survey *Muslim Voices—Hopes & Aspirations*, which was conducted by a research team at Monash University (2009b: 18), found that almost all 300 Muslim respondents (93 %) agreed with the statement 'I can be a good Muslim and a good Australian'. Many of the overseas born Muslims in this survey considered their ethnic or national origin to be an additional dimension of their identity. Nearly half the Muslim respondents born overseas (most of them in Lebanon) expressed a strong (34.4 %) or very strong (13.1 %) relationship to their country of origin and 43 % described their relationship as 'average' (Monash University 2009b: 24).

Research findings suggest that Muslims in Germany identify on average less with their country of residence and more with their country of origin than their Australian counterparts. Their sense of belonging to the German society appears to be weaker, although studies vary substantially in their conclusions. Brettfeld and Wetzels (2007: 92) found in their representative survey that a minority of Muslims see themselves only (1.7 %) or rather (10.5 %) as 'being German'. Slightly less than one-third feel equally attached to both Germany and their country of origin (31.4 %), while 56 % feel emotional ties more (28 %) or exclusively (28 %) to their country of origin.

Such a low level of self-identification with being German among Muslims has also been revealed by two explorative local studies, carried out

---

[4] Similarly high rates of identification with Australian society have been found by Markus (2012b: 15) in the 2012 Scanlon Social Cohesion Neighbourhood Report. Nine of 10 surveyed Muslims had a great (51 %) or moderate (39 %) sense of belonging in Australia.

in multi-ethnic neighbourhoods in Berlin and Hamburg. Commissioned by the Open Society Institute as part of the *At Home in Europe* project (OSI 2010a), researchers conducted 100 in-depth interviews with Muslim residents (and an additional 100 with non-Muslims) in a range of European cities. In Berlin and Hamburg, Muslims' self-identification with Germany proved to be very low—and lower than in any other of the European cities examined (OSI 2010a). Of all Muslims interviewed in Berlin (half of them holding citizenship rights), for example, only one-quarter regarded themselves as German. However, more than eight out of 10 expressed a sense of belonging to their local (multiethnic) neighbourhood (Kreuzberg), and 72 % expressed strong feelings of belonging to Berlin (OSI 2010b: 51–58). This resonates with Ruud Koopmans' observation that 'many Turkish immigrants in Berlin find it difficult to see themselves as Germans, but unproblematically define themselves as Berliners' (2004: 450).

The MLG study (Haug et al. 2009: 298) painted a more positive picture of Muslims' identification with Germany. The survey questionnaire included two separate questions on the respondents' sense of belonging to Germany or their country of origin (in contrast to Brettfeld and Wetzels, where these two dimensions were used as two ends of *one* identity scale). Almost 70 % of Muslims declared that they have a very strong (27 %) or strong (42 %) emotional connection to Germany. A further 20 % said they felt partially connected, leaving around one in 10 Muslims who felt little (7 %) or no connection at all. In addition to this identification with Germany, many Muslims continue to feel emotionally connected to their country of origin. Around 60 % of surveyed Muslims expressed strong or very strong emotional ties with their country of origin, and only around one in 10 did not (or hardly) professed such 'homeland' oriented feelings.

Qualitative studies support the widespread hesitation among Muslims to fully identify as Germans, offering insights into the perceptions and feelings among Muslims that contribute to these emotional barriers. A multi-method research study found through focus group discussion that participating young Muslims consistently stressed one reason why they did not 'feel completely German' despite holding citizenship status: 'Even if one is born here, speaks German perfectly and has achieved something in life, one will never be accepted as "real" German by "the Germans'" (Frindte et al. 2011: 491, own translation).

Negating Recognition: Experiences of Exclusion

Another dimension of citizenship as equal membership, beside legal rights and a personal sense of belonging, refers to questions of recognition as full members of society and the political community. This is where Muslims in both countries face major hurdles. In the Australian context, Kolig and Kabir (2008: 270) concluded that among the many different cultural and ethnic minority groups living in the country, 'Muslims as a 'cultural' category … face the largest difficulty meeting the criteria of acceptable citizenship'. This reverberates in the German context with the widespread feeling among Muslims of not being recognised as full member of society in Germany. According to Brettfeld and Wetzels' (2007: 108) representative survey, almost every second Muslim agrees with the general statement that Germans reject Muslims—and this proportion is even higher among Muslim secondary school students (2007: 238).

Such deficits in the acceptance of Muslims as equal citizens have been highlighted by research in Australia and Germany. Studies examining the subjective views and experiences of Muslims often pinpoint two key exclusionary mechanisms that are seen as crucial in creating barriers of belonging for Muslims and fuelling intergroup tensions in both countries. First is the public discourse on Islam and Muslims, especially in the mass media. Second is Muslims' experiences of individual and collective discrimination. Jytte Klausen (2005: 59), for example, found in her survey of active Muslim citizens ('new Muslim political elite') in several Western European countries that in Germany almost all interviewed Muslims regarded the 'negative press treatment' as a major source of problems for Muslims, followed by 'antiforeigner rhetoric' and 'everyday discrimination'.

In recent years, these exclusionary phenomena of Islam-sceptical public discourse intertwined with personal or collective experiences of anti-Muslim racism (both interpersonal and systemic) have been described by communities, human rights advocates and critical scholars with a reference to the broad term of Islamophobia (The Runnymede Trust 1997; Bleich 2011; Bouma 2011). The terminology is not unproblematic as it tends to lack clear conceptual boundaries; for this—and other sometimes polemic and political—reasons it has also attracted criticism. But despite this criticism and conceptual weaknesses, Islamophobia has become, and seems to remain for the foreseeable future, a key notion to capture the empirically undeniable, complex social phenomena of Muslims' marginalisation, linked to the contestation of their recognition as equal members of pluralistic, liberal societies in the West. In short, Islamophobia inhibits Muslims from enjoying citizenship in a truly egalitarian sense.

Media and Public Discourse as a Source of Exclusion

Research on Muslims' subjective views and experiences has consistently shown that in both countries most Muslims are extremely critical of the representation of Islam in the mainstream media.[5] Study findings in both national context often suggest that many of them assume a more or less direct—and causal—relationship between the media misrepresentation and public attitudes (Rane 2010: 104; Peucker and Akbarzadeh 2014: 90–92). The scholar Anne Aly maintains that Muslims in Australia tend to regard the media as 'a powerful moderator of public opinion with a defiantly anti-Islamic agenda' with the 'hegemonic power to turn public opinion against them' (Aly 2007: 34–35).

---

[5] One of the most researched topics in the broader context of Muslims in the West is their portrayal in the mass media. The results of these studies largely confirm Muslims' views on the predominantly biased media depiction. Some major studies investigating the situation in Australia are, for example, Brasted (2001), Isakhan (2010), Manning (2004), and Akbarzadeh and Smith (2005). In the German context, Hafez (2000), Hafez and Richter (2007), Halm et al. (2006) and Frindte et al. (2011) have examined the misrepresentation of Islam and Muslims in the media. For an overview on these and other studies, see Peucker and Akbarzadeh (2014).

The aforementioned survey among 500 Muslims in Melbourne found that the media is 'singled out as a particular source of cultural apprehension that serves as a barrier for Australia's Muslim community' (Monash University 2009a: 25). Two-thirds of the respondents expressed the view that 'almost all' or 'most media' discriminate against Muslims and a further 30 % believe that some media do. The respondents unanimously criticised the media's rigorously biased, negative and selective depiction of Islam and Muslims, which ignores the 'positive and true face' of Islam (2009a: 26). The study concluded that this skewed representation is commonly seen by Muslims as shaping the public attitudes towards them. 'This is crucial as it feeds directly into the development of informal barriers, the intangible but very real experiences of suspicion and hostility felt by Muslim Australians' (2009a: 26).

Other research studies confirm the prevalence of such views among Muslims in Australia (IDA 2007: 87; Poynting and Noble 2004: 7) Qualitative research studies have explicitly highlighted that Muslims are under the strong impression that mass media reporting demonises them (Kabir 2006: 314) and reinforces the them-and-us division between the broader society and the Muslim community. These social fractions generate, and aggravate, the outsider status of Muslims, suggesting that Muslims cannot be both Australian citizens and adherents of Islam (Aly 2007: 33–34; IDA 2007: 47)—although this stands in contradiction to the prevalent feelings of multiple belonging among most Muslims. Similarly, Gendera et al. (2012: 109) found through interviews and focus groups with 75 members of Muslim families in one metropolitan and one regional community in NSW that 'participants … stressed the negative impact of media portrayal on their sense of citizenship and social belonging'.

In Germany, Frindte and his research team (2011: 72, 101–102) found in their qualitative interviews with Muslim families that respondents also describe the depiction of Muslims in German media as biased, fuelling social conflicts and hindering the development of more positive intergroup relations. The media were seen as creating attitudes of distance and fear instead of respect towards Islam. Similarly, Zick and Heeren (2012: 45) concluded, based on focus groups with Muslims, that some Muslims hold the media directly responsible for generating or fuelling an exclusionary anti-Muslim climate within society.

Attitude Surveys: Public Climate Towards Muslims

Both in Germany and Australia, numerous surveys have examined the attitudes of the broader population towards Muslims and Islam. These studies unanimously reveal widespread negative, prejudiced views, which in many ways reverberate with pertinent media imaginaries. This applies—with some country-specific variations—to the public climate in both countries.

Negative views of Muslims are more prevalent in Australia and Germany than towards other immigrant or religious minority groups. The Australian Scanlon Foundation Social Cohesion survey series, conducted annually by Monash University researchers and the Australian Multicultural Foundation, found in 2012—consistent with previous results—that hardly any Australians hold negative views of Christians (3 %) and Buddhists (5 %), but almost one in four expressed very or somewhat negative attitudes towards Muslims (Markus 2012a: 47). Peucker and Akbarzadeh (2012) presented an overview on several other surveys confirming that Muslims face greater resentments than members of other faith groups (e.g., 2009 *Australian Survey of Social Attitudes*) and that anti-Muslim concerns are significantly more widespread among the general population than 'anti-Indigenous concerns' and 'anti-Black African concerns', as revealed by the national *Challenging Racism* project carried out by researchers from the University of Western Sydney (Peucker and Akbarzadeh 2012: 176–177).

In Germany, such negative attitudes towards Muslims seem even more widespread—and, similarly to what surveys in Australia have shown—well above the level of sentiments other minority groups are facing. According to a representative survey conducted as part of the cross-national European study *Religion and Politics*, around 60 % of Germans expressed negative attitudes towards Muslims. This proportion of anti-Muslim sentiments is not only much higher than in other European countries, but also significantly more negative than Germans' views of Buddhists, Hindus and Jews (which are still considerably high, ranging between around 20 % and 30 %) (University of Münster 2010).

What studies in Australia and Germany have highlighted is the prevalent perception of Islam as fanatical and violent, misogynistic and incompatible with 'our' Western values and Muslims being disloyal to the (Western) society they are living in—views that echo the public narratives, conveyed by the mass media. Representative surveys, like the global Pew study (2006) or the pan-European *Religion and Politics* research (University of Münster 2010), show that between 70 % and almost 80 % of Germans associated Islam with fanaticism. According to the latter study, eight in 10 Germans think of 'discrimination against women' when hearing the word Islam. Almost two-thirds associated Islam with proneness to violence, while only 22 % think that 'Islam does fit into our Western world' (University of Münster 2010). The 2006 Pew survey found that over three-quarters of German respondents shared the view that Muslims want to 'remain distinct from larger society' (Amf). According to the Gallup 2009 survey, 45 % of Germans did not think that Muslims are loyal to the country they are living in (Gallup 2009).

In Australia, studies on the attitudes towards Muslims point to a similar picture, while placing a somewhat stronger emphasis on many Australians' sense of being threatened by Islam and Muslims. In its survey of 1400 Australians, IDA (2007: 93–98) found that almost half of them expressed the opinion that Muslims have a negative impact on Australia's national security (47 %) and on the way how people in Australia get along together (48 %). More than one-third agreed that Muslims pose a threat to Australia's way of life, culture and values. One in 10 respondents indicated that many or most Muslims would support terrorism (IDA 2007: 103). A survey among almost 1000 secondary school students across Australia found that, when hearing the word 'Muslim', eight out of ten surveyed youth had negative associations, including 'terrorism', or thought of Muslims being 'different from us'. Allegations of extremism and sexism were ranking high on the list of attributes students 'like least about Muslims' (Ata 2012: 206–208).

A regional survey conducted in Queensland by a research team at Griffith University among some 500 Australians came to slightly more positive conclusions (Abdallah and Rane 2007). Seventy eight percent of the respondents stated they were comfortable with Muslims, and only

14 % expressed concerns over Muslims. Among those who were not comfortable with Muslims,

> almost one-quarter (24 percent) expressed some concern about Muslim violence, militancy, or terrorism. Thirty percent expressed concern that Muslims can't or won't "integrate" or "assimilate" as their reason. A further 14 percent of this group stated a concern that Muslims want to impose their ways on others or somehow change Australia (Abdallah and Rane 2007: 15).

Similarly, a local survey among residents of the multiethnic neighbourhood of Darebin (Melbourne) found that the majority of respondents had few concerns about Muslims in their community and felt 'empathy towards Australian Muslim communities' (Mansouri 2012: 24; Mansouri et al. 2007). However, still around 18 % somewhat or strongly agreed that Islam is not compatible with Australian values, while around one-half disagreed with this statement.

Muslims Experiences of Discrimination and Racism

Not only the media discourse and the public climate demonstrate that Muslims' citizenship is contested. Experiences of discriminatory treatment in everyday life can also reinforce a personal or collective sense of exclusion and promote self-identification as marginalised second-class citizens.

Numerous pertinent studies suggest little differences between Muslims in Australia and Germany, demonstrating that Muslims in both countries often feel discriminated against—as individuals and, on a collective level, as a community group. In the Australian context, the Monash University survey among 500 Muslims in Melbourne highlights that the vast majority of respondents—nine in 10—stated that there is discrimination against Muslims in Australia, while 56 % said they had personally experienced discrimination themselves over the past two years. The authors concluded that individual discrimination and 'more importantly the staggering proportion' of those who expressed concerns about collective exclusion of Muslims indicate 'a deep rift between Muslim Australians and the rest of the community' (Monash University 2009a: 24–25). Other studies in Australia have also revealed widespread experiences of discrimination among Muslims. Kevin Dunn and his research team found in their survey among almost 600 Muslims in Sydney that 57 % had experienced racism in at least one of several concrete social settings and public spaces (e.g., work place, education, housing market, shops) (Dunn et al. 2015: 27–28; see also Dunn et al. 2009; Poynting and Noble 2004). Jakubowicz et al. (2012: 52–53) similarly concluded in their study that two-thirds of the almost 400 surveyed young Muslims 'reported experiencing discrimination within the public sphere at least on one or more occasions'.

In the German context, surveys of ethno-religious minority groups have consistently illustrated that Muslims often experience unequal, discriminatory or abusive treatment. The cross-European EU-MIDIS survey among various ethnic and/or religious minorities conducted by the EU Fundamental Rights Agency (FRA) in 2008, for example, found that 31 % of (Turkish) self-identified Muslims in Germany had experienced discrimination in the past 12 months (on average 5.8 incidents), most commonly when looking for work (FRA 2009: 5–6). Brettfeld and Wetzels (2007: 105–106) deployed a hierarchical classification of different types of discrimination experiences in their survey among Muslims, ranging from the 'strange glance', impolite treatment and derogatory comments over racist insults and unequal treatment by authorities to physical attacks. The researchers found that just over one-third of all Muslim respondents did not report any of these experiences of discrimination. Thirty percent had been subjected to abusive comments, such as 'go back to where you come from', and around 20 % complained about unequal treatment by the authorities (e.g., police). Brettfeld and Wetzels found even more widespread experiences of discrimination among Muslim secondary school students, who were surveyed separately, with more than six out of 10 having experienced derogatory comments (Brettfeld and Wetzels 2007: 237). Other representative surveys in Germany have come to similar results, confirming Muslims' experience of unfair and derogatory treatment, and discrimination (SVR 2010; Sauer 2014).

All these studies demonstrate Muslims' subjective feelings of being treated in a discriminatory way because of their migrant or ethno-religious minority status. It is often challenging to empirically determine whether unequal treatment has actually occurred or is 'only' felt and perceived by Muslims. Booth et al. (2012) are some of the few researchers who have been able to generate reliable evidence on labour market discrimination against Muslims. Through their matched pair testing methodology, they found that in Australia a job applicant with a Middle Eastern sounding name has to submit on average 64 % more job applications to get the same number of call-backs from the potential employer as an Anglo-Saxon person with identical relevant qualifications (Booth et al. 2012: 558). Similar studies have been conducted in Germany, providing empirical evidence that job applicant with Turkish names face discriminatory barriers in the access to the labour market (e.g., Kaas and Manger 2010).

On the one hand, these labour market barriers can hamper Muslims' socioeconomic upward mobility. The persistently unequal access to relevant resources and capital may reduce the likelihood of Muslims to get actively engage in civic or political participation. On the other hand, feelings of not getting a 'fair go' and being denied equal opportunities may impact on Muslims' sense of belonging to a society, which is seen as establishing exclusionary barriers. Similar to the perceived negative media discourse and the public climate, this casts a question mark on their equal membership status in society.

***

What the existing literature clearly demonstrates is that Muslims in Australia and Germany articulate very similar experiences of individual and collective exclusion. In Germany, Muslims' feelings of social marginalisation seem to resonate with their relatively weaker sense of belonging to the 'imagined community' of the nation (Andersen 1991). Among Australian Muslims, the sense of exclusion collides with their generally strong identification as Australian citizens. In both country settings, feelings of not being recognised as equal member of society may have implications for the emergence of active citizenship. It can hamper one's eagerness to belong to the society and discourage Muslims to develop a more positive sense of identity and civic commitment. But feelings of exclusion may also trigger Muslims' resilient mobilisation and continuous participatory claim-making for recognition and for the 'desired *status* of equal citizenship' (Yasmeen 2007: 44, emphasis in original). While it is plausible to assume that feelings of exclusion are likely to have an impact on one's disposition to actively engage in certain forms of civic engagement, this interplay has hardly been systematically addressed in empirical research in Australia and Germany. Taking up this thread, the next section discusses existing research revolving various manifestations of Muslims' civic and political participation.

Performed Citizenship: Civic and Political Participation of Muslims

Contemporary citizenship is not only a static membership status, encompassing legal rights, recognition and a sense of civic belonging, but also has a strong procedural and participatory dimension, which features prominently in an analysis of active citizenship. This perspective emphasises that citizens' contributions to the public debate, civil society and the political decision-making process to advance the wellbeing of society or the neighbourhood or to promote the recognition of their community or social group. Although there is nothing that suggests that Muslim citizens are an exception here, 'the scholarship on their role as citizens attracted scant attraction' until the 2000s, as Yasmeen (2007: 42) maintains in the Australian context. This holds true also for the pertinent research landscape in Germany. The following sections explore what is known about Muslims' civic engagement[6], differentiating, mainly for analytical reasons, between the two overlapping dimensions of civic and political participation.

---

[6] Some recently concluded studies on Muslim citizenship in the Australian context, such as Harris and Roose (2014) and Chloe Patton (2014), conceptualise citizenship in very broad terms, partially borrowing from Isin and Nielsen's (2008) 'acts of citizenship'. This understanding goes beyond the notion of active citizenship as deployed in this research, for example, by including social interactions in the neighbourhood and other acts related to Muslims' developing a sense of belonging and civic recognition. Although these studies have generated innovative insights into Muslims' negotiation of identity in Australia, they have not examined civic or political participation as defined in this present research. Therefore they are not included here.

Political Participation of Muslims in Australia and Germany

Political participation can manifest itself in manifold ways, ranging from voting in general elections and running for, or holding, a political office to non-electoral, more unconventional forms of making one's voice heard in the political arena. There is a significant body of both empirical and theoretical work on political representation of immigrants and visible minorities (Bloemraad 2006; Martiniello 2005; Bauböck et al. 2006), covering especially the electoral sphere of political participation (e.g., voter turnout, party preferences/choices, candidate selection, elected legislators) (e.g., Bird, Saalfeld and Wüst 2011a). However, more specifically, for many years not much attention has been paid to Muslims' participation as voters or as elected members of parliament or local councils. This has started to slowly change with recently emerging literature on Muslim political participation in Western European countries (Nielsen 2013; Peace 2015). In Germany and Australia, research on Muslims' electoral participation continues to be lagging behind. Despite the scarcity of robust empirical evidence, existing data suggest a continuous increase in Muslims' active involvement at the top end of political representation and decision-making in both national contexts.

In Australia, where voting in general elections is compulsory, a recent study among 585 adult Muslims from Sydney, conducted by Dunn and his team (2015), found that around 70 per cent of all survey respondents voted in the last state election. This is the only statistical insight on Muslims' voting behaviour available in Australia. The research report *Political Participation of Muslims in Australia* (Al-Momani et al. 2010) uses the proportion of informal votes (i.e., intentionally or unintentionally invalid ballot papers) as a proxy indicator for citizens' electoral participation. The research team found that the 10 electorates with the highest numbers of informal votes in the 2007 federal elections, according to the Australian Electorate Commission, were located in Western Sydney suburbs with very large Muslim communities. '[T]his data suggest that areas with high numbers of informal votes are also, by and large, those with large numbers of Muslim residents' (Al-Momani et al. 2010: 15). The researchers refrained from presenting any religion-based explanation.

Instead they presumed an effect of language barriers and lack of information (cultural capital) that may disproportionately influence the likelihood of invalid voting among recent immigrants in general, many of them being Muslims.[7] 'One possible explanation … is that lower levels of English language proficiency and educational attainment correlate with lower levels of knowledge about the Australian electoral system, leading to mistakes such as misnumbering or wrongly marking ballot papers' (Al-Momani et al. 2010: 16). The research findings suggest that some of these informal votes are actually 'donkey votes'; that is, some Muslims seem to purposefully cast invalid votes out of personal 'dissatisfaction about the political options available'. One Muslim respondent stated in this context: 'The government will never do anything for us. It's a waste of time' (Al-Momani et al. 2010: 16). Moreover, a small number of respondents in the study indicated that they knew of other Muslims who consider voting to be *haram*, religiously prohibited, in a society that is not in compliance with Islamic law.

There is little systematic evidence on Muslims' representation in local councils or governments across Australia. One of the very few exceptions is Al-Momani et al.'s (2010) study on political participation of Muslims, which also sought to investigate how many Muslims were running for general elections and how many have been elected as representatives in local, state and federal government. They identified only two Muslims in state parliaments across Australia (both in the upper house in Victoria and NSW) and one member in the federal parliament in the late 2000s. Five years after Al-Momani et al.'s study was published, the number of Muslims holding a seat in the Victorian state parliament has increased to three; in NSW state parliament there were two MPs of Muslim background as of April 2015 (Peucker et al. 2014). Al-Momani et al. (2010) identified altogether 15 Muslim councillors on the local level—a number that is likely to have changed since the research was conducted –, 11 in NSW (Sydney) and four in Victoria (Melbourne). While 14 out of these 15 councillors were elected in local government

---

[7] The Scanlon Social Cohesion survey found that the participation in elections is lower among immigrants of non-English speaking background than among Australian-born; this may support the assumption that language difficulties can be a hampering factor of electoral participation for immigrants (Markus 2012b: 20).

areas with a large number of Muslim residents, all Muslim councillors who were interviewed by Al-Momani et al. (2010: 18) stressed they represent the entire constituency and not just the Muslim community. Based on semi-structured interviews with Muslims 'identified as politically active, or influential within and beyond Australian Muslim communities' (Al-Momani et al. 2010: 9), Al-Momani et al.'s study (2010) found that several Muslims 'were quite sceptical about the possibilities of advancing their political aims through formal mechanisms such as standing for political office'. Especially, Muslim women seemed reluctant to get involved in party politics, expressing doubts 'as to whether such a forum would allow them to influence policy' (Al-Momani et al. 2010: 19). Dunn et al.'s survey findings seem to support such a general reluctance towards political party engagement, revealing that just under 4 % of all surveyed Muslim in Sydney had been 'involved in an Australian political party' (2015: 37).

Several studies have explored Australian Muslims' engagement in informal political participation outside the realm of general elections in recent years. The recently survey among Muslims in Sydney (Dunn et al. 2015) found that 27 % of surveyed Muslims had been 'involved in organising or signing a petition' and 8.5 % participated in 'an organised protest' over the past 12 months (2015: 37). The Monash University (2009a) study based on a non-representative survey of 500 Muslims in Melbourne also explored, among others, respondents' involvement in various forms of non-electoral political activities. The findings indicate a fairly high level of political commitment among surveyed Muslims (Table 4.7), which in some instances (signing petition, attending demonstration, contacting politician) appears to be well above the national average for all Australians as recorded by the Scanlon Social Cohesion survey for the late 2000s (Markus 2015: 18).[8]

Especially, less time-consuming political activities, such as signing a petition, consumer boycott, donating money and attending a public demonstration, had been undertaken by more than half of the respon-

---

[8] The Scanlon Social Cohesion survey includes a question on political participation using similar items, asking respondents about their involvement in any of these activities 'in the past three years or so'. Given the different wording of the question, the responses are not fully comparable.

Table 4.7 Muslims' involvement in informal political activities

	Petition	Boycott	Demonstration	Political meeting	Contact politician	Donate money	Contact media	Internet forum
Done it in past year	38.1	33.7	24.4	22.1	14.7	35.6	19.1	19.3
Done it in more distant past	23.8	22.6	27.3	23.7	20.4	20.9	18.7	17.0
Haven't done it, might do it	23.1	24.1	31.7	33.9	43.3	25.4	40.0	38.5
Haven't done it, would never do	7.8	12.3	11.2	15.1	16.1	12.0	17.8	19.0

Source: Monash University (2009a: 43)

dents in the past year or 'in the more distant past'. Forms of engagement that tend to require more time and effort are slightly less widespread, but still far from being uncommon. More than one-third of all Muslim respondents had previously expressed their views vis-à-vis politicians or in the media and had taken part in political meetings. The relatively high proportion of those who have not undertaken such political activities yet would consider doing so in the future underscores the untapped potential of Muslims' general openness to becoming politically more active citizens in the future. Only a minority of respondents showed no interest in getting more involved in any of these activities.

Further analysis of these survey data by respondents' educational attainment yields unexpected results. Muslim respondents with a university degree appear politically less active across almost all activities covered in the questionnaire than those with only secondary school attainments. The research study concludes: 'Higher education does not seem to have facilitated a great sense of public assertiveness' (Monash University 2009a: 27)—a conclusion that contrasts with resource-oriented theoretical explanations of political participation, like the Civic Voluntarism Model by Verba et al. (1995).

The Monash University (2009a) survey further indicated that overseas-born Muslim respondents are less likely to engage in non-electoral political participation than Australian-born Muslims. Lower political engagement rates among first generation immigrants have also been discovered in other studies. The 2012 Scanlon Social Cohesion Survey (Markus 2012b: 20), for example, found lower rates of political participation (except for 'attending a demonstration') among immigrants of non-English speaking background than among Australian-born respondents.[9] These results suggest that many new immigrants may be too occupied with settlement-related social and cultural adjustment processes to be able to invest extra time in political participation and that they may lack the language proficiency needed for certain forms of political activism.

In Germany, many Muslims are legally inhibited from participating in the formal political arena of voting and running for a political office in local, state, federal or European Union parliament, as they lack full political rights to do so. The majority of Muslims in Germany have remained systematically excluded from these fundamental and arguably most powerful arenas of political participation. Reliable data on Muslims' political participation in the formal political sphere are largely absent in Germany. There are, however, some studies on the voting behaviour of first and second generation immigrants and their political participation as elected councillors or parliamentarians. These results allow some tentative proxy insights into the situation of Muslims in Germany.

The most recent empirical evidence on first and second generation immigrants' (who hold German citizenship) participation as voters in federal elections are discussed in a study by Stephanie Müssig and Susanne Worbs (2012). Based on an analysis of two large data sets, the German sub-sample of European Social Survey (ESS) and the German Longitudinal Election Study, the two researchers found that people with a (personal or family) migration background have been less likely to vote in recent federal elections (in 2002, 2005 and 2009) than the general

---

[9] The fact that the difference in political activities between all Australian-born people (including second generation) and third generation Australians is negligible tentatively suggest that factors related to the immigration situation of foreign-born non-English speaking background people and, more specifically, their (initial) English language deficits do influence the extent and proneness of political participation.

population.[10] The analysis shows, however, that these statistical gaps, which range between two and nine percentage points, narrow considerably when looking only at second generation immigrants and at those (first and second generation) migrants who are employed (Müssig and Worbs 2012: 31–33).

While robust research-based insights specifically into Muslims' political participation are lacking, several studies on the representation of migrants and minorities more generally leave little doubt that Muslims have been underrepresented in local councils and state or federal parliaments. Political scientist Andreas Wüst (2011: 253–254) found, for example, that people with a migration background continue to be severely underrepresented in state and federal parliaments and the (nationally elected) European parliament, although their numbers have been rising consistently over the past two decades, from around five in the early 1990s (of a total number of around 660 MPs) to 65 in 2008 (of a total number of around 610 MPs). Almost half of these 65 migrant parliamentarians were of Turkish descent, followed by the second biggest ancestry group from Iran (four).

Karin Schönwälder et al. (2011) found in their analysis of local councils in all 77 German cities with a population of over 100,000 that the number of local councillors with a migration background increased from 116 in the first half of the 2000s to 198 who were elected between 2006 and 2011. The proportion of those with Turkish background was with 38 % very high given that only approximately 16 % of the population with migration background who have full political (citizenship) rights were of Turkish origin (Schönwälder et al. 2011: 41).

Robust research on the number of MPs in state and federal parliaments who self-identify as Muslims does not exist. Peucker and Akbarzadeh (2014: 183) counted eight members of the Lower House (*Bundestag*, 2009–2013) who were either born in a Muslim-majority country or whose parents came from a Muslim-majority country (predominantly Turkey). These figures do not accurately reflect the number of MPs who are self-declared Muslims. The news agency idea (2013) recently pub-

---

[10] This confirms the findings of previous studies on the election participation of first and second generation migrant (Wüst 2002).

lished results from its own investigations of federal parliamentarians in the Lower House. In the 2009–2013 *Bundestag* only three MPs described themselves as Muslims and that this number has increased to eight (of a total of 630 MPs) in the current parliament (2013–2017), most of them members of the political left-wing spectrum.[11]

Despite these observations of Muslims' consistent underrepresentation in the institutions of formal policymaking, there is evidence that Muslims in Germany are interested and active within political parties. The representative study by Haug et al. (2009: 257), for example, found that 2.8 % of surveyed Muslims stated they were members of a German political party, slightly above the population-wide average of around 2 % (Gisart 2013, 361).

Muslims' engagement in informal political participation in Germany is even more under-explored than it is in Australia. While there have been several representative surveys investigating first and second generation migrants' activities within this realm of active citizenship, not a single study has focused specifically on Muslims.[12] Analysing representative longitudinal data from the European Social Survey, Müssig and Worbs (2012: 36) found that around 32 % of respondents of migration background had recently ('over the previous 12 months') participated in at least one of the following non-electoral forms of political participation, compared to 39 % among the total population:

- Signed a petition
- Contacted a politician on the federal, state or local level
- Participated in a registered demonstration
- Actively worked within a political party or group

A differentiated data analysis led to the surprising result that second generation migrants were consistently more engaged in all four types of

---

[11] This may, however, underestimate the exact number of Muslim parliamentarians as several MPs of Turkish descent either failed to respond to the journalists' query or explained that religion is a private matter, refusing to make public whether they are Muslims or not.

[12] A few older studies have examined homeland-oriented political activism of Turkish and/or Kurdish immigrants in Germany (see, for example, Ögelman 2003; Østergaard-Nielsen 2001). These studies, which draw from data collected in the 1990s, appear to be outdated and are thus considered of minor relevance for this research with its focus on Muslims' contemporary active citizenship within Germany.

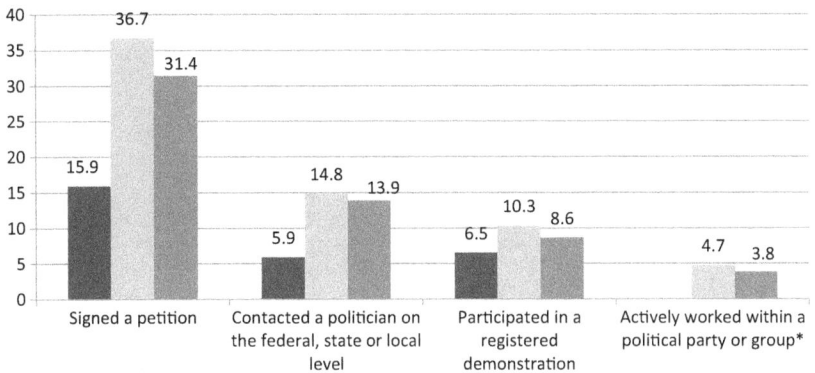

Fig. 4.6 Non-electoral political participation: First/second generation migrants, Germany
Source: Müssig and Worbs 2012: 39
* Number of first generation respondents below N=20

political participation than people without a personal or family migration history (Fig. 4.6).

Previous research on informal political participation in Germany generally confirms that, overall, people with a migration background (not differentiating between first and second generation) are involved in non-electoral political practices less often than the general average. A survey, conducted in 2008, for example, found lower participation rates across almost all forms of 'unconventional participation' (Kornelius 2010: 104). Figure 4.7 specifies the various types of participation included in this survey.

Civic Participation of Muslims in Australia and Germany

A key feature of active citizenship is civic engagement aimed at the wellbeing of the community, broadly defined as the political community or society at large, their neighbourhood or a particular social, cultural or religious community group they feel connected with. These types of activism are of less politicised nature than the aforementioned activities. Many manifes-

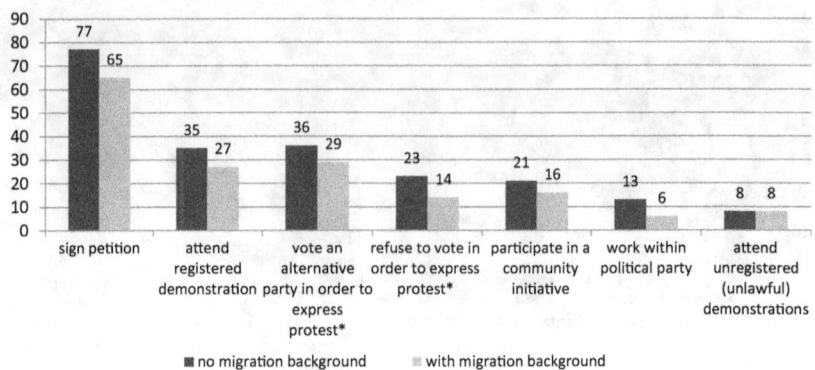

Fig. 4.7 Unconventional participation of migrants in Germany
Source: Kornelius 2010: 106
* only first/second generation migrants with German citizenship

tations of civic participation are undertaken as unpaid help and support work, within the scope of citizens' formal or informal volunteering, commonly facilitated through community groups or other non-government organisations. High volunteering rates have frequently been described as a main characteristic of a vibrant and cohesive civil society (Putnam 2000) and a fundamental manifestation of active citizenship. What is currently known about Muslims as volunteers in Australia and Germany?

In Australia, the census data quantify the extent of Muslim volunteering. In the 2011 census 9.2 % of self-declared Muslims stated that they have done voluntary work for an organisation or group; this proportion is around half of the 17.8 % in the total population (Peucker et al. 2014). While this is the only representative figure specifically on Muslims' volunteering in Australia, there are indicators that beg for a cautious interpretation of these statistics. The low volunteering rate of Muslims is, for example, partially due to the younger demographics of Muslims in Australia, with larger cohorts within those age brackets with no or lower rates of volunteering. Moreover, Madkhul (2007: 8) asserts that ethnic minority members may 'prefer a more informal and less bureaucratic approach to volunteering', which would not be sufficiently captured by the definition of (formal) volunteerism as deployed in the census questionnaire (see also Walsh and Black 2015: 10).[13] He suggested that in particular the scope of *Muslims'* voluntary contributions may be underestimated because helping others is a fundamental Islamic duty that may often not be considered to be a form of volunteering: 'It can be argued that since volunteerism is an innate behaviour to be attributed to all Muslims, voluntary activities are not specified as such by Muslims themselves' (Madkhul 2007: 27; see also CIRCA 2010: 38).

A qualitative study on volunteering among Muslim youth conducted in 2006 by Volunteering Australia (VA) and the Australian Multicultural Foundation (AMF) found evidence in support of this assumption. Through focus groups with young Muslims, the research team discovered that almost all participants have been actively 'involved in some kind of volunteering at some stage of their lives'. Such civic engagement is commonly seen as 'a significant part of being a good community member'. But many young Muslims did not describe their unpaid community work as volunteering, 'in part because they tend to feel that volunteering in Australia is a more formal experience than in their cultures of origin' (AMF and VA 2007a: 1).

The Scanlon Social Cohesion survey series (Markus 2012a, b) used a broader definition of voluntary work and consequently discovered substantially higher volunteering rates both among the total population and among non-English speaking background migrants. In the nationwide survey just over one-third of all Australian-born respondents[14] and around 30 % of non-English speaking background immigrants had volunteered at least once in the past year—defined as 'any unpaid help you give to the community in which you live, or to an organisation or group to which you belong' (Markus 2012b: 20). These results may not offer a reliable answer to the quantitative scope of *Muslims'* volunteering activities, but they suggest that a narrowly defined concept of formal volunteering may not accurately capture the reality of civic commitment of Muslims and non-Muslims in general.

---

[13] The Australian Bureau of Statistics (ABS) defines a volunteer 'as someone who, in the previous 12 months, willingly gave unpaid help, in the form of time, service or skills, through an organisation or group' (ABS 2011a: 3).

[14] This share is slightly below the 38 % of Australians aged 18 years and older who volunteered according to the 2010 General Social Survey (ABS 2011b).

As representative data on organisational setting of Muslims' volunteering in Australia are lacking, explorative questionnaire surveys and qualitative studies are the prime source of insights into the location of Muslims' civic engagement. The recent study by Dunn and colleagues found that 36 % of the almost 600 surveyed Muslims from Sydney had volunteered during the past 12 months for a faith-based organisation and 14 % for a sporting association (2015: 37). Similarly, according to the qualitative study among young Muslims by Volunteering Australia and the Australian Multicultural Foundation (VA and AMF 2007a: 1), most of the participating Muslims 'had volunteered through Muslim organisations or associations, and some had volunteered in non-Muslim organisations spanning a range of not for profit sectors'. The CALD National Survey of Australian volunteers carried out in 2003–2004 also by AMF and VA surveyed volunteers from, among others, the Arab-speaking community. While the results need to be interpreted 'with great caution' (AMF and VA 2007b: 64) due to the low response rate, they indicate that the 'most common form of activity for the volunteers from Arabic speaking backgrounds was to work with a religious group', followed by volunteering for people of their 'own cultural background'. However, there are indicators that this formal and informal[15] voluntary work includes cross-community elements, as the majority of respondents stated that their volunteering serves both the broader community and their own community; only around one in five 'worked only with their own community' (AMF and VA 2007b: 64).

These data pinpoint that Muslim volunteering takes place in a variety of organisational settings with an emphasis on Muslim community groups. The findings of the Monash University (2009b) survey among 500 Muslims support this. Instead of asking Muslims directly about volunteering, one set of questions referred to the respondents' belonging and active participation in a variety of mainstream and Muslim community organisations. Religious organisations, Muslims sports, leisure or cultural groups or other types of Muslim voluntary groups receive the highest rates (Fig. 4.8).

---

[15] Formal volunteering referred to 'time and effort' given to certain organisations, while informal volunteering was defined as 'time and effort' given 'the community outside of an organisation e.g. local neighbourhood, social networks, community networks'.

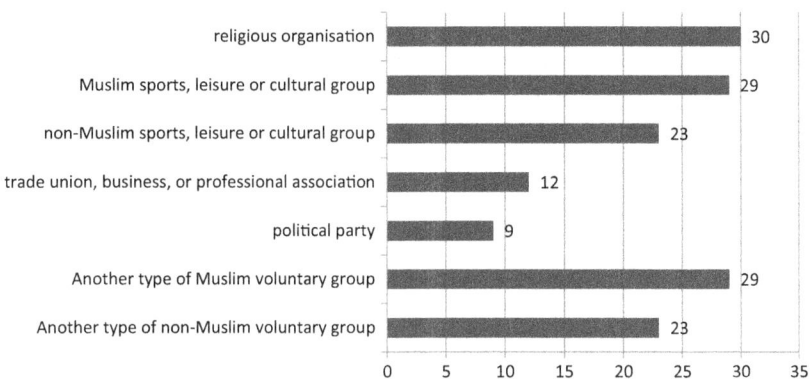

Fig. 4.8 Active participation of Muslims in selected organisational settings, Australia
Source: Monash University 2009a: 46

Overall, the findings demonstrate a high level of civic (and to some extend also political) activism, enacted within organisational settings.

In Germany, empirical evidence on Muslim civic participation and volunteering is extremely limited. The few studies on minorities' civic engagement do not refer explicitly to Muslims but focus on first and second generation migrants more broadly; and only some surveys target, more specifically, people of Turkish descent. These studies offer some tentative proxy insights into Muslims' civic participation, which need to be analysed with great caution. Results cannot simply be applied to Muslims, and those studies on people of Turkish origin may also not accurately reflect the situation of Muslims in general due to a potential 'Turkish bias'. Moreover, existing data stem from surveys carried out in the early 2000s and may be in some ways outdated in the mid-2010s.

The statistical analysis of all these surveys consistently point to lower volunteering rates among minorities and migrants compared to the general population. However, similar to the situation in Australia, there are indicators that migrants—and even more so Muslims—may often have a different understanding of civic volunteering and engagement, which can result in a skewed picture of the extent of their civic activism. Matthias Sauter (2008:200) points out in his local study on civic participation of young people in a socioeconomically disadvantaged neighbourhood in Essen (Germany) that (Muslim) migrant youth are often involved in informal voluntary activities they would not describe as volunteering and that these forms of civic volunteering commonly remain unrecorded and unrecognised.

A special analysis of the large-scale Volunteering Survey (*Freiwilligensurvey*) on civic participation and engagement of all Germans (using only a German-language questionnaire) examined in particular the responses of surveyed first or second generation migrants (Geiss and Gensicke 2006: 304–305). The study found that, while 61 % participated in one way or another in organisations or groups outsider their family and workplace (e.g. as members of a sports club), only 23 % were actively involved as volunteers in these organisational settings. The national average of the whole population was 71 % and 37 %, respectively. The longer the average time of residence in Germany, the higher was the volunteering rate among migrant respondents. The two most important organisational areas where migrant volunteering was recorded was the context of childcare and school, and sports, followed by (with much lower rates) church and religion. By far the most important target groups their volunteering was aimed at were children and youth; the second largest target group were migrants and refugees. The dominant goals of these active migrant volunteers were to help others and contribute to the common good (similar to the response pattern of non-migrants in the survey). In addition, surveyed migrants mentioned more often than non-migrants that they seek 'to work towards finding solutions', 'take responsibility', expand their experiences and skills, represent their own interests and increase personal job-related benefits.

Dirk Halm and Sabine Sauer (2005) carried out a nationwide representative survey with a very similar research design to examine specifically how people of Turkish descent (aged 16 years and older) participate in non-governmental organisations. Like in Geiss and Gensicke's study (2006), a basic differentiation between participation (in the sense of membership and involvement) and active engagement (in the sense of volunteering) was deployed. Halm and Sauer (2005: 3–4) found that almost two-thirds (64 %) of respondents participated in an organisational context (as opposed to 61 % among all migrants); however, only one in 10 stated that they actively volunteer there. This volunteering rate was much lower than in the general population, as mentioned above, and also clearly below the rate of all first and second generation immigrants (Geiss and Gensicke 2006; BMFSFJ 2010: 5).[16]

Formal educational attainments appear to have an impact on the proneness of Turkish first and second migrants to volunteer, but this effect does only partially confirm the general assumption that the engagement rate would consistently rise with higher education status. Those with a university degree were most likely to volunteer and those who dropped out of high school were least likely. However, those Turkish migrants who finished high school with the lowest possible graduation level (*Hauptschule*) more often volunteered than those with a medium or higher (but below university) degree (Halm and Sauer 2005: 83). The survey analysis also illustrates that Turkish immigrants get gradually more likely to volunteer the longer they live in Germany (2005: 88). The level of religiosity does not seem to affect the likelihood of volunteering in a significant way. The three most common thematic areas where respondents of Turkish background volunteered were religion, sport, and school and childcare, followed by music and other cultural and arts-related contexts and social (welfare) issues (Fig. 4.9).

These thematic areas also reflect the organisational settings within which this active engagement was located. The results indicate the importance of Muslim community organisations as a site of volunteering. In terms of the ethno-national composition of the respective organisational context, a majority of Turkish (first or second generation) migrant (52 %) volunteered only in a Turkish group and 29 % volunteered only in a German group; the other respondents stated that they were active in an international group (13 %) or in both German and Turkish groups (6 %) (Halm and Sauer 2005: 75).

Against the backdrop of this importance of Muslim community groups, a recent study, also by Halm and Sauer (2012), on the profile of Muslim organisations and mosques provides additional insights into the

---

[16] Halm and Sayer used a German and a Turkish version of the questionnaire, and therefore were more likely to reach those Turkish first/second generation migrants whose German proficiency was too poor to respond to the German-only Volunteering Survey (Geiss and Gensicke 2006). This has been described as a systematic bias and one of the methodology-related reasons for the extremely low volunteering rate found in Halm and Sauer's study.

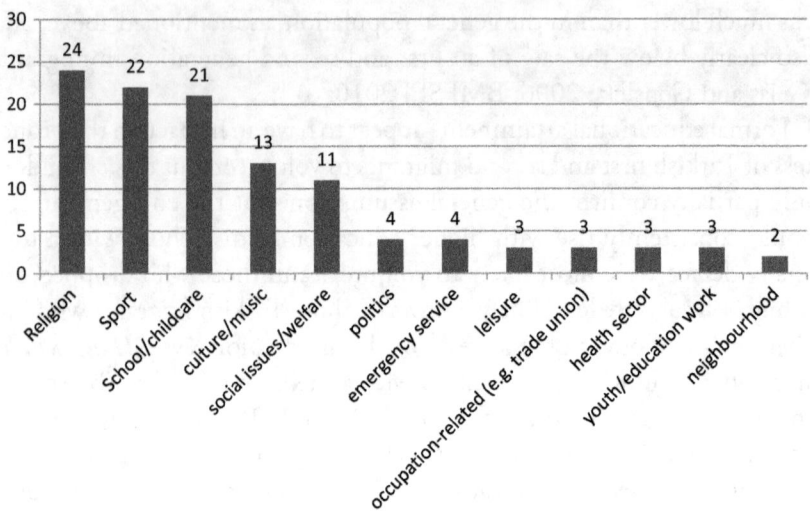

Fig. 4.9 Thematic context of organisation-based volunteering (people of Turkish origin)
Source: Halm and Sauer 2005: 7

types of activities that commonly take place within these religious organisations—and in which volunteers may become involved in. The research study, surveying 1141 Muslim community organisations, including many mosques, in Germany, found that these organisations heavily rely on Muslims' volunteering contributions.

While all organisations offer a range of religious services (e.g., religious education for children, Iftars), the vast majority of them additionally provided non-religious, social, cultural and often welfare and settlement-oriented programs (e.g., German language courses). The study identified the most commonly offered services and activities for the youth and adults. Around two-thirds of all surveyed Muslim organisations ran interreligious dialogue initiatives (65.2 %) and civics courses and excursions (66.5 %) for young Muslims (surpassed only by sport offers with 72.2 %). The most common non-religious services for adult Muslims were, except for running a tea room as part of the organisation, interreligious dialogue initiatives (60.4 %) and civics courses and excursions (48.2 %). Overall these findings suggest that volunteering in Muslim community (religious) organisations often involves cross-cultural or interreligious engagement (Halm and Sauer 2012: 77)—which resonates with the empirical evidence on Muslims' civic engagement in Australia.

***

Many questions about the scope and nature of Muslims' active citizenship in Australia and Germany remain open. Nevertheless, the existing empirical evidence points to similarities as well as divergences in the way Muslims in both national contexts enact their citizenship in a societal environment that is often seen as sceptical or even hostile towards their faith and their community. Muslims in Australia and Germany share similar experiences of social marginalisation, exclusion and public stigmatisation (although the level of anti-Muslim sentiments appears somewhat higher in Germany), which collectively denies them recognition as equal members of society and the political community. The contested nature of their citizenship is closely intertwined with—and further aggravated by—Muslims' on average socioeconomic disadvantages, inhibited social upward mobility and access to resources, including those that are assumed to enhance their inclination to engage actively in political and civic participation. Within this context of resources, however, Australian Muslims have been much more successful in obtaining high levels of education and, assumedly, civic skills than their German counterparts.

Another marked difference between Muslims in the two national settings, which is of high relevance for the way in which citizenship is being performed, is linked to their legal status and full political rights. Although Muslim communities in Australia encompass a large proportion of first generation immigrants, three-quarters of them hold Australian citizenship; this applies to only around four out of 10 Muslims in Germany. Related to this legal dimension of citizenship, the vast majority of Australian Muslims have, generally speaking, a strong sense of civic belonging and predominantly identify as both Australian citizens and being Muslim, whereas in Germany, this civic identity layer appears less prevalent.

Representative insights into the civic and political participation of Muslims in Australia and Germany are lacking, and it is extremely complicated to robustly quantify Muslims' active involvement in the (electoral and more informal) political arena or their civic volunteering. What appears to be indisputable is that Muslims are, similar to other ethno-religious minority groups, continue to be underrepresented in the powerful circles of policymaking, most importantly, in state and federal governments—despite ongoing positive developments in this realm of political representation over the past few decades. The picture of Muslims' informal political participation beyond the electoral realm is less clear, with studies in both countries suggesting that those ethno-religious minorities, including Muslims, born in Australia and Germany respectively, might even be more active in these arenas of informal political participation than the average population. Existing research suggest lower volunteering rates among Muslims in both countries, but there are good reasons to interpret these seemingly robust statistical findings with great caution due to the possible different views and personal understanding among Muslims of what volunteering actually constitutes. What research studies on Muslim volunteering in both countries discovered is the importance of religious (assumedly Islamic) organisation as a platform and location where their civic engagement is enacted. Linking this to previous studies especially in the US on the role of mosques for political mobilisation (Jamal 2005; Read 2015) and religious organisations as an 'incubator for civic skills' (Cesari 2013: 73), such a religious community-based volunteering may also have flow-on effects for Muslims' political activism and active citizenship, more broadly.

References

Abdalla, M., & Rane, H. (2007). *The impact of media representations on the understanding of Islam and attitudes toward Muslims in Queensland.* Report prepared for Multicultural Affairs Queensland. Online document viewed 23 April 2015 www.griffith.edu.au/__data/assets/pdf_file/0018/52083/MAQ.pdf

Abdullah, M. S. (1981). *Geschichte des Islam in Deutschland.* Graz: Styria.

Akbarzadeh, S., & Smith, B. (2005). *The representation of Islam and Muslims in the media (the age and Herald Sun Newspapers).* Melbourne: Monash University.

Al-Momani, K., Dados, N., Maddox, M., & Wise, A. (2010). *Political participation of Muslims in Australia.* Sydney: Macquarie University.

Aly, A. (2007). Australian Muslim responses to the discourse on terrorism in the Australian popular media. *Australian Journal of Social Issues, 42*(1), 27–40.

Andersen, B. (1991). *Imagined communities: Reflections on the origin and spread of nationalism*. London: Verso.

Ata, A. W. (2012). How Muslims and Islam are perceived in Australian public, private and religious schools: A national survey. In F. Mansouri & V. Marotta (Eds.), *Muslims in the West and the challenges of belonging* (pp. 198–235). Carlton: Melbourne University Press.

Australian Bureau of Statistics (ABS). (2011a). *Voluntary work Australia*. Canberra: Commonwealth of Australia. Online document viewed 21 April 2015 http://www.ausstats.abs.gov.au/Ausstats/subscriber.nsf/0/404350EEC6509985CA2579580013177A/$File/44410_2010.pdf

Australian Bureau of Statistics (ABS). (2011b). *General social survey. Summary results*. Canberra: Commonwealth of Australia. Online document viewed 21 April 2015 http://www.ausstats.abs.gov.au/ausstats/subscriber.nsf/0/D0B6CB77DE0BF677CA25791A00824C41/$File/41590_2010.pdf

Australian Bureau of Statistics (ABS). (2012). *2011 census of housing and population, table builder* (own calculations based on census data available at http://www.abs.gov.au/census)

Australian Multicultural Foundation (AMF), & Volunteering Australia (VA). (2007a). *Muslim youth and volunteering. Research bulletin* (June 2007). Melbourne: VA.

Australian Multicultural Foundation (AMF), & Volunteering Australia (VA). (2007b). *National survey of Australian volunteers from diverse cultural and linguistic backgrounds*. Melbourne: VA.

Bauböck, R., Kraler, A., Martiniello, M., & Perchinig, B. (2006). Migrants' citizenship: Legal status, rights and political participation. In R. Penninx, M. Berger, & K. Kraal (Eds.), *The dynamics of international migration and settlement in Europe. A state of the art* (pp. 65–98). Amsterdam: Amsterdam University Press.

Berinsky, A. J., & Lenz, G. S. (2011). Education and political participation: Exploring the causal link. *Political Behavior, 33*(3), 357–373.

Bertelsmann Stiftung (Ed.). (2008). *Religionsmonitor 2008. Muslimische Religiosität in Deutschland: Überblick zu religiösen Einstellungen und Praktiken*. Gütersloh: Bertelsmann Foundation.

Bleich, E. (2011). What is islamophobia and how much is there? Theorizing and measuring an emerging comparative concept. *American Behavioral Scientist, 55*(12), 1581–1600.

Bloemraad, I. (2006). Becoming a citizen in the United States and Canada: Structured mobilization and immigrant political incorporation. *Social Forces, 85*(2), 667–695.

Booth, A., Leigh, A., & Varganova, E. (2012). Does ethnic discrimination vary across minority groups? Evidence from a field experiment. *Oxford Bulletin of Economics and Statistics, 74*(4), 547–573.

Bouma, G. D. (2011). Islamophobia as a constraint to world peace: The case of Australia. *Islam and Christian–Muslim Relations, 22*(4), 433–441.

Brasted, H. (2001). Contested representations in historical perspective: Images of Islam and the Australian press 1950–2000. In A. Saeed & S. Akbarzadeh (Eds.), *Muslim communities in Australia* (pp. 206–227). Sydney: UNSW Press.

Brettfeld, K., & Wetzels, P. (2007). *Muslime in Deutschland.* Berlin: BMI.

Bundesministerin für Familie, Senioren, Frauen und Jugend (BMFSFJ). (2010). *Hauptbericht des Freiwilligensurveys 2009. Zivilgesellschaft, soziales Kapital und freiwilliges Engagement in Deutschland 1999 – 2004 – 2009.* Berlin: BMFSFJ.

Bundesministerium des Innern (BMI), & Bundesamtes für Migration und Flüchtlinge (BAMF). (2015). *Migrationsbericht 2013.* Nuremberg: BAMF.

Cesari, J. (2013). *Why the West fears Islam. An exploration of Muslims in liberal democracies.* Basingstoke: Palgrave Macmillan.

Cleland, B. (2001). The history of Muslims in Australia. In A. Saeed & S. Akbarzadeh (Eds.), *Muslim communities in Australia* (pp. 12–32). Sydney: UNSW Press.

Cohen, A., Vigoda, E., & Samorly, A. (2001). Analysis of the mediating effect of personal-psychological variables on the relationship between socioeconomic status and political participation: A structural equations framework. *Political Psychology, 22*(4), 727–757.

Cultural and Indigenous Research Centre Australia (CIRCA). (2010). *Civic and social participation of Australian Muslim men.* Leichhardt: CIRCA.

DESTATIS (Federal Statistical Office). (2012). *Bevölkerung und Erwerbstätigkeit. Bevölkerung mit Migrationshintergrund – Ergebnisse des Mikrozensus 2011 Fachserie 1 Reihe 2.2.* Wiesbaden: DESTATIS.

DESTATIS (Federal Statistical Office). (2013). *Bevölkerung und Erwerbstätigkeit. Einbürgerungen Fachserie 1 Reihe 2.1 – 2012.* Wiesbaden: DESTATIS.

DESTATIS (Federal Statistical Office). (2014). *Bevölkerung und Erwerbstätigkeit. Bevölkerung mit Migrationshintergrund – Ergebnisse des Mikrozensus 2013 Fachserie 1 Reihe 2.2.* Wiesbaden: DESTATIS.

Dunn, K. M., Forrest, J., Pe-Pua, R., Hynes, M., & Maeder-Han, K. (2009). Cities of race hatred? The sphere of racism and anti-racism in contemporary Australian cities. *Cosmopolitan Civil Societies. An Interdisciplinary Journal, 1*(1), 1–14.

Dunn, K., Atie, R., Mapedzahama, V., Ozalp, M., & Aydogan, A. (2015). *The resilience and ordinariness of Australian Muslims. Attitudes and experiences of Muslims report*. Sydney: Wester Sydney University and ISRA Australia.
Frindte, W., Boehnke, K., Kreikenbom, H., & Wagner, W. (2011). *Lebenswelt junger Muslime in Deutschland*. Berlin: BMI.
Fundamental Rights Agency (FRA). (2009). *European Union minorities and discrimination survey. Data in focus report: Muslims*. Vienna: FRA.
Gallup. (2009). *The Gallup Coexist Index 2009: Global study on interfaith relations*. Washington, DC: Gallup.
Geiss, S., & Gensicke, T. (2006). Freiwilliges Engagement von Migrantinnen und Migranten. In T. Gensicke, S. Picot, & S. Geiss (Eds.), *Freiwilliges Engagement in Deutschland 1999–2004* (pp. 302–349). Wiesbaden: VS Verlag.
Gendera, S., Pe-Pua, R., & Katz, I. (2012). Social cohesion and social capital: The experiences of Australian Muslim families in two communities. In F. Mansouri & V. Marotta (Eds.), *Muslims in the West and the challenges of belonging* (pp. 89–113). Carlton: Melbourne University Press.
Gisart, B. (2013). Demokratie und politische Partizipation. In Statistisches Bundesamt & Wissenschaftszentrum Berlin für Sozialforschung (Eds.), *Datenreport 2013. Ein Sozialbericht für die Bundesrepublik Deutschland* (pp. 357–362). Bonn: Bundeszentrale für politische Bildung.
Hafez, K. (Ed.). (2000). *Islam and the West in the mass media. Fragmented images in a globalizing world*. Cresskill: Hampton Press.
Hafez, K., & Richter, C. (2007). Das Islambild von ARD und ZDF. *Aus Poltik und Zeitgeschichte, 26–27*, 40–46.
Halm, D., & Sauer, M. (2005). *Freiwilliges Engagement von Türkinnen und Türken in Deutschland*. Essen: ZfT.
Halm, D., & Sauer, M. (2012). Angebote und Strukturen der islamischen Organisationen in Deutschland. In D. Halm, M. Sauer, J. Schmidt, & A. Stichs (Eds.), *Islamisches Gemeindeleben in Deutschland*. Nuremberg/Essen: BAMF/ZfTI.
Halm, D., Liakova, M., & Yetik, Z. (2006). Die öffentlichen Diskurse um den Islam in den Jahren 2000 und 2004 und ihre Auswirkungen auf das Zusammenleben von Muslimen und Mehrheitsgesellschaft in Deutschland. *Zeitschrift für Ausländerrecht und Ausländerpolitik, 26*(5–6), 199–206.
Harris, A., & Roose, J. (2014). DIY citizenship amongst young Muslims: Experiences of the "ordinary". *Journal of Youth Studies, 17*(6), 794–813.
Haug, S., Müssig, S., & Stichs, A. (2009). *Muslimisches Leben in Deutschland*. Nuremberg: BAMF.

Idea. (2013). *Zahl der Muslime steigt deutlich* (27 September 2013). Online document viewed 21 April 2015 http://www.idea.de/nachrichten/detail/thema-des-tages/artikel/zahl-der-muslime-steigt-deutlich-904.html

Isakhan, B. (2010). Orientalism and the Australian news media: Origins and questions. In H. Rane, J. Ewart, & M. Abdalla (Eds.), *Islam and the Australian news media* (pp. 3–25). Carlton: Melbourne University Press.

Isin, E. F., & Nielsen, G. M. (Eds.). (2008). *Acts of citizenship*. London: Zed Books.

Issues Deliberation Australia (IDA). (2007). *Australia deliberates: Muslims and non-Muslims in Australia*. Glenelg: IDA.

Jakubowicz, A., Collins, J., & Chafic, W. (2012). Young Australian Muslims: Social ecology and cultural capital. In F. Mansouri & V. Marotta (Eds.), *Muslims in the West and the challenges of belonging* (pp. 34–59). Carlton: Melbourne University Press.

Jamal, A. (2005). The political participation and engagement of Muslim Americans: Mosque involvement and group consciousness. *American Politics Research, 33*(4), 521–544.

Kaas, L., & Manger, C. (2010). *Ethnic discrimination in Germany's labour market: A field experiment*. Bonn: IZA.

Kabir, N. (2006). Representation of Islam and Muslims in the Australian media, 2001-2005. *Journal for Muslim Minority Affairs, 26*(3), 313–328.

Klausen, J. (2005). *The Islamic challenge: Politics and religion in Western Europe*. Oxford: Oxford University Press.

Kolig, E., & Kabir, N. (2008). Not friend, not foe: The rocky road of enfranchisement of Muslims into multicultural nationhood in Australia and New Zealand. *Immigrants & Minorities, 26*(3), 266–300.

Koopmans, R. (2004). Migrant mobilisation and political opportunities: Variation among German cities and a comparison with the United Kingdom and the Netherlands. *Journal of Ethnic and Migration Studies, 30*(3), 449–470.

Kornelius, B. (2010) Demokratie und Integration in Deutschland – Politische Führung und Partizipation aus Sicht von Menschen mit und ohne Migrationshintergrund: Ergebnisse einer repräsentativen Befragung in Deutschland. In Bertelsmann Stiftung (Ed.), *Demokratie und Integration in Deutschland. Politische Führung und Partizipation aus Sicht von Menschen mit und ohne Migrationshintergrund* (pp. 11–130). Gütersloh: Bertelsmann Stiftung (E-Book).

Madkhul, D. (2007). *Supporting volunteering activities in Australian Muslim communities, particularly youth*. Melbourne: Volunteering Australia (VA).

Manning, P. (2004). *Dog whistle politics and journalism. Reporting Arabic and Muslim people in Sydney Newspapers*. Sydney: University of Technology Sydney.

Mansouri, F. (2012). Muslim migration to Australia and the question of identity and belonging. In F. Mansouri & V. Marotta (Eds.), *Muslims in the West and the challenges of belonging* (pp. 13–33). Carlton: Melbourne University Press.

Mansouri, F., Kenny, S., & Strong, C. (2007). *Promoting intercultural understanding in Australia: An evaluation of local government initiatives in Victoria*. Geelong: Deakin University.

Markus, A. (2012a). *Mapping social cohesion. The 2012 Scanlon Foundation surveys. National report*. Caulfield East: Monash University.

Markus, A. (2012b). *Mapping social cohesion. The 2012 Scanlon Foundation surveys. Neighbourhoods report: Areas of immigrant concentration*. Caulfield East: Monash University.

Markus, A. (2015). *Mapping social cohesion. The Scanlon Foundation Survey 2015*. Caulfield East: Monash University.

Martiniello, M. (2005). *Political participation, mobilisation and representation of immigrants and their offspring in Europe*. Malmö: University of Malmö.

Monash University. (2009a). *Mapping employment & education among Muslim Australians*. Caulfield East: Monash University.

Monash University. (2009b). *Muslim voices. Hopes & aspirations of Muslim Australians*. Caulfield East: Monash University.

Müssig, S., & Worbs, S. (2012). *Politische Einstellungen und politische Partizipation von Migranten in Deutschland*. Nuremberg: BAMF.

Nielsen, J. S. (Ed.). (2013). *Muslim political participation in Europe*. Edinburgh: Edinburgh University Press.

Ögelman, N. (2003). Documenting and explaining the persistence of homeland politics among Germany's Turks. *International Migration Review, 37*(1), 163–193.

Open Society Institute (OSI). (2010a). *Muslims in Europe. A report on 11 EU cities*. New York/London/Budapest: OSI.

Open Society Institute (OSI). (2010b). *Muslims in Berlin*. New York/London/Budapest: OSI.

Østergaard-Nielsen, E. (2001). *Transnational politics: Turks and Kurds in Germany*. London: Routledge.

Patton, C. (2014). Multicultural citizenship and religiosity: Young Australian Muslims forging a sense of belonging after 9/11. *Journal for Intercultural Studies, 35*(1), 107–122.

Peace, T. (2015). *European social movements and Muslim activism. Another world but with whom?* Basingstoke: Palgrave Macmillan.

Pędziwiatr, K. (2010). *The new Muslim elites in European cities: Religion and active social citizenship amongst young organized Muslims in Brussels and London.* Saarbrucken: VDM.

Peucker, M., & Akbarzadeh, S. (2012). The vicious cycle of stereotyping: Muslims in Europe and Australia. In F. Mansouri & V. Marotta (Eds.), *Muslims in the West and the challenges of belonging* (pp. 171–197). Carlton: Melbourne University Press.

Peucker, M., & Akbarzadeh, S. (2014). *Muslim active citizenship in the West.* London/New York: Routledge.

Peucker, M., Roose, J. M., & Akbarzadeh, S. (2014). Muslim active citizenship in Australia: Socioeconomic challenges and the emergence of a Muslim elite. *Australian Journal of Political Science, 49*(2), 282–299.

Pew Research Center. (2006). *Conflicting views in a divided world 2006.* Washington, DC: Pew.

Poynting, S., & Noble, G. (2004). *Living with racism: The experience and reporting by Arab and Muslim Australians of discrimination, abuse and violence since 11 September 2001. Report to the HREOC.* Sydney: University of Western Sydney.

Putnam, R. D. (2000). *Bowling alone: The collapse and revival of American community.* New York: Simon and Schuster.

Rane, H. (2010). Media content and inter-community relations. In H. Rane, J. Ewart, & M. Abdalla (Eds.), *Islam and the Australian news media* (pp. 104–119). Carlton: Melbourne University Press.

Read, J. G. (2015). Gender, religious identity, and civic engagement among Arab Muslims in the United States. *Sociology of Religion, 76*(1), 30–48.

Sachverständigenrat deutscher Stiftungen fuer Integartion und Migration (SVR). (2010). *Einwanderungsgesellschaft 2010. Jahresgutachten 2010 mit Integrationsbarometer.* Berlin: SVR.

Sauer, M. (2014). *Integrationsprozesse, wirtschaftliche Lage und Zufriedenheit türkeistämmiger Zuwanderer in Nordrhein-Westfalen. Ergebnisse der Mehrthemenbefragung 2013.* Essen: ZfTI.

Sauter, M. (2008). Integration und Engagement bei jugendlichen Migranten – Rahmenbedingungen und Handlungsempfehlungen. *vhw Forum Wohneigentum* 4: 199–202.

Schönwälder, K., & Söhn, J. (2009). Immigrant settlement structures in Germany: General patterns and urban levels of concentration of major groups. *Urban Studies, 46*(7), 1439–1460.

Schönwälder, K., Sinanoglu, C., & Volkert, D. (2011). *Vielfalt sucht Rat. Ratsmitglieder mit Migrationshintergrund in deutschen Großstädten*. Berlin: Heinrich-Böll-Stiftung.

Smith, D., Wykes, J., Jayarajah, S., & Fabijanic, T. (2011). *Citizenship in Australia*. Canberra: DIAC.

The Runnymede Trust. (1997). *Islamophobia – A challenge for us all*. London: The Runnymede Trust.

Thielmann, J. (2008). Vielfältige muslimische Religiosität in Deutschland. In Bertelsmann Stiftung (Ed.), *Religionsmonitor 2008. Muslimische Religiosität in Deutschland: Überblick zu religiösen Einstellungen und Praktiken* (pp. 13–21). Gütersloh: Bertelsmann Foundation.

Tibi, B. (2007). A migration story, from Muslim immigrants to European "citizens of the heart"? *The Fletcher Forum of Word Affairs, 31*(1), 147–168.

University of Münster. (2010). *Germans are much less tolerant of Muslims*. Online document viewed 21 April 2015 http://www.uni-muenster.de/Religion-und-Politik/en/aktuelles/2010/dez/PM_Studie_Religioese_Vielfalt_in_Europa.html

Verba, S., Schlozman, K. L., & Brady, H. (1995). *Voice and equality. Civic voluntarism in American politics*. Cambridge: Harvard University Press.

Walsh, L., & Black, R. (2015). *Youth volunteering in Australia: An evidence review*. Braddon: ARACY.

Woodlock, R. (2011). Being an Aussie Mossie: Muslim and Australian identity among Australian-born Muslims. *Islam and Christian–Muslim Relations, 22*(4), 391–407.

Wüst, A. M. (2002). *Wie wählen Neubürger? Politische Einstellungen und Wahlverhalten eingebürgerter Personen in Deutschland*. Opladen: Leske+Budrich.

Wüst, A. M. (2011a). Migrants as parliamentary actors in Germany. In K. Bird, T. Saalfeld, & A. M. Wüst (Eds.), *The political representation of immigrants and minorities. Voters, parties and parliaments in liberal democracies* (pp. 250–265). London: Routledge.

Yasmeen, S. (2007). Muslim women as citizens in Australia. Diverse notions and practices. *Australian Journal of Social Issues, 42*(1), 41–54.

Zick, A., & Heeren, J. (2012). *Muslims in the European mediascape: Germany country report*. London: Institute for Strategic Dialogue.

5

The Muslim Community and Political Context in Australia and Germany

Civic and political participation does not occur in a societal or political vacuum. This chapter sheds light on the organisational structure of Muslim communities in Australia and Germany, and it provides insights into key dimensions of the national policy frameworks with regard to citizenship regimes, policies on managing ethno-religious diversity and church–state relations. These elaborations seek to illuminate the broader context within which Muslims enact their citizenship. Moreover, they reflect the theoretical framework of this study, according to which the performance of citizenship does not only depend on individuals' political rights, resources and skills, but is also influenced by context-specific structural and political framework conditions.

Political Framework, Collective Recognition and Church–State Patterns

Following Ireland's (1994) institutional channelling theory, an analysis of Muslims' active citizenship needs to consider the potential impact that country-specific political opportunity structures may have on the way

© The Author(s) 2016
M. Peucker, *Muslim Citizenship in Liberal Democracies*,
DOI 10.1007/978-3-319-31403-7_5

Muslims perform their citizenship. Scholars like Matthias König have argued that policy responses to Muslims' claims for recognition depend on, among others, the national 'institutional arrangements of political organization, collective identity, and religion that result from distinctive historical paths of state-formation and nation-building' (2005: 222). According to these macro-theoretical accounts, national policy frameworks, legal or institutional administrative and mechanisms, including inherited church–state patterns, directly or indirectly affect the way in which Muslims' civic engagement unfolds (Fetzer and Soper 2005; Modood 2010: 125).

The impact of national policy frameworks on participation is most evident in the policy context of citizenship and the acquisition of political rights, which entitle citizens to vote and run for political office. In addition to this legal dimension, there are a series of other policy-related factors that are likely to have implications for Muslims' citizenship. These factors may include the prevailing political stance on ethno-religious diversity, the recognition of Muslim community agency as religious and civil society stakeholders and their status within the national model of church–state relations.

Australia

During the 1970s, at a time when Muslim communities had started to substantially expand and consolidate, the Australian government ultimately abolished its hitherto racially selective immigration policies ('White Australia'), gradually replacing them by an egalitarian, proactive multicultural policy framework. Since then Australia's multicultural policies have continuously evolved, but some of its core tenets have remained in place—its appreciation of ethnic and cultural diversity, support for immigrants and minorities to maintain their cultural identity while developing a sense of belonging to the 'family of the nation' (former Immigration Minister Al Grassby, cited in Peucker and Akbarzadeh 2014: 75), and a strong emphasis on equal citizenship rights. These policy principles have continuously received broad support in the Australian society (Markus 2015) and political broad landscape—with some signs of temporary retreat, especially during the Howard years in the 2000s (and later on during Abbott's prime ministership between 2013 and 2015). The government under Julia Gillard reaffirmed its commitment to these key tenets with the 2011 multicultural policy formulation *The People of Australia* (Commonwealth of Australia 2011).

The principles of diversity, equality and citizenship within Australia multicultural policy framework are not only political rhetoric, but have been translated into concrete policies. Australia's citizenship regime, one of the key pillars of the 'genius of Australian multiculturalism' (Bowen 2011), has facilitated and promoted the acquisition of citizenship since the introduction of the Australian Citizenship Act in 1973. Children born in Australia receive citizenship status automatically by birth if at least one of the parents holds a permanent residence permit. For overseas-born immigrants naturalisation requirements have remained low compared with most other Western states—even after the minimum residence period was increased to four years and a mandatory citizenship test was introduced by the Howard government in 2007.

Since 2002 immigrants who are granted Australian citizenship have been under no obligation by Australian law to renounce their previous nationality. Hence, dual or multiple citizenship is not seen as problematic.[1] Despite the tightening of naturalisation requirements in 2007, this citizenship regime has been very successful in encouraging immigrants to become Australian citizens and obtain full political rights. Australia has one of the highest citizenship take up rates in the world; most overseas-born migrants (Smith et al. 2011) and almost all second-generation immigrants hold full political rights as equal citizens of Australia.

Such an open citizenship regime is a key reason why multicultural policies are commonly considered to have 'a positive impact on political integration' (Bird et al. 2011a: 3). In Australia, like in other countries with explicitly multicultural policies, these citizenship arrangements go hand in hand with the political appreciation of the society's cultural and ethno-religious diversity. The *People of Australia* policy describes the multicultural composition of Australia as being 'at the heart of our national

---

[1] Regarding dual citizenship, there is only one legal limitation relevant for the issue of formal political participation: Australians who hold an additional foreign citizenship are disqualified from being an elected member of the federal parliament.

identity and ... intrinsic to our history and character' (Commonwealth of Australia 2011: 2). Policy statements of this kind imply that Australia's national identity is conceptualised in an inclusive way. It emphasises the principles of equality and a 'fair go' for all and welcomes ethno-religious differences and diversity as part of the country's narrative instead of painting an exclusionary image of an ethnically defined society and polity. Since their inauguration in the 1970s Australia's multicultural policies have sought to strike a balance between celebrating cultural diversity and promoting a shared sense of civic identity (Keating 1995). Despite some political retreats during the 2000s, this two-folded policy agenda has generally been pursued quite successfully, giving immigrants and minorities space to maintain their cultural heritage and ethno-religious identity, while developing a strong sense of belonging to Australia. This is not to say that Australian society has been spared anti-immigration, nationalist racism and Islamophobic sentiments, expressions and conducts within segments of society and the political landscape. On the policy level, however, immigrants and ethno-religious minorities have generally experience comparatively high degrees of political recognition and accommodation of their cultural and religious needs.

This political responsiveness to the cultural diversification of the Australian society becomes evident also in the way the government has recognised collective representation and agency of ethno-religious minority groups as civil society stakeholders. This recognition has its historical roots in the late 1960s. Back then Australian policymakers started to rethink their previously assimilationist settlement policies, which were blind to the specific welfare needs of the growing number of non-English speaking new immigrants. It became clear that mainstream welfare organisations, such as the Good Neighbourhood Councils, were failing to effectively provide culturally sensitive settlement services to these new arrivals. Instead of relying on these ineffective mainstream welfare provisions, an informal system of self-help within immigrant and minority communities, based on existing kinship and village community networks, emerged, trying to absorb 'the pressure and pain of the settlement process' (Jakubowicz 1989: 9).

The government realised that neither the mainstream welfare agencies nor the informal assistance system was suitable to offer adequate support to these newcomers and to prevent the looming deterioration of urban poverty. As a reaction, the government decided to reorganise the entire welfare system with 'a transfer of responsibility for direct services … from government onto ethnic collectivities' (Jakubowicz 1989: 10). Responding to the vocal claim-making of already well-established minority communities (e.g., Greek or Jewish community), the government implemented a grants-in-aid funding model to systematically assisted these migrant and minority community organisations in professionalising and expanding their welfare services for their respective cultural or ethno-religious clientele. Muslim communities, still very small at the time of this paradigm shift in the welfare landscape, were not directly involved in these claim-making activities, but they soon began to benefit from the restructured welfare system with its allocation of funds and responsibilities to minority organisations (Peucker and Akbarzadeh 2014: 148).

Immigrant and ethno-religious minority organisations, among them also some mosques, soon became formally recognised welfare providers, receiving 'grants from both State and Federal governments … for providing a variety of welfare and educational services' (Humphrey 1988: 240). These minority organisations were not only expected to offer efficient settlement services for their community members, but also to act as representative agency who can speak on behalf of their community on the political stage (Humphrey 1988: 240). While this restructured multicultural welfare system triggered tensions and internal competition between different Muslim community organisations over state funding and recognition, it prepared the path for Muslim agency to become 'ordinary' civil society stakeholders, representing their communities vis-à-vis the state and other non-Muslim civil society groups.

Muslim community groups have also been recognised as *religious* organisations within Australia's inherited model of church–state relations without triggering fundamental political problems. This seems to be attributed to, among other factors, the historically grown political tolerance—or indifference—towards religion in general and the state's secular, non-interventionist stance towards faith groups. By the time Muslim communities started to emerge in significant numbers within Australia's multi-religious landscape, the previous 'sectarian rivalries' (Bouma 1999: 289) between the Anglican-Protestant and the Catholic Churches had been settled. The constitutional principle of religious freedom, which had previously been of 'marginal legal utility in the defence of minority religious groups' (Bouma 1999: 285), has been realised in social practice. And it has been extended—almost by default under Australia's equity-based multicultural policy paradigm—to other denominational groups, including Islamic organisations. Consistent with this constitutional principle of state's secular, non-interventionist stance on religious matters, there has been no mechanism in place to formally recognise (or deny recognition for) religious organisations. 'Anyone could set up his church and every religion could flourish … you just had to show that you were not for profit', as the Australian sociologist Andrew Jakubowicz put it (cited in Peucker and Akbarzadeh 2014: 149).

Thus, the Australian model of secularism—in combination with the multicultural policy principles of equality and support of cultural maintenance—has been quite accommodating for religious minorities, despite the lack of strong institutionalised relationships between state authorities and religious organisations. However, despite this relaxed political framework, as Gary Bouma argues, Muslims 'have been singled out in public as 'others' whose difference is too great or as a religious group to be feared' and have thus 'progressed towards full acceptance more slowly' (2012: 48) than most other denominational groups.

This snapshot examination of some key aspects of the political opportunity structures in Australia illuminates the prominent policy principle of recognition of Muslims and their faith on both the individual as well as on the collective agency level. On the individual level, Australia's citizenship-based multicultural policies with their explicit appreciation of ethno-religious, cultural and linguistic diversity offer an inclusive platform for Muslims' identification as equal Australian citizen of Islamic faith. On the collective level, many Muslim organisations have acted for several decades as 'ordinary' community stakeholders in Australia's vibrant civil society, where different interest groups mobilise for their community agenda and struggle for their respective viewpoints and claims in the public and political negotiation process. The main challenge to this supportive and accommodating policy framework has been the attitudinal climate within substantial segments of the population, which are reluctant to accept Muslims and Islam as an inherent part of Australia's society

Germany

The political opportunity structures for immigrants' and ethno-religious minorities' civic engagement in Germany stand in many ways in stark contrast to the Australian policy setting. This is particularly evident in the context of the national citizenship regime and the policy approach to integration and cultural diversity. Moreover, it applies to the persistent political reluctance to recognise Muslim organisations as civil society actors and as a religious community within Germany's formalised corporatist model of church–state relationship.

Until the 1990s, Germany's citizenship regime was not geared towards the incorporation of immigrants and ethnic minorities into the political community. Immigrants faced almost insurmountable hurdles in acquiring German citizenship, and their children, even those born in Germany, also commonly remained foreign subjects without full political right. These restrictive and ethnically-based citizenship provisions[2] reflected the prevalent political view that the many million foreigners, who had moved to Germany since the 1960s, would sooner or later return to their 'home' country and should not become equal members of society with citizenship right. During the 1990s, the political refusal to accept the large and diverse immigrant communities and the permanent nature of their settlement ('Germany is not a country of immigration') started to dwindle. The national citizenship regime underwent major changes, especially with the 1999 naturalisation reform, which introduced substantial improvement for immigrants who seek to acquire German citizenship.

The amended naturalisation law lowered the basic requirement for naturalisation; the minimum duration of legal residence in Germany, for example, was reduced from 15 to now eight years. The most ground-breaking legal changes refer to the acquisition of citizenship by birth (*ius soli*). Children born to non-German parents now obtain German citizenship (in addition to their parents' citizenship) automatically by birth provided at least one parent has resided legally in Germany

---

[2] Ethnic German immigrants (*Spätaussiedler*) primarily from Eastern Europe, Russia and other regions of the former Soviet Union receive German citizenship upon arrival in Germany. Although they have not lived in Germany for many generations, they are considered ethnically German and thus are automatically eligible for citizenship and considered legally German.

for eight years and holds permanent residence permit. These so-called *ius soli* children are, however, obliged to choose between their German and their other nationality before they turn 23. If they fail to explicitly opt for their German citizenship in time, they automatically lose their full citizenship rights.[3] This much-debated provision is consistent with the government's general reluctance to allow dual, or multiple, citizenship. According to the 1999 citizenship act reform, would-be citizens are required to renounce their previous nationality unless it is legally or practically impossible to do so.

Although the citizenship take-up rate increased after the legal amendments came into effect in 2000, it has remained quite low compared with many other Western societies. While the majority of foreigners seem to legally qualify for naturalisation, the eagerness to become German is relatively weak, especially among the large Turkish population. Various attempts of the political opposition to urge the government to overcome its restrictive views on dual citizenship, erase the *ius soli* provisions for those born in Germany and reduce the minimum residence requirements have met with the strict refusal of the ruling conservative-liberal government until most recently (see footnote 3). The main argument put forward by the supporters of this restrictive citizenship regime has been that citizenship needs to be earned by immigrants and be regarded as the 'crowning' prize for a successful integration trajectory and not as a tool to promote participation, inclusion and a sense of belonging (Jurado 2008).

The development of Germany's citizenship regime is indicative of the changing political stance on ethno-religious pluralisation of the society. Until the 1990s, the majority of policymakers held on to the conviction that immigrants and their families (many of them having come to Germany under the guest workers scheme) would eventually leave Germany. Accordingly, the cultural, linguistic and religious diversity was not seen as a permanent feature of society and, consequently, received little political attention. When this illusion gradually eroded, the new political challenge was to find appropriate strategies to respond to these

---

[3] This legal provision that granted German citizenship to German-born second or third generation immigrant youth under the condition that they renounce their parents' citizenship when they turn 23 was abolished in 2014—after the interviews for this research were conducted.

diversification processes. German policymakers have come to accept the immigration-related demographic changes. But, in contrast to Australia's policy shifts in the 1970s, they have not created a fundamentally positive narrative around society's factual diversity. In various policy papers and public announcements on migrant integration (see, for example, the preface to the National Integration Plan, German Government 2007), immigration and cultural diversity is being portrayed as a potential source of problems, conflicts and social tensions unless managed properly by the state. In other words, diversity is only an asset under the condition of successful integration as defined by the government.

In the academic discourse the German government's prevalent understanding of migrant integration has often been described as an assimilationist concept aimed at the reduction of otherness (Häußermann and Siebel 2004: 192) rather than the celebration of diversity. Accordingly, multiple identities are not seen as normal phenomena in pluralistic modern societies, but are generally problematised and viewed with political suspicion—the 'urge to unambiguity' prevails, as the German social anthropologist Werner Schiffauer (2008: 93) puts it. Contrary to the national narrative in Australia, which revolves around the country's immigration history and diversity, the dominant self-image advocated by German policymakers within the conservative political camp often refers to the anti-pluralistic notion of a German 'leading culture' (*Leitkultur*) that immigrants and minorities have to subscribe to. Tellingly, this assimilationist *Leitkultur* has been introduced into the political debate almost simultaneously to the above described naturalisation law reform. While the legal changes opened up the political community to cultural and ethno-religious minorities, the political discourse moved more towards the culturally assimilationist end of the integration spectrum. Although it has remained unclear what exactly this 'dominant culture' encompasses, except for constitutional principles, human rights and the rule of law, this notion has become a common reference in political debates about immigrants' integration and their duty to adapt to this ill-defined set of values, allegedly based on Judeo-Christian tradition and an idealised version of liberalism and humanism.

The political lack of appreciation of diversity and the pressure to adapt have created an exclusionary political climate that has hampered the development of a positive sense of civic belonging. This is supported by the findings of various surveys among immigrants that highlight the often fairly low level of emotional identification with Germany as their home country (see Chap. 4). The national citizenship regime is tied to this in two ways. First, the political reluctance to accept dual citizenship is indicative for the sceptical political stance on diversity, difference and multiple identities (Bös 2002). Second, the unwillingness to apply for citizenship among those foreigners who meet the legal requirement for naturalisation point to the often-lacking desire to become German citizens, attributed to the unwelcoming and diversity-adverse political climate, which discourages immigrants and minorities to develop a sense of belonging and civic identity.

The political reluctance to regard immigrants and ethno-religious minorities as equal citizens has manifested itself, on the collective level, in the poor recognition of immigrant and Muslim organisations as stakeholders in Germany's civil society and corporatist welfare system. Instead of promoting and enabling minority organisations to act as welfare providers for, and representatives of, their community members, the government commissioned mainstream welfare agencies to take responsibility for providing social assistance to the growing number of foreign workers and their families since the 1960s and 1970s. This paternalistic welfare system, which was formally abolished only in the early 2000s, has had hampering implications for the development of representative structures and civic recognition of ethno-religious minority communities. The social scientist Uwe Hunger (2002) argues that mainstream welfare agencies did not only provide social support to their migrant clientele; they also acted as a political voice, trying to speak on behalf of 'their' immigrants—without incorporating minority members into their institutional structures and decision-making processes. Hunger maintains that this paternalism of welfare agencies has 'created an artificial dependence' (2002: 4) between these mainstream institutions and their migrant clientele and has undermined for many years the emergence of political and civic engagement of immigrants (see also Kraus and Schönwälder 2006: 212).

A similar system of patronising representation has been established within the political arena. The problem of political disenfranchisement of immigrants—who were regarded as temporary sojourners even after many years in Germany—was recognised by policymakers already in the 1970s. However, little effort has been made to strengthen migrant and minority organisations in effectively representing their community in the political discourse. Instead, the government set up ombudsman offices, commissioned to represent immigrants and speak on their behalf, such as the Federal Commissioner for Foreigners' Affairs (established in 1978) on the national level and coordination councils in numerous larger cities (Hunger and Candan 2009: 9).

On the local level, these councils were soon replaced by local foreigners' councils (*Ausländerbeiräte*), which comprise of, and are elected by, usually non-German local residents. Although these migrant representations only have advisory status and no political power in the local decision-making process (Didero 2013: 39), they 'can be regarded the first form of political participation of immigrants on the local level' (Hunger and Candan 2009: 9). However, the establishment of these local councils has done little to advance the political recognition of migrant and ethno-religious community agencies, for the elected members of these advisory councils act as individuals and not as formal representatives of a community organisation.

The long-standing political ignorance towards migrant organisations as negotiation partners in the political process and as providers of settlement support to their community members has diminished since the mid-2000s. Since then numerous migrant organisations have been invited by the government to discuss their role as facilitators of integration, and government-funded programs have been launched to assist these community organisations in professionalising their integration-related services. This changed political attitude has also led to some forms of cooperation with Muslim organisations (e.g., German Islam Conference, collaborations between mosques and police departments) and very few funding projects for mosques (e.g., training programs for imams and for dialogue commissioners in mosques). Despite these recent developments towards a greater acknowledgement of Muslim agency, the cooperation between the government and Islamic organisations has often been characterised by mutual suspicion and regularly erupting controversies over the government's securitisation agenda and its domesticating interference in internal religious affairs (Humphrey 2009).

The government's scepticism towards Muslims as collective actors in civil society and as political negotiation partners is directly intertwined with its denial to formally recognise Muslim or Islamic groups as a faith-based corporation under public law (*Körperschaft öffentlichen Rechts*). This statutory recognition is a key component of Germany's secular model ('positive neutrality') and the relationship between religious entities and the state. Although the German Constitution obliges the state to be religiously neutral and establishes a separation of state and church, 'the constitution secures cooperation between the two institutions in such areas as education and social welfare' (Fetzer and Soper 2005: 105). Within these arrangements, religious organisations have been assigned an important role as civil society stakeholders and as a religious voice in the political and public discourse. Acting as formal partners of the state within this institutionalised church–state cooperation, religious organisations enjoy various financial benefits (e.g., church tax collected by the state, tax breaks) and other entitlements including the right to provide religious education in public schools and chaplaincy programs in state institutions, privileges in the context of urban planning and designated seats in public committees (e.g., state broadcasting committees).

However, this privileged status is limited to those denominational groups that are formally recognised by the individual state government as public corporations. The German Constitution specifies in section 140 the basic organisational requirements, which have over time been further specified through several court rulings: Any religious societies (*Religionsgesellschaft*) shall be granted this status 'upon application if their constitution and the number of member give assurance to their permanency'. Currently the two traditionally dominant Protestant and Catholic Churches, as well as the Jewish community and several smaller (mostly Christian) denominational groups but no Islamic organisation (except for Alevis in some states) have received statutory recognition. According to Joel S. Fetzer and J. Christopher Soper, this church–state relationship model also provides 'Muslim groups in Germany a model to which they can point in arguing for state support for their religious institutions...[It] legitimates their demands for public recognition' (2005: 19). However, all attempts of Muslim religious organisations to apply for this formal status as public corporation since the 1970s have thus far failed and have been rejected by state governments on structural grounds (e.g., insufficient membership registration, lack of hierarchical structures). This political denial has been criticised by many Muslim and non-Muslims scholars in Germany as being indicative of a political strategy that puts pressure on Muslim community organisations to structurally assimilate and adopt church-like hierarchical organisational structures, which are traditionally foreign to Islamic communities (Peucker and Akbarzadeh 2014: 69–73).

As a consequence, Muslim community organisations have been missing out on financial benefits, collective participatory rights and the advantages that come with a formalised privileged and equal-footing partnership with state authorities—special rights that other religious groups have been enjoying. This puts Muslim agency in a disadvantaged position in public claim-making and contributes to the collective sense within Muslim communities of being treated as a second-class religion by a state that in principle promises both religious neutrality and a positive recognition of faith groups as stakeholder in society and the political discourse. The hesitant engagement of state authorities with Muslim organisations, overshadowed by a general climate of mistrust, reflects the political stance on ethno-religious diversity in general and, on the individual level, the continuously restrictive access to citizenship rights and the political reluctance to accept the reconcilability of civic and Islamic identities. Against this backdrop, and compared to Australia, the political opportunity structures in Germany appear to be less likely to foster Muslims' civic engagement.

Muslim Community Structures

Muslim organisations play an important role in facilitating Muslims' civic and political participation. They are places where Muslims do voluntary community work, and they may serve as mobilising and empowering platforms for active engagement within civil society and the political arena (Read 2015; Jamal 2005). Previous research has stressed that the organisational structure and connectedness of ethno-religious minority communities and the range of activities of these organisations (Tillie

2004: 531) as well as issues revolving around community leadership may affect the impact of collective agency on Muslims' active citizenship.

While a detailed analysis of the organisational landscape of Muslim communities in Australia and Germany is beyond the scope of this chapter, the following paragraphs offer a snapshot of the organisational structures, addressing key dimensions relevant for the emergence of Muslims' active citizenship. This includes the activity profile of major Muslim community groups, their internal (bonding) and external (bridging and linking) connectedness and, related to the latter, their public standing and recognition within the political structures.

Australia

The Muslim community in Australia is characterised by its enormous internal heterogeneity and fragmentation especially along ethno-cultural lines, which makes it more appropriate to speak of communities in plural. This multitude of Muslim voices within traditional Islamic organisations and other civil society groups has contributed to a very vibrant Islamic life and a comparatively strong public presence of Muslim stakeholders.

The basic structure of the traditional organisational landscape evolved in the 1970s as a three-tier system encompassing the local, state and federal level. On state level, Islamic Councils were established as state peak bodies, which represent numerous affiliated local mosque associations (often called Islamic Societies) and other Muslim grassroots groups. While many of these local organisations have been dominated by a single national or ethnic group (Humphrey 2001), they have usually been open to all Muslims regardless of ethnicity and national origin (Bouma et al. 2001). The Islamic Councils in each state or territory formally gather under the umbrella of the Australian Federation of Islamic Councils (AFIC), established in 1976 as the predecessor of the Australian Federation of Islamic Societies (founded already in the early 1960s). AFIC praises itself for its genuinely diverse, multicultural composition and its democratic structures and procedures (Humphrey 2001: 40). The flipside of this diversity is that the relationship between the three levels—

local mosques and grassroots community groups, state councils and the federal peak body—has often been rather loose.

Internal tensions and disagreements between various organisations within this established three-tier system have been the rule rather than the exception, which has challenged and weakened the authority of AFIC over time (Saeed 2003: 140). Individual Muslim organisations, such as the Lebanese Muslim Association (LMA) in Lakemba (Sydney) or the Islamic Council of Victoria (ICV) in Melbourne, have obtained a particularly strong political standing and have been much more visible in the public debate than AFIC itself. Far from all Muslim organisations are affiliated with an Islamic Council and/or with AFIC. Countless local (often multi-ethnic) grassroots groups, Muslim women's, youth, student and other civic society advocacy organisations have been established over the years, many of them by Australian-born Muslims, *outside* these traditional three-tier community structures. These Muslim community groups all pursue their own specific agenda, but they are vastly committed in one way or another to supporting Muslims and advancing the recognition and accommodation of Islam as inherent part of Australia's multicultural society. Cooperation with Islamic Councils or other traditional Islamic organisations (e.g., mosques)—as well as with other non-Muslim civil society groups—has become increasingly common among many of these grassroots Muslim groups.

This organisational complexity indicates that Muslim communities are highly fragmented and multi-vocal. By default, this applies also to Muslim leadership, which has been—and still is—a 'contentious issue for many Muslim immigrant communities as well as the Australian Governments' (Humphrey 2001: 42). Despite the intra-community fractions along ethnic, sectarian (and other) lines and competition over political recognition, power and resources, there has been a 'considerable amount of cooperation between different Muslim ethnic groups' (Bouma et al. 2001: 63). In his historical analysis of Muslim community life in Australia Bilal Cleland (2001) emphasises that both division and unity have been dominant features for many decades. The dynamics between fragmentation and cooperation persist until today. Muslim communities have remained 'place[s] of competition, conflicts and collaboration, where groups form and reform and leaders struggle for power and influence'

(Jakubowicz et al. 2012: 46). Regardless of their disagreements and tensions, they have been able to activate cross-communal ties, for example, when the recognition of Islam in Australia or their co-religionist overseas are seen to be under political attack or to face severe physical threats (e.g., Iraq war, humanitarian situation in Palestine, Syrian civil war).

Intergenerational changes within Muslim community groups have had implications for the loosening of ethnic boundaries and the advancement of a new pragmatism. Australian-born Muslims, who have recently gained more prominent positions in traditional community circles and other Muslim agency groups, appear less concerned with retaining their (or their parents') cultural and ethnic ties. Their views and motives for civic engagement are predominately shaped by their experiences of growing up as Muslims in Australia. Many of these second-generation, often well-educated Muslims (see Chap. 4) have not hesitated to work together with other Muslim groups irrespective of their different ethnic origin. The multicultural composition and cross-ethnic collaboration within Islamic Councils and the ethnically diverse classrooms in Islamic schools are only two of many examples to illustrate the diminishing ethnic fragmentation and growing collective social capital of Muslim communities in Australia.

The generational leadership changes and the enhanced cross-community networks are not the only recent developments within Muslim communities in Australia that may have lasting ramification for their facilitating and empowering role in the context of Muslim active citizenship. Until the break of the twenty-first century, most Muslims community groups were predominantly concerned with maintaining their Islamic faith, defending it against external pressure and lobbying for the accommodation of their religious needs (Peucker and Akbarzadeh 2014: 146–157). This predominantly inward-looking agenda changed fundamentally in the wake of the 9/11 terrorist attacks, when Islamophobic hostility and intergroup tensions between Muslims and parts of the wider Australian society soared. Increasingly more Muslim community figures became acutely aware that they had to do more to actively tackle mutual misconceptions and break down ignorance and prejudice. In an interview in 2012, then ICV president Elsayed described the 11 September events as a 'wake-up call' that 'slapped us [Muslims] in the face … [we realised] we have to outreach, we have to do our part … everyone realised we all have to be part of the solution' (cited in: Peucker and Akbarzadeh 2014: 162). Opening up to, and cooperating with, non-Muslim groups and stakeholders of the mainstream society and politics is now seen as vital for the future of Muslims in Australia. This new agenda of public engagement and civic activism has unfolded in many Muslim community organisations (Amath 2013).

Subsequently, Muslims' political, media and community involvement in multi-faith and cross-community dialogue and outreach activities have expanded to an unprecedented degree (Bouma et al. 2007). Numerous empowerment and leadership or mentoring programs, sometimes set up in cooperation with university departments, have further contributed to groom a new and articulate Australian Muslim leadership, capable and motivated to act as intermediaries between Muslim communities and the wider society (Peucker et al. 2014). As a consequence of all these efforts, broader and more robust intercommunity networks have emerged and fruitful relationships with the media, universities, non-Muslim religious organisations and other civil society groups have intensified (Peucker and Akbarzadeh 2014: 162–167)

In recent years, not only the relationships with these non-governmental groups have grown stronger, but many Muslim organisations have also enhanced their cooperation and communication networks with authorities (e.g., police) and political decision-makers. For many Muslim community organisations, especially the more established ones, this was not entirely new territory. Some of them have been liaising with authorities since the late 1970s and 1980s within Australia's multicultural welfare system, in which cultural and ethno-religious community organisations could apply for government funding (grants-in-aid) to set up welfare and settlement services for their community members (Jakubowicz 1989). As mentioned above, these minority organisations, including many mosque associations, have been expected to not only provide culturally appropriate services for their clients but also to act as political intermediaries and represent their community vis-à-vis the government (Humphrey 1988: 256).

A consequence of these institutionalised links between government and community organisation within Australia's multicultural welfare system is that Muslim organisations, including larger mosque associations, have already been recognised for several decades within government circles as ordinary civil society actors and welfare providers. Against the backdrop of the Muslim community post-9/11 outreach paradigm, these cooperation networks with government officials, local councils, policymakers and authorities (e.g., police) have further intensified—also as a result of the growing political eagerness to cooperate with Muslim communities within the government's social cohesion program and counter-terrorism agenda. This urge to engage with Muslim communities is inherently linked to the unprecedented level of securitisation that Muslim communities have experienced as a result of 'increased state surveillance and public discourse that constructs Muslims as a potential terrorist threat' (Cherney and Murphy 2015: 403). On the one hand, Muslim communities have been constructed through counterterror legislation and the pertinent political rhetoric as a 'suspect community' (Cherney and Murphy 2015). On the other hand, governments have sought their support and cooperation in countering radicalisation and violent extremism. Against the backdrop of these ambivalent post-9/11 developments, the status of Muslim community organisations as ordinary stakeholders in a multi-ethno-religious civil society has become more contested (Grossman 2014).

Notwithstanding this arising ambivalence, longstanding cross-community cooperation and resilient lobbying and engagement with various civil society groups and political stakeholders, especially over the past decade, have resulted in a relatively high level of connectedness among broad segments of Muslim communities. The hitherto rather insular and isolated nature of Muslim organisations has substantially diminished, as multiple networks both within Muslim communities (Tillie 2004) and with non-Muslim groups and individuals have been established, expanding Muslim communities' linking and bridging social capital (Putnam 2000). This level of collective recognition of Muslim agency (Woolcock 2001) appears to be a solid basis for the mobilisation of Muslims into various forms of civic and political participation and cross-community engagement—despite the most recent deterioration of relationships with the Commonwealth government under Prime Minister Tony Abbott.

Germany

The organisational landscape of Muslim communities in Germany is no less complex and fragmented than the one in Australia. In contrast to the situation in Australia, this has been attributed not primarily to its internal ethnic diversity but, rather the opposite, to the tensions within the quantitatively dominant group of Muslims of Turkish origin. When Muslim community life started to evolve in the late 1960s and early 1970s, several Turkish Sunni Muslim groups set up separate organisational umbrella structures in Germany, each one trying to gain control over local mosque associations and competing over members and influence within the large Turkish Muslim community. These intra-communal power struggles revolved around political conflicts in Turkey and thus remained oddly disconnected from the everyday lives of Turks in Germany (Peucker and Akbarzadeh 2014: 168–174). Instead of cooperatively lobbying for the accommodation of religious needs in Germany, these Turkish exile organisations, many of them banned in Turkey, used Germany as a safe haven for their homeland-oriented mobilisation (Yükleyen and Yurdakul 2011). The three most important Islamic organisations at the time were the politically active *Milli Görüş* (later: *Islamische Gemeinschaft Milli Görüş* (IGMG)), affiliated with several consecutively banned Islamist parties in Turkey, headed by Necmettin Erbakan (Schiffauer 2007: 173), the mystical Islamic *Süleymanci* based *Islamische Kulturzentren* (IKZ, later: VIKZ) and, a few years later, Turkish-Islamic Union for Religious Affairs (DİTİB), run by the Turkish state's directorate for religious affairs *Diyanet* (Doomernik 1995: 51).

While the political and religious agenda, institutional outlook and internal activity profile of these Muslim organisations varied broadly, none of them was initially committed to assisting their clientele with their social or political integration in Germany. Besides the homeland-oriented political agenda, which lost prominence in the late 1980s, they provided a very basic religious infrastructure for Turkish 'guest workers' and their families, who considered their stay in Germany to be temporary. Consequently, mosque associations and other Muslim umbrella organisations for many years did not lobby for sustainable accommodation of religious needs, and they did not invest much effort in reaching out to the wider community. Direct interaction between Muslim groups and mainstream civil society organisations or government officials hardly occurred—not in the neighbourhood or with the local council and even less so on the state or national level. Networking and cooperation between Muslim community groups were vastly limited to the emerging vertical structures within national or supranational umbrella organisations, like DİTİB, IKZ or the *Milli Görüş*-dominated *Islamrat*, at the top and their affiliated local mosque association on the ground. For many years, horizontal networks between these Turkish Sunni Muslim groups were rare, and communication with the growing number of non-Turkish Muslim community organisations (e.g., Bosnians, Moroccans, multi-ethnic) was almost entirely absent. Needless to say, the relationship between Turkish Sunni groups and the many Turkish Alevis, which as a group suffered persecution and discrimination in Turkey and were thus extremely critical towards other Turkish groups, have been characterised by utter avoidance. Although this profound lack of collective social capital, leadership and community bridging ties of Muslim organisations in Germany has diminished since the late 1980s, it has had hampering implications for the emergence of both inter- and intra-community networks and communication channels until the present day.

Towards the end of the twentieth century the Muslim community landscape underwent significant changes as a result of a series of interrelated developments. With the easing political crisis in Turkey, the homeland-oriented mobilisation of Turkish exile organisations in Germany diminished. At the same time, many of these groups realised that more needed to be done to lobby for religious accommodation and to assist Muslim immigrant families in their settlement process. This new insight was driven by a mentality change that gained prominence among many Muslims. The vast majority of them had come to Germany as supposedly temporary guest workers with no intentions to stay permanently. This previously prevalent mindset began to change during the 1990s as more and more Muslims abandoned their plans of eventually returning to their country of origin.

Especially, the quickly growing second generation of Muslims considered Germany their home country, and they were less willing than their parents to accept the status of second-class residents without full citizenship rights. These changes coincided with an unprecedented ethno-religious diversification of Muslim communities following the arrival of large numbers of refugees from the Balkan, various corners of the Arab and Central Asian regions and other Muslim-majority countries. All these factors contributed to major shifts in the organisational landscape and activity profile of Muslim communities.

The number of newly established mosques, especially those set up by non-Turkish Muslim groups (e.g., Bosnians) and by multi-ethnic Muslim associations, not dominated by a particular nationality group, rose significantly. Moreover, a wide range of independent Muslim civil society organisations including Muslim women and youth associations have formed since the 1990s. This ongoing diversification process has reduced the previously almost hegemonic influence of the major Turkish-Sunni peak organisations, like DİTİB, VIKZ and IGMG, and it contributed to an emergence of a multitude of Muslim community voices. During the 1990s, Muslim community leaders became acutely aware that more cooperation and strategic alliances between different Muslim groups were vital for their efforts to improve the religious and social situation of their community members. Several attempts to set up a multi-ethnic Muslim representative body were undertaken—the foundation of the Central Council of Muslims in Germany (ZMD) being one of the initially most promising ones—but failed to achieve their main goal of speaking with one voice in lobbying for recognition and a greater degree of accommodation of Muslims' religious needs. Nevertheless, these developments mark the beginning of a new era of cross-community networking between Muslim organisations as well as between Muslim agency and state actors on local, state and federal level.

The endeavours of Muslim organisations to enhance inner-community networks have been driven to a considerable degree by external pressure, directly or indirectly exerted by the state or federal governments. In several states, Muslims community groups have joined forces since the late 1990s and established state-wide representative organisational structures—the so-called Schuras—to act as points of contact and negotiation partner for state governments in regard to the accommodation of Muslim needs (in particular Islamic instruction at school). Especially since the 2000s, cooperation initiatives between representatives from Muslim groups and non-Muslims civil society actors and authorities (e.g., police, government officials, internal security agency) at the state level have expanded slowly but continuously. These state-level exchange and discussion processes have been regarded as vital since some of the most pressing issues surrounding the accommodation of Muslim needs fall within the responsibility of state government. In several states they have already proven to be a practical and effective means of Muslims' lobbying for recognition, as the recent signing of formal state contracts (*Staatsverträge*) between Muslim organisations and the state governments of Hamburg and Bremen demonstrated.

On a local level, too, the cooperation between different Muslim organisations and mosque associations has increased and in many instances led to the formation of new local Islamic networks, which represent Muslim issues vis-à-vis civil society groups and local government (Lemmen 2009). Local Muslim civil society organisations and mosque associations have increasingly opened up to other non-Muslim community groups and broadened their engagement in intercultural and interfaith dialogue activities and the promotion of Muslim social integration. A recent study by Halm and Sauer (2012), who surveyed more than 1100 mosques, shows that most mosques in the twenty-first century are no longer isolated prayer places without links to the broader community. The study findings reveal that well over 60 % of all surveyed mosques are involved in interreligious dialogue initiatives, and more than eight in 10 mosques have participated in the annual community outreach initiative Open Mosque Day (Halm and Sauer 2012: 77–82).

On the national level, the launch of the high-profile German Islam Conference (DIK) in 2006, a government-initiated dialogue platform between Muslim organisations (and unaffiliated individuals) and government officials, marked a watershed moment in the relationship between Muslims and the German state (Peter 2010; Peucker and Akbarzadeh: 2014). Despite its many flaws and procedural shortcomings, the Islam Conference has had far-reaching ramification for the consolidation of Muslim communities, their leadership, public visibility and their cooperation—as recognised negotiation partners—with the state. In the run-up to the first DIK phase in 2006, the four DIK participating Muslim peak organisations DİTİB, Islamic Council, ZMD and VIKZ undertook an unprecedented step of joining forces to establish the Muslim umbrella organisation, Coordination Council of Muslims in Germany (KRM), which claims to represent around 80 % of all mosque associations (Lemmen 2009: 8). Although the KRM is less visible in public and political debates than some member organisations (especially the ZMD), the foundation of the KRM illustrate the shift towards more pragmatic and intensified cooperation between Muslim peak bodies and for a significant tightening of intra-communal ties within Muslim organisations. One key goal of the KRM that is yet to be achieved is formal recognition by the state as a religious community representation according to Germany's constitution (see below). This formal status as public corporation would grant the KRM enhanced legal, political and financial benefits (e.g., right to provide Islamic education in schools), similar to other religious communities, like the major (and various smaller) Christian denominations or the Jewish community.

Similar to the situation in Australia, the 9/11 terror attacks and, even more so, the 7/7 London bombings, have had major ramifications for the status and experiences of many Muslim community organisations in Germany. On the one hand, the debates arising about social integration have narrowed their focus specifically on Muslims and have put Muslim communities under an unprecedented degree of public scrutiny and suspicion (Schiffauer 2012). On the other hand, this magnifying political attention diminished the previous lack of visibility of Muslim community organisations. In this post 9/11 climate, ignoring Muslim communities was no viable political option any longer; the launch of the aforementioned DIK is the most significant marker of this development. Muslim communities that were previously largely ignored were now viewed more than ever with suspicion, but at the same time governments started to expect them to 'function as integration facilitators, as 24-hour contact partners for politics and media, and as counter-terrorism activists' (Rosenow-Williams 2013: 759). This ambivalence between increased recognition, expectations, and heightened suspicion has fundamentally changed the context within which Muslim community organisations attempt to negotiate their place in Germany's civil society and vis-à-vis policymakers.

Although these changes within the Muslim organisational landscape in Germany have entailed a major increase in the internal and external connectedness of Muslim communities, the recently emerging networks and communication channels with government officials and mainstream stakeholders have remained far less viable than among Muslim communities in Australia. Cooperation and lines of communication with public opinion leaders, the media and other prestigious institutions (e.g., universities) are still under-developed. Moreover, the relationship with government officials has often been overshadowed by mutual scepticism and has been dominated by the government's mistrust towards more orthodox expressions of Islam and the state's interventionist domestication attempt (Humphrey 2009) to mould a German Islam according to its own liberal ideals. This prevalent mistrust is vividly reflected by the fact that some Muslim organisations, most importantly the large 'post-Islamist' IGMG (Schiffauer 2010), are under surveillance by the German intelligence agency and officially considered to be in opposition to constitutional values, despite their active commitment to interfaith and cross-community initiatives, integration and civic engagement (Yükleyen and Yurdakul 2011).

While today's Muslim communities in Germany seem much more capable of encouraging and facilitating active citizenship among Muslims than a decade ago, their collective social capital and public standing are clearly less advanced than among their Australian counterparts.

References

Amath, N. (2013). The impact of 9/11 on Australian Muslim civil society organisations. *Communication, Politics & Culture, 46*, 116–135.
Bird, K., Saalfeld, T., & Wüst, A. M. (2011a). Ethnic diversity, political participation and representation: A theoretical framework. In K. Bird, T. Saalfeld, & A. M. Wüst (Eds.), *The political representation of immigrants and minorities. Voters, parties and parliaments in liberal democracies* (pp. 1–21). London: Routledge.
Bös, M. (2002). Das bedrohte Fundament nationaler Identität? Staatsangehörigkeit und Migration in Deutschland und Europe. In H. Kaelble, M. Kirsch, & A. Schmidt-Gernig (Eds.), *Transnationale Öffentlichkeiten und Identitäten im 20. Jahrhundert* (pp. 237–262). Frankfurt a.M.: Campus.
Bouma, G. D. (1999). Social justice issues in the management of religious diversity in Australia. *Social Justice Research, 12*(4), 283–295.

Bouma, G. D. (2012). Minority religious identity and religious social distance in Australia. In J. Pietsch & H. Aarons (Eds.), *Australia: Identity, fear and governance in the 21st century* (pp. 47–60). Canberra: ANU E Press.

Bouma, G. D., Daw, J., & Munawar, R. (2001). Muslims managing religious diversity. In A. Saeed & S. Akbarzadeh (Eds.), *Muslim communities in Australia* (pp. 53–72). Sydney: UNSW Press.

Bouma, G., Pickering, S., Halafoff, A., & Dellal, H. (2007). *Managing the impact of global crisis events on community relations in multicultural Australia*. East City (QLD)/Melbourne: Multicultural Affairs Queensland, Department for Victorian Communities.

Bowen, C. (2011). *The genius of Australian multiculturalism*. Address to the Sydney Institute, 17 February 2011. Online document viewed 23 April 2015 http://www.chrisbowen.net/media-centre/speeches.do?newsId=4154

Cherney, A., & Murphy, K. (2015). Being a "suspect community" in a post 9/11 world – The impact of the war on terror on Muslim communities in Australia. *Australian and New Zealand Journal of Criminology, 46*(3), 403–421.

Cleland, B. (2001). The history of Muslims in Australia. In A. Saeed & S. Akbarzadeh (Eds.), *Muslim communities in Australia* (pp. 12–32). Sydney: UNSW Press.

Commonwealth of Australia. (2011). *The people of Australia. Australia's multicultural policy*. Canberra: Commonwealth of Australia.

Didero, M. (2013). Muslim political participation in Germany: A structurationist approach. In J. S. Nielsen (Ed.), *Muslim political participation in Europe* (pp. 34–60). Edinburgh: Edinburgh University Press.

Doomernik, J. (1995). The institutionalization of Turkish Islam in Germany and the Netherlands: A comparison. *Ethnic & Racial Studies, 18*(1), 46–63.

Fetzer, J., & Soper, J. C. (2005). *Muslims and the state in Britain, France, and Germany*. New York: Cambridge University Press.

German Government (Bundesregierung). (2007). *Nationaler Integrationsplan*. Berlin: Bundesregierung.

Grossman, M. (2014). Disenchantments: Counterterror narratives and conviviality. *Critical Studies on Terrorism, 7*(3), 319–335.

Halm, D., & Sauer, M. (2012). Angebote und Strukturen der islamischen Organisationen in Deutschland. In D. Halm, M. Sauer, J. Schmidt, & A. Stichs (Eds.), *Islamisches Gemeindeleben in Deutschland*. Nuremberg/Essen: BAMF/ZfTI.

Häußermann, H., & Siebel, W. (2004). *Stadtsoziologie. Eine Einführung*. Frankfurt a.M: Campus.

Humphrey, M. (1988). Community, mosque and ethnic politics. *ANZ Journal of Sociology, 23*(2), 233–245.

Humphrey, M. (2001). An Australian Islam? Religion in the multicultural city. In A. Saeed & S. Akbarzadeh (Eds.), *Muslim communities in Australia* (pp. 33–52). Sydney: UNSW Press.

Humphrey, M. (2009). Securitisation and domestication of Diaspora Muslims and Islam: Turkish immigrants in Germany and Australia. *International Journal on Multicultural Societies, 11*(2), 136–154.

Hunger, U. (2002). *Von der Betreuung zur Eigenverantwortung. Neuere Entwicklungstendenzen bei Migrantenvereinen in Deutschland* (Working paper). Münster: Westfälische Wilhelms-Universität Münster.

Hunger, U., & Candan, M. (2009). *Politische Partizipation der Migranten in der Bundesrepublik Deutschland und über die deutschen Grenzen hinweg*. Münster: Westfälische Wilhelms-Universität Münster.

Ireland, P. (1994). *The policy challenge of ethnic diversity. Immigrant politics in France and Switzerland*. Cambridge: Harvard University Press.

Jakubowicz, A. (1989). The state and the welfare of immigrants in Australia. *Ethnic and Racial Studie, 12*(1), 1–35.

Jakubowicz, A., Collins, J., & Chafic, W. (2012). Young Australian Muslims: Social ecology and cultural capital. In F. Mansouri & V. Marotta (Eds.), *Muslims in the West and the challenges of belonging* (pp. 34–59). Carlton: Melbourne University Press.

Jamal, A. (2005). The political participation and engagement of Muslim Americans: Mosque involvement and group consciousness. *American Politics Research, 33*(4), 521–544.

Jurado, E. (2008). *Citizenship – Tool or award? The role of citizenship policy in the process of integration*. London: Policy Network.

Keating, P. J. (1995). *Opening address at the Global Cultural Diversity Conference Proceedings, Sydney*. Online document, viewed 24 April 2015 https://www.dss.gov.au/our-responsibilities/settlement-and-multicultural-affairs/programs-policy/a-multicultural-australia/programs-and-publications/1995-global-cultural-diversity-conference-proceedings-sydney/opening-address

König, M. (2005). Incorporating Muslim migrants in Western nation states – A comparison of the United Kingdom, France, and Germany. *Journal of International Migration & Integration, 6*(2), 219–234.

Kraus, P. A., & Schönwälder, K. (2006). Multiculturalism in Germany: Rhetoric, scattered experiments and future chances. In K. Banting, & W. Kymlicka (Eds.), *Multiculturalism and the welfare state. Recognition and redistribution in contemporary democracies*. Oxford: Oxford University Press.

Lemmen, T. (2009). Engere Kooperation. Die islamischen Organisationen und der Staat. *Herder Korrespondenz Spezial, 2*, 6–11.
Markus, A. (2015). *Mapping social cohesion. The Scanlon Foundation Survey 2015*. Caulfield East: Monash University.
Modood, T. (2010). Multicultural citizenship and Muslim identity politics. *Interventions: International Journal of Postcolonial Studies, 12*(2), 157–170.
Peter, F. (2010). Welcoming Muslims into the nation. Tolerance politics and integration in Germany. In J. Cesari (Ed.), *Muslims in Europe and the United States since 9/11* (pp. 119–144). London: Routledge.
Peucker, M., & Akbarzadeh, S. (2014). *Muslim active citizenship in the West*. London/New York: Routledge.
Peucker, M., Roose, J. M., & Akbarzadeh, S. (2014). Muslim active citizenship in Australia: Socioeconomic challenges and the emergence of a Muslim elite. *Australian Journal of Political Science, 49*(2), 282–299.
Putnam, R. D. (2000). *Bowling alone: The collapse and revival of American community*. New York: Simon and Schuster.
Read, J. G. (2015). Gender, religious identity, and civic engagement among Arab Muslims in the United States. *Sociology of Religion, 76*(1), 30–48.
Rosenow-Williams, K. (2013). Organising Muslims and integrating Islam: Applying organisational sociology to the study of Islamic organisations. *Journal of Ethnic and Migration Studies, 40*(5), 759–777.
Saeed, A. (2003). *Islam in Australia*. Crows Nest: Allen & Unwin.
Schiffauer, W. (2007). From exile to Diaspora: The development of transnational Islam in Europe. In A. Al-Azmeh & E. Fokas (Eds.), *Islam in Europe. Diversity, identity and influence* (pp. 156–178). Cambridge: Cambridge University Press.
Schiffauer, W. (2008). *Parallelgesellschaften. Wie viel Wertekonsens braucht unsere Gesellschaft? Für eine kluge Politik der Differenz*. Bielefeld: transcript.
Schiffauer, W. (2010). *Nach dem Islamismus. Eine Ethnographie der Islamischen Gemeinschaft Milli Görüş*. Berlin: Suhrkamp.
Schiffauer, W. (2012). Before the law: Priorities and contradictions in the dialogue between the German state and Muslims in Germany. *European Journal on Criminal Policy and Research, 18*(4), 361–383.
Smith, D., Wykes, J., Jayarajah, S., & Fabijanic, T. (2011). *Citizenship in Australia*. Canberra: DIAC.
Tillie, J. (2004). Social capital of organisations and their members: Explaining the political integration of immigrants in Amsterdam. *Journal of Ethnic and Migration Studies, 30*(3), 529–541.

Yükleyen, A., & Yurdakul, G. (2011). Islamic activism and immigrant integration: Turkish organizations in Germany. *Immigrants and Minorities, 29*(1), 64–85.

Woolcock, M. (2001). The place of social capital in understanding social and economic outcomes. *Isuma: Canadian Journal of Policy Research, 2*(1), 11–17.

6

Types and Trajectories of Muslims' Activism

Active Muslims interviewed for this study were selected based on their active involvement in one or two forms of civic or political participation (see Table 2.2. and 2.3 in Chap. 3). This selection process sought to ensure a maximum diversity of manifestations of active citizenship. It was aimed at covering independent as well as collective forms of civic engagement pursuing either Muslim community (e.g., within a Muslim community organisation) or other group-related objectives (e.g., within trade union) or republican goals revolving around advancing the wellbeing of society at large. These neatly defined selection categories served their purpose as guidelines for the sampling process, but they turned out to be too rigid to capture the multi-faceted manifestation of active citizenship of most of the interview partners. This points to the first key finding: the majority of interviewed Muslims in Australia and Germany have been involved—often simultaneously—in various civic-political activities within an organisational context as well as independently, and many have pursued both communitarian and republican goals without expressing conflicts between both agendas.

What adds to this complexity is that most interview partners demonstrated an extensive history of active citizenship that evolved over time, with no immediate end in sight; and most of these civic careers of interviewed Muslims have seen substantial shifts. Although each of the 30 individual Muslims had their unique story to tell, the qualitative analysis of the interview data revealed certain trajectory patterns that occurred more commonly than other patterns.

This chapter begins with a descriptive discussion of the various types of civic engagement of the 30 interviewed Muslims. This reflects to some extent the choices made in selecting interview partners based on their involvement in specific forms of civic or political participation. This analysis of the location of Muslims' active citizenship also demonstrates, however, that their multifaceted engagement tends to go beyond the forms of participation that they were initially chosen for. After the examination of the different locations of their activism, the chapter presents an analysis of the civic trajectories and related personal experiences of the interviewed Muslims and explores the transition moments within these citizenship careers.

Locations of Muslims' Active Citizenship

Muslims interviewed for this study have been active in a range of different contexts. The analysis of the location of their civic engagement differentiates between their (1) civic participation within Muslim community structures, (2) engagement in mainstream civil society context and (3) formal or informal political participation, including media activism. This categorisation serves as an analytical structure to describe interviewed Muslims' active citizenship; it does not reflect their often multifaceted and dynamic civic biographies, which will be examined in detail in the second part of this chapter.

Civic Participation in a Muslim Community Context

The vast majority of interview partners described the Muslim community as an important reference point or organisational location of their civic and/or political participation. This confirms previous research findings in both countries pinpointing that the religious organisational context is a key site where many Muslims are actively involved as volunteers (Monash University 2009b; Halm and Sauer 2005). The prevalence of the Muslim community context as the place of civic engagement, as discovered in this study, is not merely a result of the interview selection process, for even some of those chosen due to their active role within mainstream institutions also mentioned forms of civic participation within the Muslim community context. These community-based types of activism manifest themselves in a variety of ways. Muslim organisations, ranging from traditional Islamic community and umbrella organisations and local mosque associations to independent Muslim youth, student or women's organisations, often serve as a platform that encourages and channels Muslims' active citizenship.

The vast majority of interview partners in both country samples have more or less intensive personal ties to Muslim organisations, and these ties have often played a crucial role in their civic, and sometimes also, their political engagement. In the Australian fieldwork, although half of the 14 interviewed Muslims were chosen mainly based on their activism outside the Muslim community, 12 stated that their civic or political engagement has taken place at least partially within or in conjunction with Muslim community groups. Only two interview partners (AUS1, AUS13) explained that they had never been involved in any Muslim community related forms of activism. For eight of the 12, civic participation has been and still is primarily rooted in their affiliation with Muslim community organisations, such as mosque associations, Muslim women's or youth groups or Muslim representative (umbrella) organisations. One interview partner, Ms Sabbagh (AUS5), whose civic engagement has been predominantly located in the Muslim community context, even set up her own grassroots organisations. The first formed together with her religious teacher and her husband is the *Young Muslims of Australia*, which is now the oldest Muslim youth group in Australia. The second and more recent is *Benevolence*, a community organisation for Muslims 'dedicated to serving the Australian community through the teachings exemplified and inspired by the Prophet Muhammad (peace be upon him)' (website).

In the German sample, there were also only two interview partners who did not mention any connections with the Muslim community sphere during their civic career, although several interviewed Muslims were selected because of their active engagement in the trade union or in political parties. In eight of the 16 civic biographies of participants in Germany, Muslim organisations constituted the main context for their current civic participation. Most of the others mentioned Muslim community organisation either as a previous or as a current but secondary context. Three interview partners—all women—established their own community organisations. Ms Theißen (AUS3), a German convert, set up a Muslim women's support and empowerment organisation in 1996. Ms Dogan (DE8) co-founded the women's organisation *Fraueninitiative für Bildung und Erziehung* (FIBEr, Women's Initiative for Education), which focusses on education-related issues for Muslim and non-Muslim women, and the local political party *BIG*, which she represented in the local council as an elected council member. The third woman, *Alev* (DE11), established a local organisation that is primarily active in the area of interfaith and intercultural dialogue, associated with the Gülen movement.

This relevance of the Muslim community as the context of active citizenship, even for some of those whose active citizenship is geared towards republican or other non-Muslim community goals (on which basis they were selected) is an important finding of this study. This holds true for both the Australian as well as the German sub-sample. *Burak* (DE1),[1] for instance, was chosen due to his active participation as political party member and elected local councillor. During the interview it was learned that he used to be a board member of a Turkish-Islamic (mosque) association. Another example in the German sample was *Onur* (DE16), a full-time representative of a workers' council (similar to a shop steward; *freigestellter Betriebsrat*) in a large manufacturing company. He was interviewed because of his active role in the trade union. Besides some other civic activities in a non-Muslim context, *Onur* also stressed that he often 'acts as an informal point of contact' for many local Turkish-Islamic community organisations. Although he does not hold a formal position there, he 'of course also helps out' (DE16) in the mosque where is father is

---

[1] Names of interview partners written in italics indicate that the names are pseudonyms; these interview partners preferred not to be named and to remain anonymous.

chairman, and he has personal contacts with many other local mosque communities.

In the Australian sample, there were also several participants selected due to their engagement for broader social issues not immediately linked to the Muslim community. It turned out during the interviews that the active involvement of some of them has been focussed, at least partially, on the advancement and support of Muslim community. Mr Kamareddine (AUS7), for example, a civil engineer with a recently awarded PhD, was initially selected on the basis of his candidature in the 2012 local council elections in Hobson's Bay (Melbourne). While it was clear at the time of his selection that his political candidature was endorsed by the local Islamic Society in Newport (Melbourne), the interview revealed that Mr Kamareddine's active citizenship was *primarily* located within the Muslim community, including an Islamic school, where he was board member, the local mosque, where he was actively involved in youth work, and as volunteer supervisor of the construction of the new Newport mosque.

Civic Engagement in a Mainstream Community Context

The analysis of the diverse forms of civil society engagement of interview partners in both country samples highlights that active Muslim citizens can rarely be described as *either* Muslim community *or* mainstream-based activist. It was very common that the individuals' engagement falls within *both* categories. Around one-half of the 14 interviewed Muslims in Australia have been involved in civic participation within the mainstream community context, not including political forms of activism (see below). For some of them, this mainstream-based activism has been complemented, sometimes simultaneously, by active engagement in Muslim community organisations.

Mr Sattar (AUS8) has been a board member of the Muslim organisation Mission of Hope, where he has also been active for the project Hayat House Street Outreach offering support to at-risk youth in the Bankstown area in Western Sydney. Prior to his role at Mission of Hope, Mr Sattar volunteered for a range of mainstream organisations. 'My active citizenship started, working with the Cancer Council, raising money through street charity fundraisers', which he got involved in as a high school student. He also mentioned his 'passion for human rights', which made him go 'to protests fighting for people's rights … [and against] anything that I found to be oppressive. Aboriginal rights, land rights, (…) the Northern Territory Intervention'. During his early years at university he continued volunteering for mainstream organisations; he stated as an example that 'we were doing cupcake stores for AIDS awareness and stuff like that' (AUS8).

Ms Saleh (AUS10) was asked to participate in this study due to her position as public relations manager at amnesty international Australia, but her civic engagement activities turned out to predominantly revolve around her volunteering work and leadership role within Mission of Hope. She also stated during the interview that she had previously volunteered for UNICEF (although doing only basic administrative work). Other interview partners who actively participated in mainstream civil society institutions are Mr Dellal (AUS4), executive director of the Australian Multicultural Foundation in Melbourne, and Ms Abdo (AUS9), manager of the United Muslim Women's Association (UMWA) in Sydney. Both of them have, for example, been on the board of the public broadcasting service SBS.[2] Moreover, Ms Abdo has represented the UMWA within the Sydney Alliance, a cross-community initiative in Sydney's west, officially launched in 2007. This coalition of community groups, religious organisations, unions and schools has run various activities seeking to 'make the city a better place to live' (website). The Alliance has been advocating for, among other goals, better public transport, housing and employment opportunities. These forms of cross-community collaboration, bringing together various community groups to work towards joint goals, highlights the blurry boundaries between civic engagement in a Muslim community and a mainstream context. More generally, it reflects the shifts and overlaps between republic and communitarian manifestations of

---

[2] SBS, the Special Broadcasting Service, is a public and hybrid-funded radio and TV broadcaster specifically established with the aim of, and dedicated to, promoting and catering for a multicultural Australian society. Mr Dellal was director of the SBS Board at the time of the interview.

active citizenship, where the needs of certain communities dovetail with the greater good of society as a whole.

Mr Merhi (AUS1) was one of two interviewed Muslims in the Australian sample who did not mention any involvement in a Muslim community context. He has been active in the trade union as well as in various grassroots civil society organisations, for example, as a volunteer Football (AFL) coach for several junior teams (often disadvantaged youth). He also mentioned his involvement in an initiative providing breakfast for 'poor primary school students' (AUS1). Moreover, he stressed his volunteering as youth mentor within a project, run by a local church group (Uniting Church), where he was looking after young kids, some of them Indigenous and 'orphans who did not have a father figure' (AUS1). Ms Faruqi (AUS13), member of the NSW state parliament (Upper House) for The Greens, is the second person in the Australian sample who has never been involved in Muslim community work during her active citizenship career in Australia. Her civic engagement has unfolded primarily within various environmentalist community groups, for which she has volunteered for many years in different roles.

The analysis of the German sample paints a similar picture. Half of the 16 Muslims in the German sample mentioned at least some level of engagement in a mainstream civil society context. This ranges from independent (unaffiliated) 'good citizen' contributions, for example, as lay jury members at court (*Schöffe*; DE4, DE16) or as election poll volunteer (*Wahlhelfer*; DE4, DE13), to active engagement within mainstream organisational settings. The latter has taken place in a range of non-Muslim (and non-ethno-religious or migrant) organisations. *Burak* (DE1), for example, has been a volunteer in the local fire brigade and used to be actively involved in his German hometown's international sister city partnership initiative. *Esra* (DE7), selected for her participation in a Muslim youth network, volunteered for the local branch of a socialist youth organisation, where she ran various support programs for socioeconomically disadvantaged youth in the neighbourhood and subsequently moved up into a leadership position. Ms Dogan (DE8), a local councillor in Bonn, has been involved in interfaith dialogue initiatives and a local multiethnic Muslim community group (*Rat der Muslime*), where she was initially involved in setting up a Muslim women's subgroup. As the cross-community activities of this Muslim women's group evolved, Ms Dogan eventually established a new local women's initiative for education, led by a multicultural team of women, offering activities for Muslim *and* non-Muslim women in the neighbourhood. Lastly, the interview with Mr Yerli (DE14), chairman of the local mosque in Penzberg (Bavaria), revealed that he has also acted as official workers' representative (*Betriebsrat*) within his company and trade union representative—similar to *Onur* (DE16) who has been an active trade union representative at local, regional and national level.

Political Participation

While all interviewed Muslims in Australia, and all but two (DE6, DE12) in the German sample, have been involved in some forms of civic participation, a significant number of interview partners have also become politically active. This may encompass political party work, running for (or holding) a political office or acting as member of a committee and board within the political landscape, but it may also involve more informal and less institutionalised forms of making their voice heard in the public discourse, for example in the media.

In the Australian sample, half of all interview partners elaborated on their political participation. Three of them have run for a political office on local or state level, either as member of a political party (in both cases, The Greens; AUS3, AUS13) or as an independent candidate in the local council (AUS7) or state election (AUS3). Although none of them won a seat in the elections, Ms Faruqi (AUS13) obtained a political mandate later, being internally elected by her party to fill a vacant seat in the NSW Upper House. Mr Ahmed (AUS3), an African community activist with political ambitions, ran as a member of The Greens for a seat in the Victorian state elections and as an Independent candidate in the Melbourne by-election.

The dominant form of political participation in the Australian sample, which applies to five of the seven politically active Muslims, is sitting on mostly government-initiated boards, committees or advisory councils, which give a voice to civil society representatives from various groups and communities within the political decision-making processes. Most of these committees or advisory councils are characterised by their multicultural profile. This often reflects their specific agenda, as it is the case with local multicultural councils, the national Multicultural Advisory Council or the (temporary) government-initiated Muslim Reference Group. In other cases (e.g., Victorian Human Rights Commission), the committee's diverse composition is rather the result of the pertinent organisations' general endeavour to represent the pluralistic Australian civil society.

Several interviewed Australian Muslims considered their committee work an effective and worthwhile political exercise. Only one interview partner, Ms El Matrah (AUS2), expressed some criticism about this kind of political participation. Mr Galil (AUS11), an imam who represented an Islamic Society in Melbourne's east at the Knox Multicultural Advisory Committee between 2007 and 2013, praised the work of this advisory committee and the official recognition it enjoys:

> It was a marvellous time, we've had a number of recommendations been implemented by the Council, which was terrific. We usually had two or three councillors attending the meeting … as well as the council staff! It shows that the council is really serious about it.

Ms Abdo (AUS9), community worker and manager of the Muslim Women's organisation UMWA in Sydney's west, has been heavily involved in political committee work for many years, representing the views of the Muslim community (and of Muslim women in particular) as members of the greater society. She remarked: 'I was on various advisory committees, and I was sitting on a ministerial advisory committee … engaging on all these levels … You know, sport and recreation, safety for Muslim women, women only swimming spaces [and so on]' (AUS9). She also mentioned as an early example her involvement in a local council-led advisory group in Bankstown (Western Sydney), dating back some 15 years, which dealt with, among others, issues revolving around problems of 'sexual violence at the local level' (AUS9).

Ms Abdo's political collaboration with policymakers and local and state governments has also another facet outside the institutional context of advisory committees. As UMWA representative she has over the years established direct lines of communication with key policymakers, which have recently been utilised more effectively: 'We engage with government a little bit more. We engage with the government and ask them what are your stands on [a particular] issue'. As an example, Ms Abdo mentioned the heatedly discussed issue of Muslim women being obliged to take off their face covering for police checks. This problem was ultimately resolved by the NSW government with new legislation, for which UMWA and other Muslim organisations were directly consulted and which was positively acknowledged by these Muslim community groups (Peucker and Akbarzadeh 2014: 162). Ms Abdo elaborated on the negotiation and discussion process: 'At that time we had an election here, so we were talking to the Premier of the previous government, and then talking to both parties about what we want as Muslim women'.

Ms El Matrah (AUS2), representative of the Australian Muslim Women's Centre for Human Rights in Melbourne, also elaborated on her active membership of a number of boards (e.g., Victorian Human Rights Commission) and high-profile advisory committees, including the Muslim Reference Group. Reflecting on her involvement in this political engagement, she pointed to the government's endeavour to get especially Muslim women on board of these consultation processes: 'The government people have been a little bit better [after 9/11], sometimes for the wrong reasons, but they have worked really hard to bring women around the table with men'.

The analysis of the political activities of Muslims in Australia revealed that a majority were also involved in media work. Although none of them was chosen as an interview partners primarily because of their media activism, 10 of the 14 interview partners mentioned that they have made active contributions to the media, by either publishing opinion pieces or other newspaper articles (often on request), by giving interviews or by cooperating with the media as public relations officer of a Muslim community group. Most of them have done so without any formal media training. Some interviewed Muslims have been engaged in alternative media outlets (e.g., an Arabic-English newspaper for Muslims in Australia; AUS7) and online platforms (e.g., blogs; AUS12, AUS14). Others have occurred occasionally—and some quite regularly—as commentators in the mainstream news media, voicing their views on various

Muslim or migrant-related issues, often (indirectly) representing shared perspectives within segments of their community (AUS2, AUS3, AUS9 and AUS12).

Mr Ahmed (AUS3), a political and African community activist in Melbourne, for example, explained that in addition to his main civic engagement in the political and community sphere he uses the media as a platform to contribute to the political and public debate. Convinced that the media reporting 'creates a picture' that other people generally consider to be true, he explained: 'I use the media to reach out … I advocate in the media about refugee issues, about integration problems, I speak loudly in the mainstream, but I also speak within the communities'. He links his media power directly to his civic efficacy, elaborating that politicians contact him personally to hear his political views and to take them on board because of his community leadership and media presence: 'I'm visible in the media. If I write something against [politicians], it will hurt them. So it is better for them to "neutralise" me'.

Mr Tabbaa (AUS12), board member of the Islamic Council of Victoria (ICV) at the time of the interview, where he was in charge of media and youth, started his media activism informally with a blog on Facebook in 2011. 'Since then I've been going to different [alternative media] outlets … and I have a better idea now which outlets might be better, and I also have a few that would always accept [my articles]'. He recalled that out of frustration mainly about developments within the Muslim community he used to write down his views, but he 'didn't know what to do with … I tried to publish it, but it wasn't successful, nobody would know what to do with it. I contacted different organisations but nothing happened'. But since one of his opinion pieces was finally published by a major Australian newspaper, the Sydney Morning Herald, attracting a large number of online viewers ('That was the big article, got 80,000 hits in one day'.), he has been requested to write articles several times and has published a few more.

In the German sample, nine of the 16 interviewed Muslims spoke about their current or previous engagement in the political sphere. However, at least three of them stated that they deliberately stopped their political activism (DE3, DE7, DE9). Dissatisfied with the political processes or the internal structures of political parties, they abandoned the political path in their civic careers. A fourth interview partner, Mr Aydin (DE10), renounced his party membership due to his disagreement with the party's negative view on the accession of Turkey to the European Union, but continued to politically participate as a member of the local migrants' representative advisory council (*Migrationsrat*).

Engagement within these local advisory councils, a politically weak institution, set up by the local council, comprising of migrant representatives elected by a city's foreign or migrant population (see Chap. 5), was the dominant form of institutional political participation in the German sample. Four Muslims were either currently (DE4, DE10) or previously (DE7, DE11) involved in one of these local institutions of political representation. These advisory councils were also criticised by several of these interview partners. *Esra* (DE7) and Mr Fetić (DE4), for example, lamented their political ineffectiveness and lack of influence and decision-making power—a view that echoes a general assessment prevalent among integration experts (Hunger and Candan 2009: 10–11; Cyrus and Vogel 2008: 30–31; Didero 2013: 39). *Esra* put it very bluntly: 'The whole system of these [advisory] councils is really idiotic, because one does not have a voice there, because this is all tokenistic politics' (DE7). In the same vein, Mr Fetić described the political advisory work in these councils as tokenistic forms of political participation: 'I have always described it as a "sandpit", which politicians give to immigrants, where they can play with each other … this is actually some kind of self-occupation therapy'.

Altogether eight interviewed Muslims in the German sample have (or had previously) been active members of a political party (three of them no longer), but only two of them stated they have run as a candidate in an election—both of them secured a political mandate in the local council (DE1, DE8). It is worth noting that one of them, Ms Dogan (DE8), held a seat in the city council of Bonn as an elected member of a political party that she herself co-founded with the goal to create an alternative political voice on issues around migrant integration, education and the recognition of ethno-religious diversity. Two other interviewed Muslims, *Miran* (DE12) and Mr Fetić (DE4), have had active leadership roles in certain sub-groups within mainstream political parties, set up primarily for people of minority background. *Miran* was a coordinator of the

Turkish migrant initiatives *SPD ve biz* within the Social Democratic Party in the state of Baden-Wuerttemberg, and Mr Fetić represented the *Grüne Muslime* (Green Muslims) initiative of the Green Party in the state of North Rhine-Westphalia (NRW), focussing especially on advancing the recognition of Islam and Muslims.

Only very few interview partners in the German sample mentioned the media as a relevant site of their (political) activism. One of them, Mr Cicek (DE9), a young student of Turkish descent, started his civic career by setting up an online blog to contribute to the political debate on Muslim integration. He has also worked as a journalist for several overseas newspapers on various topics. Mr Şenol (DE6) was selected as an interview partner because he has been running a successful online news platform to add an alternative voice to the political discourse on integration, citizenship and cultural diversity.

Concluding Analysis: Locations of Active Citizenship

The diverse sites of civic participation among interviewed Muslims echo previous research findings on their organisation-based active membership and volunteering in a civil society context in Australia and Germany (Chap. 4). In both national contexts previous studies have revealed that Muslims are actively involved in a range of Muslim and non-Muslim organisational settings, with religious community organisations being the most prominent site of their participation (Halm and Sauer 2005; Haug et al. 2009; Monash University 2009a). This explorative research confirms these findings—but it also draws a much more complex and dynamic picture of Muslims' organisation-based engagement, highlighting that many Muslims have been active in various organisations, both religious and non-religious, either simultaneously or consecutively over the course of their civic biographies. These shifts within their civic pathways will be discussed in more depth in the second part of this chapter.

Comparing the different contexts of *political* participation of interviewed Muslims in Australia and Germany allows tentative conclusions on the political opportunity structures, which appear overall more favourable in Australia. The only institutional platform (outside of political parties) politically active interview partners in Germany mentioned was the rather powerless local migrant advisory councils. No other types of committees or boards where they could have added their voice to the political debate were mentioned. In contrast, politically active Muslims interviewed in Australia have been involved in a range of different committees and advisory boards. They appear to have better chances to actively contribute to debates and decision-making processes as recognised civil society stakeholders, be it independently or as representatives of their community organisations. The cross-national comparison suggests that these institutional sites of decision-making for civil society stakeholders are not only more common, but also more inclusive and accessible for Muslims in Australia than they are in Germany. Moreover, while some Muslims in Germany described their political involvement in these local advisory councils as tokenistic, Australian Muslims were generally more positive about their political engagement in boards and committees.

Media activism was mentioned very often as an additional form of informal political engagement in the Australian sample, but it played only a marginal role among Muslims interviewed in Germany. While the two national sub-samples are in no way representative, these observations reverberate with the findings of a recent study by Peucker and Akbarzadeh (2014). The two researchers concluded that 'Australian Muslim voices have become much more present in the mainstream media over the past decade or so', whereas in Germany 'the presence of Muslim voices in the media is, albeit growing, still very limited' (Peucker and Akbarzadeh 2014: 121–122). This difference is also reflected by the general research interest in Muslims' media activism. There have been several studies in the Australian context—but none in Germany—that have explored Muslims' active participation in the media as a struggle for recognition and equal citizenship.

The Australian researcher Tanja Dreher was one of the first to systematically examine attempts of 'speaking up and talking back' (2003) in the media and 'community media intervention' (2010) of ethnic and religion minorities, including Muslims in Australia. Dreher's research focusses on the way in which Muslim communities have responded to skewed media reporting on Muslims, particularly since the 9/11 terrorist attacks. 'Media racism', Dreher (2010: 186) argues, 'creates a heavy workload for community organisations and community representatives, who are called upon to defend their communities by responding to intense scrutiny and media demands'. According to Dreher's observations, Muslims' media activism has contributed to a 'far greater diversity of representations of Muslims in Australia' (Dreher 2010: 195),[3] improved reporting in the mainstream media and to a general sense of empowerment among participating Muslims (Dreher 2010: 186). However, this media engagement continues to be a rather reactive and responsive 'command performance' (Dreher 2010: 196), in which Muslims rarely get a chance to set the agenda and are rather urged to explain and respond to accusations and prevalent stereotype (see also Carland 2012).[4]

The findings of the present study paint an ambiguous picture of Muslims' political participation within parties and the formal (electoral) political system. On the one hand, political party membership was mentioned very often in the German sample—much more commonly than in the Australian sample. Only three of them (in the German sample) were chosen due their political party engagement, which suggests that political parties might often be an additional space where Muslims seek to become politically active. This resonates with the finding of the representative MLG survey that a relatively high proportion of self-declared Muslims in Germany were members in political parties—2.8 % of all surveyed Muslims (Haug et al. 2009: 260), which is slightly above the 2 % level of the total population (Gisart 2013: 361). What also stands out in this cross-national comparison is that two of the politically active interview partners in Germany, who both have never tried to win a mandate, hold a leadership role within party sub-groups specifically targeting party members of Muslim (*Grüne Muslime*, DE4) or Turkish background (*SPD ve*

---

[3] The above mentioned study *Political Participation of Muslim in Australia* (Al-Momani et al. 2010: 22) lists a range of Muslim public figures, community leaders and opinion makers in Australia, among them Muslim academics, authors or other professionals, who have 'achieved a public voice' in the media who by, for example, writing co-eds for major newspapers, giving interviews to journalist and participating in broadcasted debates on TV or the radio.
[4] Dreher's conclusion about the empowering effect of active media work stand in some contrast to the arguments of other Australian researchers (Aly 2007; Posetti 2010) who have maintained that Muslims' continuous use of mainstream media would reinforce their sense of victimhood and hamper their feelings of belonging. Instead, these latter studies argue, Muslims can gain a sense of self-empowerment by deliberately disengaging with the mainstream media.

biz, DE12). Such institutional sub-structures for minorities, which have proven to be effective stepping stones on the way to more powerful positions within the party and eventually the parliament, have not been mentioned in the Australian sample.

On the other hand, party membership among interviewed Muslims in Germany does not necessarily indicate serious political ambitions or effective political participation. Only half of all eight interviewed Muslims with a current or previous party membership described the political party work as an important aspect of their current civic engagement; among those only two had ever tried to obtain a political mandate, both successfully and both on the local level (DE1, DE8). It is noteworthy though that one of them, Ms Dogan (DE8), sat in the Bonn city council not as a representative of a mainstream party but of the alternative political initiative *Bündnis für Innovation und Gerechtigkeit* (*BIG, Alliance for Innovation and Justice*), which pursues a deliberately multicultural agenda (Didero 2013; Peucker and Akbarzadeh 2014: 183). Several interviewed Muslims who mentioned a party membership in the German sample had abandoned these political ambitions due to dissatisfaction with some of the party's viewpoints or internal party dynamics and/or their personal acceptance within the party.[5] All this suggests that mainstream political parties might be perceived as not very inclusive of Muslims (and possibly other ethno-religious minorities); their suitability as sites for effective and active political engagement of Muslims appears limited.

The analysis of the German sample data also pinpoints the hampering impact of Germany's citizenship regime and naturalisation regulations on some interviewed Muslims' formal political participation. Mr Aydin (DE10), who does not hold German citizenship (although he has been living in Germany for 40 years), for example, criticised that he cannot become German citizen unless he renounces his Turkish citizenship—which he is not prepared to do. He stressed that without this restrictive legal provision on dual citizenship he would apply for citizenship, re-commence his party membership again (which he had previously

---

[5] Ms Theißen (DE3), who did not pursue her membership with the Greens because of a lack of time, also mentioned that her husband—a Muslim who came to Germany as a refugee—tried to get involved with the local Social Democrats but did not feel welcome by the other party members.

abandoned) and become politically much more active. Several other interviewed Muslims also mentioned these hampering opportunity structures for electoral political participation, referring to Germany's restrictive citizenship regime, in particular the political reluctance to accept dual citizenship.

Another rather peculiar administrative practice within the Germany's citizenship regime has been an additional hurdle for some Muslims' active political engagement. Any person who is or has previously been active within community groups affiliated with certain Muslim organisations, such as *Milli Görüş* (IGMG) or the Islamic Community Germany (*Islamische Gemeinschaft Deutschland, IGD*), which are monitored by the German domestic intelligence agency (*Verfassungsschutz*) due to suspicion of partially anti-constitutional tendencies,[6] is usually denied citizenship. Mr Yerli (DE4), who used to be affiliated with a local IGMG-run mosque (back then the only mosque in his home town), applied for citizenship but his application was rejected—in his views because of his leading role in youth work at the IGMG-affiliated and another independent mosque. He reported that many other Muslims who have been active within Muslim community organisations and mosques have had similar experiences of political disenfranchisement. Not holding German citizenship and thus lacking full political rights has hampered Mr Yerli's political ambition to become more actively involved in local politics, for example as member of the city council.

In the Australian sample, such structural or legal hurdles of political participation were not mentioned. In contrast to Muslims interviewed in Germany, none of the Australian Muslims who have been actively involved in political parties have abandoned their political ambitions. To the contrary, the two interview partners who spoke about their party membership have also run for political office and consider their political participation to be quite successful. Similarly, the third interviewed Muslim who ran for a seat in the local council as an Independent expressed positive views about his candidature. Ms Faruqi (AUS13) described her and

---

[6] The cultural anthropologist Werner Schiffauer (2010) offers an in-depth study of more recent developments *within Milli Görüş* in Germany; his findings fundamentally question the allegations of the German *Verfassungsschutz*.

her party's election results as very satisfactory and a great success for The Greens, although she did not win the seat. And Mr Ahmed (AUS3), an African community and political activist, considers himself very successful in having used the preferential voting system in Australia to achieve his political goals for the advancement of his community—without ever having won a political mandate.

Trajectories: Dynamic Shifts in Muslims' Civic Careers

Most interviewed Muslims demonstrated a more or less extensive career as active citizens, and many of them have experienced significant shifts during their civic biographies. The analysis of the 30 individual civic trajectories led to the identification of two interrelated themes, which typically characterise the changes of Muslims' active citizenship over time.

- *Shifting locations*: This refers mainly to the (sometimes blurry) differentiation between civic participation in community groups and civil society more broadly, on the one hand, and political participation on the other. A typical pattern detected in the interviews is that many Muslims move from civic engagement to more political forms of active citizenship.
- *Shifting activity focus*: The engagement may either solely revolve around intra-community commitments and supporting other Muslims, or it is located within the Muslim community context with strong outreach and cross-community collaboration components. Or, as a third typical focus, it may lack any connections to the Muslim community and encompass only activities of mainstream civic or political engagement. The analysis of interview data demonstrates that Muslims' active citizenship usually shifts between these types, often with a prevalent tendency towards cross-community activities or mainstream engagement. There was not a single interview partner—not even among those who were chosen for their Muslim community engagement—who has not been involved in at least some form of cross-community or mainstream community related participation.

Pathways of Civic Activism: Shifts from Civic to Political Participation

Many of the interviewed Muslims' began their career as active citizens in the area of civic participation and subsequently moved towards more political forms of active citizenship, usually complementing—not replacing—their civil society or Muslim community based commitment. This was the most prevalent pattern discovered in the analysis of Muslims' civic trajectories, especially within the Australian sample, and they resonate with the findings of previous studies in Australia and Germany. A qualitative study on Muslims' political participation in Australia, conducted by Al-Momani et al. (2010), for example, discovered that for some of the politically active Muslims in the study 'the first step to political engagement [was] engaging in civil society' (Al-Momani et al. 2010: 38). The authors further posited that this non-political participation may help Muslims overcome disengagement and feelings of alienation and thus pave their way into political participation. In the German context, Schönwälder et al.' (2011) study on local councillors of (first or second generation) migrant background in Germany similarly found that many of the surveyed councillors had previously been active in various civil society groups, grassroots (mainstream) initiatives (*Bürgerinitiativen*) or trade unions (Schönwälder et al. 2011: 4).[7]

The pathway from civic to political participation was evident among most of the eight politically active Muslims in the Australian sample. Their active engagement in civil society, most commonly in a Muslim community context, was the entry point to their active citizenship career. The analysis of the interviews conducted for the present study further explored the pathways from civic to political engagement in Australia. Typically, interviewed Muslims initially become active as volunteers in a grassroots community organisations (usually within the Muslim com-

---

[7] Research in the UK on Muslim councillors (Purdam 2000) has come to similar results, confirming that participation in the formal political system is often preceded by citizens' active participation in civil society and community organisations. A telephone survey among 111 Muslim councillors, conducted in the mid-1990s, showed that the interviewees 'have had voluntary experiences in various anti-racist agencies, community action groups and advice centres' (Purdam 2000: 49), before they got elected as local councillor.

munity); their community-based civic engagement subsequently results in their enhanced public profile as a community stakeholder and eventually leads to their invitation—often as representatives of the respective community group—to join political advisory boards. This specific pattern was detected among at least five Muslims in the Australian sample (AUS2, AUS4, AUS7, AUS9, AUS11).

Mr Galil (AUS11), for example, an imam and Muslim community leader in Melbourne, explained how he became member of the Multicultural Advisory Committee of the Knox Council in Melbourne's east. The mosque association, for which he temporarily served as imam, had initially asked him to represent the mosque community in the council-initiated Knox Interfaith Network, which has a generally non-political agenda. He accepted, and his participation in this interfaith initiative then 'led to me representing them again in the Knox Multicultural Advisory Committee' (AUS11), where he served for the maximum of two terms between 2007 and 2013, effectively contributing to the local political discussion and decision-making process.

Ms Abdo (AUS 9), Executive Officer of the Muslim women's organisation UMWA in Sydney, initially focussed her activism on Muslim community work, more specifically on settlement service, leadership and empowerment programs for Muslim women. Eventually she moved up within the UMWA from an ordinary volunteer to president. Holding this leadership position, her civic engagement gained more and more political dimensions as she was invited to various political advisory boards and committees. She emphasised that she was nominated for these political advisory roles in her capacity as UMWA president, but also due to the public profile as an active community figure, which she had acquired through her civic participation in the community and beyond.

Mr Kamareddine's (AUS7) civic biography also illustrates how community engagement paves the way into the political realm of active citizenship. Shortly after he immigrated to Australia in 2007 to pursue his PhD studies he became actively involved in volunteer youth work at the local Islamic Society in Newport (Melbourne). His role within the Muslim community led to his appointment to the local Multicultural Advisory Group (Hobsons Bay), where he represents the Islamic Society and, together with other minority community representatives, gives 'advice to the elected councillors and the council on the concerns of the community' (AUS7). Mr Kamareddine's active community involvement encouraged him to also undertake another form of political activism: In 2012, he ran as an independent candidate for a seat in the local council election. Although he did not win, he described this as an 'excellent opportunity'. He explained:

> I feel that the Muslim community should contribute more to the political life of Australia and Victoria. We live in Victoria, so we need to have a voice. And I found that the existing parties don't represent the people. So I thought I start as a councillor.... I thought I should raise my hand to say I want to run for councillor and that was a big challenge, especially for my community.

The civic trajectory of Ms El Matrah (AUS2), representative of the Melbourne-based Australian Muslim Women's Centre for Human Rights, underscores how civic community work—in her cases, advocacy for migrant women (which has also been part of her paid role)—facilitates political participation as member of advisory boards and committees. She elaborated that she has been invited to these committees and boards either directly because of her active role within the Muslim Women's organisation or because of her general public profile, which developed also as a result of her active role within this organisation. It is worth noting that Ms El Matrah was the only interview partner in the Australian sample whose civic career seems to veer away from political participation again. She stated she would not 'go on boards anymore' due to the generally poor efficacy and lack of impact. She explained: 'Very little changes, unless you speak to the bureaucracy the way bureaucracy likes. But that is a very distinct culture that is very disconnected from how things are on the ground' (AUS2).

Only two Australian interview partners, Mr Ahmed (AUS3) and Mr Taabba (AUS12), became politically active before or parallel to their community-based civic engagement. Mr Ahmed, who arrived in Australia as a refugee in the mid-1980s, joined the Australian Labor Party (ALP) in 1993, because he considered the political sphere to be 'the place to influence policies' (AUS3). After renouncing his ALP membership and becoming a member of The Greens, he ran for state election in 2004 and, later on, as an Independent for the office of Melbourne Mayor. These political ambitions unfolded parallel to his community commitment, which led Mr Ahmed to co-founding the African community advocacy organisation African Think Tank in 2005. Mr Taabba's (AUS12) prime engagement focus has been on advancing the wellbeing of the Muslim community. He has pursued this aim through, among others, political commentary in blogs and subsequently in local and national media outlets—parallel to his volunteering in Muslim community organisation, including a mosque, a Muslim student association at university and the Islamic Council of Victoria.

The analysis of the German sample of active Muslims paints a less consistent picture of the paths towards political participation. The trajectory pattern from civic engagement in Muslim community organisations to political participation has also been detected, but it appears less common than in the Australian sample.

Three of the nine Muslims interviewed in Germany who elaborated on their political activism did not mention any substantial forms of civic participation prior to or during their political activism. Mr Şenol (DE6), a media activist, began as a political blogger and then established his own online media platform to contribute to the political and public debate on migration, integration and citizenship. Mr Fetić (DE4) has been a member of a local advisory council and chairperson of the Greens party's sub-group *Grüne Muslime*, and *Miran* (DE12), a university student, began her civic engagement as an active member of a Turkish sub-group of the Social Democratic party, where she soon assumed a leadership role.

Further two Muslims in the German sample (DE9, DE11) were active primarily in the sphere of civic and community area, but also mentioned some political engagement. Both spheres of activism were, however, not or only very loosely connected. In these two instances, civic participation did not serve as a gateway to political participation. *Alev* (DE11) started her civic career in 1995 as a volunteer, tutoring young Turkish high school students. Soon after that, without any links to this volunteering, she decided to run for a seat in the local advisory council for foreigners. Mr Cicek (DE9), a university student from Bochum, has a short but already quite complex history of civic engagement, shifting between political and civic participation. He entered the arena of active citizenship via the pathway of informal political participation in 2010, setting up the online blog *Integrationsblogger* as a platform to discuss integration-related issues. He described this as his 'entry point to the public … it was the first time that I tried to add my voice to the debate. That was primarily of … political nature' (DE9). Soon after that he became member of the youth organisation of the Social Democratic Party (SPD) at his university, where he participated for a short while in the Students' Parliament, the highest student representative body at university. However, he soon renounced his membership due to ideological arguments within the Jungsozialisten (JUSO), and his political engagement (including his blog activities) ceased. Mr Cicek then moved more towards civic participation primarily within a Turkish and Muslim community context. He volunteered as a tutor for high school students of primarily Turkish background within an organisation led by a group of well-educated people of Turkish origin. He also became actively involved in a local intercultural dialogue initiative, loosely linked to the Gülen movement, and joined the Muslim youth network *Zahnräder*. In addition, Mr Cicek successfully applied to participate in an initiative called Young Islam Conference (*Junge Islamkonferenz*), coordinated by the Humboldt University (Berlin) and the Mercator Foundation, which brings together Muslims and non-Muslims to discuss how the German state should engage with religious minorities. Among others, they develop recommendations, pass them on to the Federal Ministry of the Interior and discuss their work with high-profile opinion leaders and policymakers.

Except for the three politically active Muslims without prior civil society based activism and those two whose civic and political participation efforts were not connected, the examination of the German sample also found evidence for the trajectory from civic to political participation. This pattern appears, however, less consistent than it in the Australian sample. That is, the link between civic and political engagement is often less clear and more indirect. Moreover, the pathway from, more specifically, Muslim community engagement to political participation was much less common in the German sample. Only two of all nine politically active Muslims (DE10, DE8) entered into the arena of political activism *because* of their civic participation within the local Muslim community and the public profile, recognition and networks they gained as a result of this community work.

Mr Aydin (DE10) has had a long track-record of engagement within various Turkish-Muslim community groups (e.g., mosques, Turkish parents' initiative) in Ingolstadt (Bavaria). He stated that he was personally approached by several organisations and local opinion leaders, asking him to participate in the local advisory council (*Migrationsrat*)—'because if someone is so active, he should also be in this council' (DE10). The second interview partner whose political activism can be described as a result of her civic participation within the Muslim community is Ms Dogan (DE8), an active figure in the local Muslim community and interfaith initiatives in Bonn (NRW) for many years. Due to her local community activism, she has been asked several times to become involved also in the local integration/migrant advisory council (*Integrationsrat*). She consistently rejected these requests, arguing that the *Integrationsrat* was not the right platform for her activism as it would only concentrate on foreigners. Such a narrow focus would collide with her eagerness to advance the wellbeing of *all* people regardless of their national, religious or ethnic background. She was, however, open to the suggestion of a Muslim community friend, who she had cooperated with on various occasions within the scope of her Muslim community engagement, to establish a new political initiative to participate in the upcoming election of the city council in 2009. She explained how this idea was finally implemented:

> [Against the backdrop of the upcoming general council election], all of a sudden politics has become a topic, I don't know, ... also because we have had bad experiences with the City of Bonn, and we thought we somehow need to make sure that people get into the council who have a heart for people with a migration background, also for Muslims, and who cooperate with us better. Mr [Y.] told me that he had a look at all the party programs ... and then he said: "Actually we should do that [set up a political party] ourselves". And I thought, oh, again one of his ideas ... I'm already busy enough.

Shortly after that, the political party BIG (initially named BFF; see Didero 2013) was formally inaugurated, just in time to take part in the general council election. Both Ms Dogan and Mr Y. were elected in the Bonn City Council as BIG representatives. This transition from civic to political participation suggests that neither the local advisory council nor mainstream parties was considered an apt platform for contributing to the political debate; an alternative political group was deemed more suitable to get involved in the local political decision-making.

Two other interviewed Muslims in Germany have become politically active primarily as a result of their civic engagement in *mainstream* (non-Muslim) organisations. *Burak* (DE1) was recruited by the mainstream political party to run as a candidate for the local council election, primarily due his active engagement in various local civil society groups and initiatives, among those the city's international sister-city partnership initiative. *Esra* (DE7) was asked by the chairperson of the local migrant advisory council (*Integrationsrat*) to participate in that advisory council because she has been known for her active civic commitment, especially for the local group of the socialist youth organisation. She accepted this invitation and was elected. After a few years of committed (but in her view not very effective) work at the advisory council, however, she decided—also for reasons of frustration with the advisory council's work and political disillusionment—to not pursue this political advisory path any longer. She lamented the political voicelessness of this kind of political platform for foreigners and stated that she realised soon 'that I was just meant to be the token woman'.

The analysis of Muslims' trajectories from civic to political participation sheds light on the crucial role of civil society organisations as facilitator of political engagement. This empirical finding supports the argument put forward in the Civic Voluntarism Model (Verba et al. 1995: 369). This study does not only confirm the general gateway function of civil society organisations, but also points more specifically to the role that civic engagement within Muslim community groups can play in paving the way into Muslims' active involvement in the political landscape. This confirms arguments and empirical findings of several studies, like Jamal (2005), Foley and Hoge (2007), and, most recently, Read (2015), Fleischmann et al. (2015), and McAndrew and Voas (2014), which all revealed mobilising effects of active involvement within a Muslim community context, usually the local mosque, on Muslims' broader civic and political engagement. These findings resonate with Amanda Wise and Jan Ali's (2008: 20) conclusion in their Australian study on Muslims' grassroots strategies to improve inter-community relations: 'The mosque … becomes a central focus and serves as a base for the mobilisation of Muslim immigrants within a political arena'.

The comparative analysis of the German and Australian sample suggests that this pathway towards political participation via Muslim community organisations is much more common among interview partners in Australia. This seems attributed, at least partially, to the country-specific opportunity structures and the status of many Muslim community groups. In Australia, there has been a generally higher level of recognition for ethno-religious minority community as civil society stakeholders (Humphrey 1988; Peucker and Akbarzadeh 2014: 148–9), which has resulted in traditionally more institutional collaborations and hence more opportunities for personal contacts between Muslim community groups and mainstream stakeholders in the political sphere. This has led to (and is further reinforced by) a broader variety of—accessible—advisory committees in Australia that offer civil society actors, including Muslim community representatives, a platform to contribute to political debates.

In Germany, there appears to be a more pronounced disconnect between Muslim community-based engagement and the mainstream political landscape and its institutions and representatives. Muslim community organisations have experienced a lower degree of recognition as ordinary voices in the political debate, and the opportunities to gain access to political boards and councils appear more restricted. This may also be linked to the lack of formal recognition of Muslim religious organisations as faith-based corporation under public law (*Körperschaft öffentlichen Rechts*), which puts them in a disadvantaged position compared to other religious groups, denying them the right to represent their community in various political decision-making committees. Overall, the analysis of the German sample shows that Muslims (and supposedly also other minorities) with political ambitions have often only one participation option outside the formal electoral political context: the tokenistic participation in the politically weak local advisory councils.

Shifting Activity Focus of Participation and Engagement

Closely connected to—but not congruent with—these shifting locations of Muslims' activism (e.g., civic participation within Muslim or mainstream community context, political activism) are the changes in the specific activity focus of their civic and political participation, moving between intra-community, cross- or intercommunity and mainstream engagement (Fig. 6.1).

Although the Muslim community context is the single most important location of interviewed Muslims' active citizenship, not a single interview partner described their current civic activities as being solely intra-community focussed and as having no cross-community interaction elements. This analysis illustrates the complex and dynamic nature of active citizenship, shedding light on how Muslims' activity focus has evolved and shifted between intra-community, cross-community and mainstream engagement. Two, sometimes overlapping, trends in the interviewed Muslims' trajectories as active citizens can be identified. Firstly, the activity focus has shifted over time towards increasingly cross-community or mainstream-based engagement; this pattern applies to the majority of Muslims in both national samples. Secondly, some Muslims have expanded their commitment to intra-community activities within the Muslim community, often complementing their mainstream-oriented engagement.

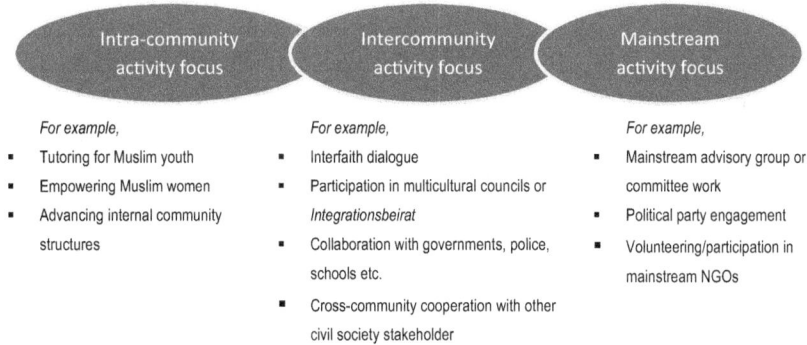

Fig. 6.1 Illustration of three overlapping types of activity focus

The above outlined analysis of shifting locations illustrates the processes in which Muslims in the German and, even more so, in the Australian sample have often moved from (Muslim) community based civic participation into political activism (e.g., councils, advisory committee work). These changing locations of active citizenship have commonly gone hand in hand with a shift in the activity focus towards more cross-community and or mainstream engagement. However, even without such a location shift, intercommunity and mainstream activity foci have gained prominence in the civic biographies of many interview partners. A prevalent pattern among several Muslims is that their civic engagement begins with intra-community activities aimed at supporting or assisting other Muslims and then moves towards more cross-community collaborations and intercommunity engagement—often without changes in their primary location of activism. In many cases this development has been caused primarily by the changing profile and agenda of the respective Muslim organisation. In some instances, however, it was primarily a result of the personal eagerness of the individual to reach beyond Muslim community boundaries and get more involved in cross-community activities.

The data analysis does not point to major differences between the interviewed Muslims in Germany and Australia. In both sub-samples, the majority of those Muslims whose civic careers have seen relevant shifts in their activity focus over time explained how their initially predominantly intra-community activism eventually opened up and expanded towards intercommunity and, in some cases, mainstream engagement. In the Australian sample, this pattern applies to all Muslims whose primary location of civic participation was the Muslim community context.

Mr Galil (AUS11), for example, has been actively involved in Muslim community work since he came to Australia in 1969 (e.g., helping build the Preston mosque). After he retired in 1992 he accepted the offer to become imam at a mosque in West Heidelberg (Melbourne). Soon after his appointment he, together with some other representatives of the mosque, responded to a public 'call from some synagogues in Kew, searching for a Muslim group to interact with … We started that journey [of interfaith dialogue] here in Australia'. Mr Galil highlighted that 'my concentration was in the Muslim community before I retired and interfaith [engagement] came afterwards'. Intercommunity dialogue quickly became his main activity focus (in addition to his ongoing role as imam), as his engagement in the 'interfaith movement' continuously expanded—from initially informal interfaith meetings to active involvement in various activities and leadership roles (including president) within the Jewish-Christian-Muslim Association (JCMA, established in 2003). Mr Galil's cross-community engagement continuously grew not only as a result of his personal decisions but also due to the expansion of the JCMA's agenda and activities, which now also encompasses a school program, aimed at countering religious and racial stereotypes, discrimination and misunderstanding among students. Moreover, Mr Galil's interfaith engagement with JCMA has been the catalyst for other cross-community forms of his civic and political participation within the local council-initiated Knox Interfaith Network and the Knox Council Multicultural Advisory Committee.

Ms Sabbagh's (AUS5) civic pathway similarly illustrates how organisational changes as well as personal ambitions have led active Muslim citizens from primarily intra-community engagement for fellow Muslims to cross-community dialogue and collaboration activities. Ms Sabbagh's initial activity focus was on young Muslims. At the age of 16 she organised her first community program, a camp for young Muslim girls, and she explained that she has been in community work ever since. In the 1980s, she co-established the organisation Young Muslims of Australia (YMA) with the aim of bringing together Muslim youth and offering them a 'support structure … to practice their faith *and* be part of Australian culture'. While YMA explicitly sought to empower young Muslims, the organisation—and Ms Sabbagh herself as a key figure at YMA—soon got involved in various types of cross-community collaborations, for example with schools, governments and the police. In the early 2000s, she decided to follow 'a slightly different calling'. She left YMA and pursued her own projects independently. A key driver was her eagerness to enhance her cross-community commitment.

> I wanted to work with the wider community, so YMA is particularly [for] young Muslims, and I broke away and started teaching on my own. There are many projects that I worked on. I worked on the *My Dress, My Image, My Choice* show, which is a fashion show that I created … to bring com-

munities together to discuss what is Islam really about … to demystify the hijab and to engage and really discuss why women dress the way they do. That's one point, but it was really about: *Let's talk*! The hijab was just a means to engage. Because this show was so successful, it only finished in 2011. So ten years, it was an ongoing show, it travelled all around Australia.

Ms Sabbagh continued working with schools, governments and the police after she left YMA, 'but on my own now', as she explained. Moreover, after she established a new Muslim community organisation, *Benevolence*, her interfaith and cross-community engagement, especially with other women, has not ended:

But has [the foundation of Benevolence] changed my work? No! I'm still doing the same things. Just, now, I'm training other women to do the same thing. And we're more organised in doing it. My talks at church groups is still there … my engagement with schools is still there. I work for Women's Forum Australia, which is a non-religious group that is very passionate about creating a change in the … images of women in the public sphere, sexualisation of girls, pornography, all those issues …, creating policies and changes. I joined that because I love that … I don't always have to work with Muslims, you can find like-minded people that aren't of the same tradition.

In contrast to Ms Sabbagh's and Mr Galil's personal eagerness to participate in cross-community activities, the sole driver behind Mr Tabbaa's (AUS12) activism has been the advancement and wellbeing of the Muslim community. His personal agenda is reflected in his previous and current civic activities. He volunteered, for example, for a mosque teaching Arabic to young Muslims, and he was president of the Islamic (student) Society at LaTrobe University and sat (at the time of the interview) on the board of the Islamic Council of Victoria (ICV). 'I see the priority for me is Muslims', Mr Tabbaa emphasised. Notwithstanding this engagement focus, his leadership roles within different Muslim community groups have also led him into cross-community activities. During his time as president of the Islamic Society at LaTrobe University 'we actually made it a priority to focus on Muslims on campus', but he was also actively involved in outreach activities: 'we'd give pamphlets, talks, dialogues … with the general public at LaTrobe'. As ICV board member, he became more involved in cross-community communication, for example, 'dealing with multicultural groups [and] multi-faith groups'.

The civic trajectories of several other Muslims in the Australian sample, such as Ms Abdo (AUS9), Mr Kamereddine (AUS7) and *Serap* (AUS6), further underscore the prevalence of this pattern of civic engagement, mainly located within Muslim community organisations but with increasing engagement in cross-community activities. This observation also holds true for many in the German sample. Here, too, a majority of interviewed Muslims began their activism within a Muslim community context, with more or less pronounced—and expanding—elements of cross-community engagement. Ms Taraji (DE5), for example, has been active in several Muslim community organisations for many years; she did not mention any other locations of civic activism. She established a Muslim women's organisation, has been involved in organising annual conferences of the Islamic Community Germany (IGD) and has volunteered for the Central Council of Muslims in Germany (ZMD), where she was in charge of the portfolio of women and families. Ms Taraji explained that she 'grew into this Muslim community life' and soon began to take a more active role (especially within the IGD). Despite the Muslim community being her sole location of civic participation, cross-community and interreligious elements eventually complemented Ms Taraji's intra-community engagement. She explained that these cross-community activities occurred later in her civic career: 'First, one has to find stability for oneself, it's only then that one can try to reach out'. She further elaborated that these more recent facets of her activism unfolded as a result of institutional developments within the Muslim community organisations she has been involved in. Ms Taraji agreed that this has also led to personal changes:

> We at the IGD, for example, ran the NEIGHBOUR campaign last year. Opening up and introducing yourself to your neighbours. Well, there have been several [such] projects … It is not enough to stick together, to live in a parallel society, but we really want to enrich society and thus we need to open up.

For *Asim* (DE15) and Ms Al-Ammarine (DE2), too, the profile of the Muslim community organisation they are active in directly shaped their cross-community engagement and collaborations. *Asim* has been active in the Muslim youth organisation *Muslimische Jugend in Deutschland* (MJD), and was recently elected a MJD board member. His Muslim community-based volunteering initially had an intra-community focus. Subsequently, as a MJD representative, he has cooperated not only with other Muslim community groups, but has also been increasingly involved in interfaith projects with non-Muslim (mainly Christian) youth groups. Moreover, he has been invited by schools to give talks on various aspects of Islam and Muslims in Germany and has directly cooperated with government representatives within state-funded community projects. It is the MJD's activity agenda that has drawn him into cross-community engagement and enabled him to build personal networks with political decision-makers and civil society stakeholders.

Similarly, Ms Al-Ammarine's (DE2) Muslim community-based civic participation has broadened over time to include more cross-community activities, for example, at her mosque, where she became involved in the regular interfaith meetings with women from different church groups. Ms Al-Ammarine's main location of activism has been the Muslim women's organisation *Begegnungs- und Fortbildungszentrum muslimischer Frauen* (BFmF; Meeting and Training Centre of Muslim Women) in Cologne. Initially she ran religious (Qur'an) courses as a BFmF volunteer before she started her job as a social worker, in charge of, among others, the settlement support program for recent immigrant women. Her activity focus evolved over time to include various cross-community collaborations, which she performs partially as a representative of the BFmF and partially independently:

> For years I have given talks across Germany on education, on women in Islam … For me, this is about raising awareness… I have been active for many years in dialogue initiatives, between Jews, Christian and Muslims … Moreover, I have been invited by schools [to speak] at History or Religion classes, where they deal with Islam.

This pattern of growing cross-community engagement among active Muslims associated with Muslim organisations similarly applies to other interview partners in the German sample. Considering also those who moved from civic community to more political participation and, as a result, became more involved in cross-community (or mainstream) forms of activism, not a single interviewed Muslim in Germany was solely active in intra-community engagement. And, similar to the majority of interviewed Muslims in Australia, almost all of them demonstrate continuous, more or less extensive shifts towards these bridge-building manifestations of active citizenship.

A minority of interviewed Muslims, especially those who initially volunteered, or continue to do so, for mainstream organisations, have in some ways moved into the opposite direction. Their civic activism has shifted towards more engagement within the Muslim community and closer contacts with Muslim community groups—usually not at the expense of their mainstream activism. In some of these cases their political or civic (cross-community) participation directly led to more collaboration with Muslim communities; other interviewed Muslims decided to become more actively involved in a Muslim community context independent of their previous forms of civic activism. Examples for this shifting activity focus were found in the civic trajectories of a small number of interviewed Muslims in Australia and Germany.

The civic career of the young Australian Muslim *Ashtar* (AUS14) used to have no personal connections to Muslim community groups prior to her work for a state government commission on multiculturalism and community relations. Although she had been religious all her life, as she stressed,

> I didn't get [Muslim] community exposure until I started my role in government... That's when my two co-workers, both from the Muslim community, started to introduce me to all these organisations. And I needed to know this because this is the area I was now going to work in. I was thrown in the deep end very quickly.

In her role as a project coordinator within this government commission she was required to build and strengthen relationships between various communities, including the Muslim community. Thus, she was urged to develop better insight into Muslim community structures. This resulted also in her becoming more actively involved within this community sphere. She explained:

> The first year at the [commission] was a matter of observing, to see how things are done and to find out what's going on in the [Muslim] community. I went to a lot of community events, where people started to recognise me ... So over time, they started to ask me: "Can you do this event? Can you to that ...?" So I started to do a lot of volunteer work, and I did a lot of volunteer work with refugees, asylum seekers in Villawood detention centre, and I did a lot of volunteer work with the Lebanese Muslim Association. So I became very active and I found myself to have no time but help the community.

Mr Sattar (AUS8) is the second person in the Australian sample whose activity focus moved from mainstream towards cross-community engagement—however, without a direct connection between both. His civic career can be divided into two separate phases. During his time as a high school student and his first few years at university, Mr Sattar volunteered for a number of mainstream organisations (e.g., Cancer Council) and various mainstream causes (e.g., HIV awareness raising), and attended public protests for human rights (e.g., Aboriginals' rights). His second phase of active citizenship began rather abruptly when he was around 25 years old and decided that he wanted to fundamentally change his life:

> I was just sick of partying every weekend ... and I had nostalgia for being this 17 year old kid that had a passion for helping people and a passion for applying the principles of my religion ... so I returned to my roots, which is my religion, and I found a spiritual connection again. But then I was faced with a problem: I did not have a single Muslim friend.

At that point in life, Mr Sattar came across a Facebook post by a Muslim community leader and representative of the Muslim organisation Mission of Hope, inviting people to volunteer for a community project. He successfully applied and has since been actively involved in the project Hayat House Outreach—a cross-community initiative, run by Mission of Hope with the aim to support at-risk youth in Sydney's west regardless of their faith or background. Mr Sattar soon became project coordinator and Mission of Hope board member. In this leadership role, he has communicated and engaged with government departments, police, schools and other mainstream institutions—all facets of his cross-community engagement.

In the German sample, this trajectory pattern of moving towards *more* Muslim community engagement or cooperation as a main aspect of someone's civic activism also applies only to a small minority of interviewed Muslims. Mr Fetić (DE4), for example, has been primarily active in the political sphere, as a member and later on chairman of a local migrant integration advisory council (*Integrationsrat*) and as an active representative of the political initiative *Grüne Muslime*, a working group within The Greens in the state of NRW. As part of these roles he has liaised and engaged with local Muslim communities. He stated that every member of the working group, including himself, is active in their own local context trying to encourage Muslims and their organisations to become more actively involved in the political sphere and in society more broadly—'to get out of their own circles, to join [mainstream] clubs and associations and interest groups'. While Mr Fetić has been a passive member of a Bosnian mosque association for many years, his political activism within the Green party (and to some degree also in the local advisory council) has resulted in intensified and broadened collaboration and contacts with representatives of various mosques and other Muslim organisations.

In contrast to Mr Fetić, whose political participation led directly to increased contacts and cross-community cooperation with Muslim community groups, *Esra*'s (DE7) expanded engagement within the Muslim community sphere unfolded independently of her previous civic activism. *Esra* volunteered for the local branch of a socialist youth group and was active in the local integration advisory council. Both facets of her active citizenship were largely disconnected from Muslim community organisations (although she worked with, among others, Muslim individuals). Separate from this engagement, she became involved in a network of young Muslim students and professionals called *Zahnräder*, which runs annual conferences to strengthen networks among mostly well-educated Muslims and to work 'as Muslims for the society at large', as she put it:

I went to their first conference… I had never been at a Muslim event before, with so many Muslims, where everything was about Muslims … At this conference I was totally thrilled. Great, there were so many smart people and they were all like that. I was positively shocked! Great projects, great people who all came along with the goal to run a project for society.

Esra joined the *Zahnräder* team, within which she assumed responsibility for developing the visual communication strategy for the network. She stated that she invested a lot of time, 'like everyone else', over a period of one and a half years. As a result of this civic activity focus on Muslim issues, parallel to her other ongoing forms of civic engagement, her networks and personal friendships with other fellow Muslims has substantially expanded.

The longitudinal analysis of interviewed Muslims' civic trajectories and, more specifically, the shifting locations and activity foci underscores that Muslims' activism is highly complex and dynamic, and anything but an isolated intra-community engagement exercise. Cross-community activities and collaborations prevail—even among those whose primary location of participation is the Muslim community context. Muslim community organisations often function as accessible sites of active citizenship and subsequently as gateways to other forms of civic and political participation. Previous studies have detected that religious organisational settings are important sites for Muslim volunteering (Halm and Sauer 2005; Monash University 2009a), but have not been able to illustrate the prevalent shifts towards cross-community nature of this civic engagement.

A key finding of this study is that the organisational structures, agendas and cross-community connectedness of Muslim community organisations, both within and across community boundaries, play a crucial role for the unfolding of Muslims' active citizenship. On the one hand, these factors become the basis for the mobilisation of Muslims into political participation (especially in Australia) and, on the other, they serve as facilitating platforms for cross-community engagement. While Muslim communities in Germany appear less successful in the political mobilisation of their members than in Australia, communities in both countries seem well positioned to play the role as facilitator of cross-community civic engagement. Although some Muslim community organisations continue to shy away from liaising with other civil society groups or political representatives (these were not present in this study's sample), the majority of them seem to have left behind their self-occupied and inward-looking past and have increasingly strengthened their outreach and intercommunity engagement agenda. This has been confirmed by recent research studies both in Australia (Amath 2013; Underabi 2015; Peucker and Akbarzadeh 2014: 159–165) and Germany (Halm and Sauer 2012: 77; Peucker and Akbarzadeh 2014: 186–191)—and it directly affects the nature of Muslim's community-based active citizenship.

Transition and Recruitment

The previous elaborations on Muslims' civic pathways highlighted the dynamics of active citizenship careers. This observation draws attention to the transition processes from one form of activism to another. How do people shift their engagement focus towards new civic or political challenges? Do they make a deliberate decision or do they feel 'dragged into activism' by the circumstances? And what role does recruitment and invitation by a third party play? The analysis of the interview data revealed many similarities between the German and the Australian sample, but also some nuanced differences regarding these issues of transition.

An obvious precondition for active citizenship that applies to all interviewed Muslims is their general willingness, readiness and, in most cases, eagerness to become involved in civic or political participation. In addition to this basic personal prerequisite, the examination of the activism transition processes commonly points to a combination of external and internal factors. While the former refer primarily to direct recruitment or encouragement by a third party and a set of (often seemingly coincidental) circumstances, the latter revolve around personal decisions to seek certain forms of engagement or 'to put up their hand' when the opportunity arises. Usually internal and external factors are inherently intertwined. For example, external circumstances may generate a situation that offers opportunities for civic engagement, which the person then actively takes up, or accepts the invitation by someone else to do so. Importantly, many of the investigated civic careers cannot simply be classified as a whole; some transitions within someone's civic biography may have been more internally driven, while others have been triggered primarily by external factors.

The data analysis underscores the complex nature of the interplay between external and internal factors, which presents itself differently in each transition phase for each individual interview partner. This complexity can be located on a continuum oscillating between, on the one hand, those who feel entirely—and almost involuntarily—'thrown' into their active participation and, on the other hand, those who have made proactive decisions without describing 'the circumstances' or third-party influence as relevant. The vast majority of Muslims interviewed for this study mentioned a combination of both internal and external factors. Only in a few cases, Muslims have become actively engaged solely based on their personal decision to deliberately pursue a certain type of civic activism without any external encouragement or recruitment. It has been a widespread view among interview partners that their active engagement career 'just happened' and unfolded due to the circumstances and external factors rather than as a result of thoroughly weighted or even strategic decisions.

External Encouragement and Recruitment

Recruitment and encouragement by a third party plays a key role for most interviewed Muslims' ways into civic and/or political participation. This holds true for the majority of Muslims in the German sample and almost all Australian interview partners. Being encouraged, invited or even urged to become involved in certain civic or political activities can manifest itself in many different ways: the following three factors characterise this recruitment:

- *Location of previous civic engagement*: The person may be recruited due to his or her previous civic engagement within the Muslim or the wider (non-Muslim) community context.
- *Location of new civic engagement*: The person may be invited to take up new forms of civic engagement located within or beyond the Muslim community context.

- *Recruiter*: The recruiters may act as a private person (e.g., friend, colleague) or in their capacity as representative of an organisation either within the Muslim community or mainstream civil society or the political arena.

One common pattern of recruitment by representatives of mainstream society organisations, which has been mentioned particularly often in the Australian sample, has already been described earlier: Several interviewed Muslims have been invited by government and representatives of other mainstream institutions to join government-led or other committees, councils and advisory groups as a result of the public profile they had gained through their active role *within* the Muslim community. Similarly, some other Muslim community activists have been invited and encouraged by mainstream society institutions to engage in cross-community collaboration outside this institutionalised realm of committee work. Ms Sabbagh (AUS5), the co-founder of Young Muslims of Australia (YMA), for example, has established close relationships with, among others, the police, government and schools during her time at YMA. These relationships have built the foundation for her invitation to ongoing cooperation with these institutions even after she had left YMA.

Mr Dellal's (AUS4) civic biography illustrates a slightly different version of this external recruitment into various forms of political and civic (mainstream) engagement, for he developed this public profile and activist reputation *outside* the Muslim community. Starting off as a teacher at a Catholic school, where Mr Dellal soon became active in, among others, curriculum design, he eventually got involved in, as he explained, 'much broader areas of promotion of diversity through the arts and then later on through policy … it just grew from there. You know, working with ministers, working with government, working with local governments, a whole range of things'.

Recruitment does not only play an important role for the transition into collaboration and consultancy work in a mainstream context, but also *within* the Muslim community sphere. The active citizenship career of *Serap* (AUS 6), an English teacher and volunteering PR officer at a young Muslim women's organisation in Melbourne, is an illustrative example. From an early age on *Serap* has demonstrated willingness to participate and to take on responsibilities primarily within the Muslim community (e.g., Islamic student association at university), but also beyond (e.g., running for school captain in Year 12). Despite her personal eagerness, she emphasised that her civic engagement within the Muslim community has unfolded as a result of external recruitment:

> I was led into these things. I was never actively looking for it. It was always by invitation that I got into it. That's how it always happened....It was never out of me getting up, it was all on invitation. It was all based on "oh, we know you can do this". That's how it always was.

When in 2008 the leaders of the local mosque decided to set up a subgroup for Muslim girls and young women, *Serap* was among those who were directly approached:

> It was the [mosque] elders that got the youth together, the three, four main young girls, well, we were all young professionals ... So it was the elders who choose who they wanted to run this group. I got a visit from the mosque board, the female board ... and they said they had been doing a bit of research on responsible young women in the community. [They said] "your name was mentioned quite a lot of times ... So we want you to be part of our mosque and start an establishment for our youth".

According to *Serap*, her previous contacts and activities within the local Muslim community—especially as a teacher in a private Islamic school—led to this recruitment into her PR role. This pattern of community-internal recruitment into civic participation based on someone's reputation within the Muslim community also applies to the way in which Mr Kamareddine's (AUS7) civic activism has evolved rapidly within a short period of time. Mr Kamareddine held a range of volunteer positions. At the time of the interview, he managed the construction of the new Newport Mosque in Melbourne's west, was in charge of youth work at the mosque, wrote for an Arabic-English newspaper for a primarily Muslim audience in Australia, sat on the boards of the national umbrella organisation AFIC and of an Islamic school in Tarneit (Melbourne) and represented the Muslim community in the multicultural advisory group of the local council. Similar to *Serap*, Mr Kamareddine did not actively seek these roles; his multi-faceted active citizenship expanded rather coincidentally, but also as a result of his willingness to contribute.[8] Asked about his active decisions to take on all these roles, he replied:

> It just happened actually ... I started at the [Newport] mosque giving lectures and talks. People say: "oh that's good, do you want to write an article with me". And ... Newport [Islamic Society] is part of AFIC. And you go to meetings and see you can do some work. But I did not look for it, it has just happened. And when I saw that I can do something, I jumped.

Mr Tabbaa (AUS12) similarly described the trigger for his active engagement within the Muslim community as a combination of personal willingness and capacity, coincidental circumstances and external encouragement. While studying at university, he was, for example, asked by the then president of Islamic Society at LaTrobe University (Melbourne), who was about to resign, to become the new president—a request that Mr Tabbaa accepted. Later on, he was urged by several Muslim community members to run as a candidate in the Islamic Council of Victoria (ICV) board elections, after he had publicly criticised the ICV for its community management and lack of grassroots representation. He explained that

> a lot of people contacted me and said I should run for the ICV board ... When they said to me I should run for the board, I said: I probably should. It's not good enough to complain and leave the opportunity. So I said: OK, I will, I don't know if I will get in ... but yes, I run ... And I got in very comfortably.

According to Mr Tabbaa, circumstances have often urged him to become active. He stated that in 'probably every organisation' he worked for there was someone who tapped him on the shoulder asking him to

---

[8] In contrast, Mr Kamareddine's political ambitions to run as an Independent candidate in the local council elections in 2012 were not a result of coincident or external recruitment. He stressed that 'rais[ing] my hand to say I want to run for councillor' was my 'own decision': 'I thought we need to have someone. I would like to stand up and give it a go'.

take on an active role.[9] But he emphasised that 'I have also put myself out there to tap ... I guess [it is] a mixture'.

The analysis of the German interview data revealed similar recruitment patterns in the civic trajectories of interviewed Muslims, but also suggest some differences. Like in the Australia sample, the majority of interview partners considered external factors—including coincidence—to play a crucial role for the way in which their civic engagement has evolved. Again these recruitment processes have unfolded in various directions. Mr Aydin (DE10), for example, began his civic activism career within the Muslim community (e.g., mosques, Turkish parent group). Through this volunteering work he gained public recognition and developed a public profile that led mainstream stakeholders to encourage Mr Aydin to participate in the local cross-community volunteering network *Brueckenbauer* and the local migrant advisory council (*Migrationsbeirat*). He explained that he was approached and persuaded by several local associations and public opinion leaders to participate in the *Migrationsbeirat* due to his active role in the local community.

Similarly, *Esra* (DE7) was asked to run as a candidate for the local advisory council (*Integrationsrat*), assumedly, as she asserted, due to her reputation as an active volunteer in a local youth group of a socialist organisation, unrelated to any Muslim or ethnic minority community:

> The chairman of the *Integrationsrat* approached me, he apparently thought "she's active; she would like to do that". He also said they need more women and young people ... I found that quite interesting at the time because I thought, cool, you can change things there, you can achieve something.

A few Muslims interviewed in Germany have transitioned into new forms of civic engagement in more complex ways of recruitment and external encouragement. Mr Yerli (DE14), for example, has played an active leadership role for many years in both the local Muslim community and as an elected member of the work council (workers' representation

---

[9] However, Mr Tabbaa's engagement also encompasses contributions as a critical media commentator, which started independently of external invitation by a third party.

within a company; *Betriebsrat*) and the trade union. His civic engagement began when the local mosque decided to set up a youth group, and Mr Yerli offered to take on responsibility for this new group. He said that 'no one else was really taking care of it', and he has always considered it important to become active himself instead of merely demanding others to do something. Later on, he was encouraged by members of another local mosque association in a neighbouring town to run a similar youth group there. He accepted this request and subsequently became more and more involved in this mosque association, also due to the personal contacts with many of the mosque members who Mr Yerli knew from his workplace. This coincided with the mosque chairman's moving to another city, and Mr Yerli began to informally represent the mosque. After a while members of the mosque association proposed that Mr Yerli (who was only in his mid-20s at the time) should become the official chairman. Yerli accepted this invitation and has been chairman of this mosque in Penzberg (Bavaria) ever since.

This pattern of external encouragement, coupled with the willingness to take personal responsibility, is also reflected in Mr Yerli's way to become an elected workers' representative in his company's work council (similar to a shop steward in Australia) and an active member within the trade union. Here, too, his engagement started rather informally without an official position; and it is noteworthy that this civic participation at the workplace was related to his active role in the Muslim community (on the importance of the workplace for political mobilisation, see Verba et al. 1995). He explained:

> What happened at work is that, also because of my activities within the Islamic community and as its chairman, I have been asked again and again about my views on certain things. I've been trade union member from the beginning … initially without actively participating … I've been asked repeatedly about certain topics, especially when it concerned Muslims … so I was confronted with these topics. And finally a colleague of mine approached me, asking if I would like to become actively engaged in the work council.

Mr Yerli was elected in 2006 and this civic engagement subsequently expanded as he was also elected as a trade union representative acting within the company (deputy *Vertrauenskörperleiter*) and as a trade union's delegate on the regional level.

What stands out in Mr Yerli's civic career is that he has been encouraged to take on new active roles by colleagues and friends rather than by representatives of Muslim or mainstream institutions. This pattern of informal recruitment through personal acquaintances also occurred in the trajectories of several other Muslims in the German sample; it was much less prevalent, however, in the Australian sub-sample, where interview partners were commonly invited through more formal and institutional channels to engage in new forms of civic activism. The German university student, *Miran* (DE12), for example, used to be not interested in any form of civic or political participation until her mother, an active member of the Social Democratic Party (SPD), suggested to her one day attending a meeting of the Turkish-German sub-group *SPD Ve Biz*. This visit started *Miran*'s active political participation with this group, where she soon assumed a leadership position. Similarly, *Asim*'s (DE15) first encounter with the Muslim youth group MJD, within which he later became very active and took on leadership roles, was initiated by a friend he knew from the local mosque. *Asim* explained that he did not go to the mosque for religious, but rather for social reasons. 'And one day a friend who was also there invited me to join him at one of the meetings of the local network of the MJD… I had just finished high school, so I started to go there'.

Ms Dogan's (DE8) multiple forms of civic and political participation have also predominantly been initiated by invitation and encouragement by friends and acquaintances. Ms Dogan's involvement in the local Muslim-Christian dialogue initiative began 'by chance', as she put it: 'Some acquaintances have invited me'. Another personal acquaintance, a local community activist, played a key role in encouraging Ms Dogan to participate in other civic and political activities within and beyond the Muslim community. He invited Ms Dogan, together with several other Muslim women, to take part in a Muslim women's group within the new local Council of Muslims (*Rat der Muslime*).[10] The same person encour-

---

[10] She left this Muslim women's group eventually to establish her own cross-community women's organisation (named FIBEr), which targets women of all faiths and backgrounds. In contrast to her other externally encouraged forms of civic activism, Ms Dogan decide herself to set up this new organisation.

aged Ms Dogan to join him and other local (Muslim and non-Muslim) activists in setting up a new local political party as an alternative voice in the political landscape. Ms Dogan actively contributed to the process of registering the new party in time for the council election and to the election campaign itself. She was, however, initially not interested in becoming politically active. However, when one of the party's top candidates withdrew her candidature, the other party members urged her to fill the vacancy:

> Initially, I did not offer to [stand as one of the top candidates], but then the others said that if there is anyone who has the guts to do this, it's you. And I thought, well, we won't get [elected] anyway, I have to admit, I did not expect us to [win a council seat].

These elaborations underscore the crucial importance of external recruitment and encouragement for the way in which the civic trajectories of active Muslims have unfolded and changed directions. This applies to both the Australian and the German sample. A common factor of these recruitment processes is the prevalent perception among many interview partners that these transitions in their civic careers often 'just happened by chance'. A more analytical interpretation of these views, however, suggests that, while coincidental constellations may also have been at play, these external recruitment and invitation processes are often indicative of the—less coincidental—operation of existing personal and/or institutional networks.

This conclusion resonates with previous research findings on the importance of network structures and collective social capital of minority community for the mobilisation of community members into civic activism (Tillie 2004; Fetzer and Soper 2005). Previous studies on Muslim and Arabic-speaking volunteers in Australia have particularly emphasised the recruitment within Muslim community circles through 'Muslim community sources' (AMF and VA 2007a: 2) and 'word of mouth methods of recruitment, such as through family or community groups' (AMF and VA 2007b: 68–69). While the interview analysis of this present study confirms such patterns, it also found evidence for cross-community recruitment into new forms of (political) participation, often by representatives of mainstream organisations. In the German sample, recruitment occurred more commonly through personal networks and was thus based mainly on the individual's social capital. Interview partners more frequently mentioned friends, family, colleagues, and other acquaintances as those who encouraged them to get involved in new forms of participation. This confirms previous representative survey findings on volunteers of Turkish origin (Halm and Sauer 2005), which identified friends and acquaintances as the most important recruitment agents (Fig. 6.2). Moreover, it resonates with Verba et al.' (1995: 369) general argument that the workplace, in addition to church groups and voluntary organisations are site of citizens' mobilisation.

Among Australian interview partners, existing institutional networks (both within the Muslim community and beyond) and lines of communication and cooperation are particularly influential—in addition to personal connections. The prevalent pattern of cross-community recruitment of active Muslim citizens in Australia into multicultural and mainstream committee and advisory work appears to be due to the (in comparison to Germany) more extensive institutional networks between Muslim organisations and mainstream stakeholders—linking social capital in Woolcock's (2001) terminology. The invitation by Muslim commu-

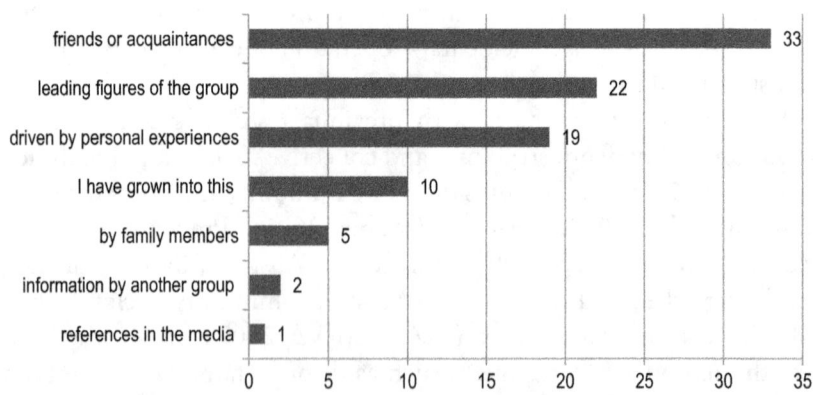

Fig. 6.2 Initiation and recruitment of volunteering (Turkish background migrants) in Germany
Source: Halm and Sauer 2005: 107

nity representatives, instead of friends and acquaintances, to play active roles *within* Muslim community structures point to more closely knit networks (collective social capital) within the Muslim community (Tillie 2004). These institutional connections serve as important catalysts of civic engagement as they provide access to a range of civic and political participation. While this is not to say that private networks are irrelevant for external recruitment processes, institutional networks provide additional, and more systematic, opportunities for Muslims who are willing to become active, and they rely less on informal (and more coincidental) personal networks and on having the 'right' friends, acquaintances or colleagues.

Independent Decisions

While independent efforts to choose and pursue certain types of civic activism—supposedly without external invitation—have been the exception in both sub-samples, they have been slightly more common among interviewed Muslims in Germany than among their Australian counterparts. These differences may tentatively point to less developed or less effective recruitment structures in Germany. This also resonates with the findings in the previous section, suggesting that there is a more systematic impact of institutional networks on the external recruitment on Muslims' civic activism (e.g., from civic to political participation) in Australia.

Only one interview partner in Australia, Mr Ahmed (AUS3), described his civic career as a series of strategic personal decisions, made independently of external invitations. Driven by his strong desire to 'actively participate in the greater social good' and 'to speak on behalf of the people that I know can't speak', Mr Ahmed has been a political activist and African community leader in Australia since the 1990s. He stressed that he has never been approached or asked by others to become active: 'No, from the day I started it was myself'. Considering the political party sphere to be the most effective place 'to influence policies', he joined the Australian Labor Party in 1993. In 2000, he left the party due to disagreements on the Gulf War and the party's unwillingness to change its policy stance. But Mr Ahmed did not give up his political ambitions: 'I joined The Greens in 2001/2002, because I found some similarity and I could work on the issues I wanted to work on at the time, because I wanted Labor to change their policies'. A few years later, he left The Greens again and continued his political career as an Independent. Mr Ahmed underscored that his political commitment has primarily been driven by his goal to push for changes 'for the good of the country [and] for the good of the world'. Through his political engagement, he has deliberately sought to develop and enhance his public profile and visibility in order to increase the efficacy of his civic engagement: 'If you don't have the visibility, you don't have the power to change … If my profile is going to help people at the end of the day, I may [well use it]'.

Mr Ahmed's second area of active citizenship is related to his role as an African community leader, most prominently as the co-founder and chairman of the African Think Tank (Melbourne). It was his own decision to establish and lead this advocacy organisation, which seeks to unite African communities in Victoria and Australia and educate them about mainstream Australia as well as to inform 'governments, corporates and mainstream Australian about the culture, the background of Africans': 'So I have a role to play—and this is where the African Think Tank comes in: creating a platform to reach out to mainstream Australians to understand more about Africans'. Mr. Ahmed's civic career is the absolute exception in the Australian sample in the way it unfolded based on personal decisions and without external recruitment. In the German sample, however, this pattern applies to the civic trajectories of around one quarter of all 16 interviewed Muslims.

The media activist Mr Şenol (DE6), founder and editor-in-chief of the online media platform MiGAZIN, for example, did not mention any third party recruitment in his civic activism. He began his engagement career as a law student, independently setting up an online blog called JurBlog, where he wrote about primarily legal issues revolving German integration and citizenship policies. The trigger for Mr Şenol's decision was his personal outrage about a specific legal provision that led to his parents—together with some 50,000 other citizens of Turkish origin—losing their German citizenship status two years after they had been naturalised.

It really made me feel terrible that so many people had to live in fear and uncertainty [because of this legal provision]. I simply wrote in the JurBlog what I found out and taught myself. This is how JurBlog … began. I had written a lot of things but did not know what to do with it. I had no access to the media or journalists. So the easiest way was to set up an internet page, I did not even think that anyone would read it.

As his media activism as an online blogger continuously expanded, Mr Şenol sought to increase the impact and readership of his media work and to enhance his contribution to the public and political debate by setting up a new format of online media platform. This led him to establish the media outlet MiGAZIN in 2008:

I started working on this, I looked for like-minded people in my social circles, people who were able and eager to write and were somewhat familiar with this topic [of integration]. I put together a small team and created the MiGAZIN website all by myself.

He has since then further expanded the MiGAZIN website and developed it into a popular and widely recognised alternative voice in the media landscape in the area of migrant integration, racism and diversity.

Another interview partner in the German sample whose activism evolved primarily as a result of his personal decisions is Mr Cicek (DE9). His civic biography started when he began his university studies in 2010, which coincided with a heated public debate on the allegedly failed integration of Muslims, following the publication of a controversial book by Thilo Sarrazin. Mr Cicek described this public debate as the trigger for his active citizenship career. He set up the online blog *Integrationsblogger* with the deliberate intention to contribute to this public debate and to correct the misrepresentation of Muslims. 'This was the first time I tried to add my voice [to the public debate]'. He further elaborated:

It was initially very emotional. That is very important. It wasn't like I had intellectual input, but instead it really hit me personally. If I hadn't been so concerned, I would possibly not participate in society to the extent I do it today.

What defines Mr Cicek's civic trajectory after he handed over the online blog to his colleagues is a series of deliberate choices to become active, trying out various forms of involvement. He joined the Social Democratic Party (SPD) and attended the weekly party meetings, but stopped going there due to a lack of time. He became member of the JUSOS [Young Socialists] university group and participated for a short period of time in the Student Parliament (*Studendenparliament*), but soon decided to not pursue this any further. Later on he applied to present his online blog project at the annual national conference of the young Muslim network *Zahnräder*. This conference attendance was the beginning of his civic engagement within this Muslim network: 'I tried to participate in the internal team [of *Zahnräder*], initially in the media team, then in the team in charge of finances and now I want to organise the next conference'. During this time, he also came across a Facebook announcement of the so-called *Junge Islamkonferenz* and successfully applied to participate in this political discussion initiative.[11] Although he viewed this project with scepticism as rather tokenistic he wanted to become involved:

> To be honest, I did not have a lot of experience with this, but it is basically always the same. One develops [recommendations], and then nothing happens. But I thought I'd rather be involved myself than leaving it up to other people to do this.

Ms Theißen (DE3), a teacher by training and Muslim community activist, is another illustrative example for the emergence and expansion of civic activism as a result of personal, independent decisions. From the beginning of her civic engagement, which spans now more than three decades, she has actively looked for ways to participate and contribute. External recruitment or invitation seems to have played no role in her civic career. In the early to mid-1980s (which was prior to her conversion to Islam), when job prospects for graduated teachers like herself were difficult, she decided to teach German in a centre for recently arrived

---

[11] The *Junge Islamkonferenz* is a joint initiative by the Humboldt University in Berlin and the foundation Mercator, bringing together Muslims and non-Muslim to discuss how the German state should engage with religious minorities.

Vietnamese boat people and later for asylum seekers. After her conversion to Islam, she

> went to the mosques to find out what kind of social work there was. At first I tried to run tutoring classes for school kids in an Arabic mosque. I wanted to set something up between the local council's youth department and the parents, but that didn't work out.

After two years, she decided to end her volunteer work with this Arabic-dominated mosque and went to a Turkish mosque to teacher German to Muslim women. When she realised that many of these mostly young women did not have a secondary school degree, she started to offer tutoring to help those who were interested in acquiring a high school degree. During this time she also set up a girls-only swimming initiative for Muslim high school students, in cooperation with a local swimming pool and ten high schools across Cologne; being trained and qualified as a PE teacher, she also ran the swimming lessons herself. Eventually, Ms Theißen's developed the more ambitious plan to establish an independent centre for Muslim women. She asked friends and other acquaintances to support her initiative, and printed and distributed flyers; she collected enough donations to rent a small office and, in 1996, registered the association BFmF (Meeting and Training Centre of Muslim Women), which she still represents as director. Since then the BFmF has grown and expanded enormously, also thanks to her tireless networking and lobbying for funding and official recognition.

Concluding Remarks: Trajectories and Transitions

The analysis of the transition processes into, or between different forms of, civic engagement among active Muslim citizens provides insights into the interplay between their personal dispositions, goals and capacities, on the one hand, and external recruitment and encouragement, on the other. While the former (internal) factors typically form the basic prerequisite for their engagement, the latter (external) factors appear paramount in opening up avenues and in facilitating specific forms of civic or political participation. Usually, the institutional *structures* of engagement (e.g., advisory committees, boards, community projects seeking volunteers) exist already before the individual person decides to get involved in certain civic/political activities. It was the exception that interviewed Muslims created these structural opportunities of engagement themselves, for example by establishing their own organisation. This pinpoints the importance of country-specific opportunity structures for the nature of Muslims' active citizenship. Two intertwined determinants and processes that shape these opportunity structures of active citizenship can be identified.

First, Muslims' personal networks and bonding social capital (Putnam 2000: 22) and the collective social capital and intra-community interconnectedness of Muslim groups (Tillie 2004) affect the availability of and access to civic engagement opportunities *within* the Muslim community context. The data analysis suggests that interviewed Muslims in Germany rely often on informal networks (e.g., friends, colleagues) (see also Halm and Sauer 2005: 107), while their Australian counterparts are commonly recruited by community representatives. This might be attributed to more closely connected Muslim community structures at least on the local level in Australia. Further research is necessary to gain better insights into these facilitating intra-community factors of Muslims' civic participation, which has consistently resulted in interviewed Muslims' extended cross-community engagement and intensified civic or even political participation.

Second, cross-community networks between Muslim communities and mainstream institution in civil society or the political landscape (linking social capital) influence the opportunities for many Muslims to become involved in civic or political participation and, more specifically, in institutions of public discourse *outside* Muslim community boundaries. These cross-community lines of collaboration have traditionally been more advanced among Muslim community groups in Australia than in Germany, where Muslim communities continue to struggle for their recognition as civic society stakeholder (Peucker and Akbarzadeh 2014). The commonly discovered transition of Australian Muslim community activists into political advisory work as invited members of multicultural and mainstream sites of public discourse (e.g., advisory groups, boards, committees) suggest that these platforms of active citizenship may be more accessible in Australia. The established lines of communication between Muslim community groups and (state and local) governments and other relevant mainstream institutions (e.g., Human Rights Commissions, public broadcaster) in Australia reflect more inclusive political opportunity structures that facilitate certain types of political engagement. This sits well with Ireland's institutional chanelling theory, highlighting the 'influence of host-society institutional structures on … political mobilization' (Ireland 1994: 8) of immigrants and, by extension, ethno-religious minorities such as Muslims.

More generally, the analysis of interviewed Muslims' types and trajectories of civic and political participation underscores the complex dynamics of Muslims' active citizenship. The vast majority of interview partners demonstrated an intensive multi-faceted career as committed citizens, characterised by shifts over time—often from civic to political and towards cross-community activities—, at times simultaneous forms of participation, and in most cases with no immediate end in sight.

What this empirical analysis further reveals is the paramount role that Muslim community organisations play for the emergence and development of Muslim active citizenship in Australia and Germany. Volunteering within a Muslim community context, according to these explorative findings, is anything but a barrier to active citizenship. It does not only constitute an 'ordinary' manifestation of civic participation in a pluralistic civil society, of which Muslim community groups are an inherent part. The empirical data also leave little doubt that active involvement in this community context serves as a facilitator of a range of cross-community forms of civic engagement. This gateway function applies—without exception—to all Muslims interviewed in Australia as well as Germany.

Despite these vital convergences, important country-specific differences have also been detected. In the Australian sample, a substantial number of interview partners have gained a public profile and reputation through their Muslim community work that has led to their invitation to, in some cases, relatively powerful institutions of public debate and political decision-making. This phenomenon emerged only rarely in the German sample, where Muslim community engagement has also paved the way to more cross-community civic engagement and collaborations, but not into more powerful institutions of public discourse. This is not to say that interviewed Muslims were entirely absent from these institutions, but their (previous) Muslim community engagement has done little to foster their pathway into these political powerhouses.

The findings indicate that civil society structures and institutions of political and public discourse affect the way in which active citizenship processes of some Muslims unfolds. This resonates with Ireland's argument that 'institutional gatekeepers … control … access to the avenues of political participation' (Ireland 1994, 10). Although some of the interviewed Muslims have become actively—and successfully—engaged in political parties and other institutions of public discourse, others have encountered difficulties in entering these circles of political decision-making. Especially among Muslims interviewed in Australia positive views prevail. Those who have represented their local Muslim community in political advisory councils have expressed positive experiences, and those who have been active in party politics or ran for a political office have also described this in very positive terms.

Barriers to effective political participation, indicating less supportive political opportunity structures for political integration of minorities, have been mentioned in particular by interview partners in Germany who have sought (mostly with very limited success) to become active in the political landscape. The most common type of political participation among Muslims in the German sample was their involvement in local advisory integration councils. However, local institutions were described by several Muslim in the German sample as a rather tokenistic and ineffective form of political participation for non-citizens.

Mainstream political party structures were seen as not conducive for minorities to participate, which seems to be one of the reasons why several interview partners have abandoned this political party oriented path of active citizenship. This is supported by the fact that the few Muslims in the German sample who did articulate successful participation within political parties have been active either within minority sub-groups of mainstream political parties (e.g., the SPD Turkish subgroup *Ve biz* or the Green's group Green Muslims) or in a newly founded alternative party at the local level. The one local councillor in the German sample who represented a mainstream political party (*Burak*; DE1) stressed the unusually strong local support from within his local party branch. He highlighted that he had only been nominated as a candidate for the local council elections because the mayor has been particularly committed to cultural diversity within the political decision-making landscape—an indicator that political opportunity structures in a certain local context may differ decisively from the national setting (Koopmans 2004).

References

Al-Momani, K., Dados, N., Maddox, M., & Wise, A. (2010). *Political participation of Muslims in Australia*. Sydney: Macquarie University.

Aly, A. (2007). Australian Muslim responses to the discourse on terrorism in the Australian popular media. *Australian Journal of Social Issues, 42*(1), 27–40.

Amath, N. (2013). The impact of 9/11 on Australian Muslim civil society organisations. *Communication, Politics & Culture, 46*, 116–135.

Australian Multicultural Foundation (AMF), & Volunteering Australia (VA). (2007a). *Muslim youth and volunteering. Research bulletin* (June 2007). Melbourne: VA.

Australian Multicultural Foundation (AMF), & Volunteering Australia (VA). (2007b). *National survey of Australian volunteers from diverse cultural and linguistic backgrounds*. Melbourne: VA.

Carland, S. (2012). Silenced: Muslim women commentators in the Australian media. *The La Trobe Journal, 89*, 140–150.

Cyrus, N., & Vogel, D. (2008). *Förderung politischer Integration von Migrantinnen und Migranten. Begründungszusammenhänge und Handlungsmöglichkeiten*. Oldenburg: University of Oldenburg.

Didero, M. (2013). Muslim political participation in Germany: A structurationist approach. In J. S. Nielsen (Ed.), *Muslim political participation in Europe* (pp. 34–60). Edinburgh: Edinburgh University Press.

Dreher, T. (2003). Speaking up and talking back: News media interventions in Sydney's 'othered' communities. *Media International Australia Incorporating Culture & Policy, 109*, 121–137.

Dreher, T. (2010). Community media intervention. In H. Rane, J. Ewart, & M. Abdalla (Eds.), *Islam and the Australian news media* (pp. 185–205). Carlton: Melbourne University Press.

Fetzer, J., & Soper, J. C. (2005). *Muslims and the state in Britain, France, and Germany.* New York: Cambridge University Press.

Fleischmann, F., Martinovic, B., & Böhm, M. (2015). Mobilising mosques? The role of service attendance for political participation of Turkish and Moroccan minorities in the Netherlands. *Ethnic and Racial Studies, 39*(5), 746–763.

Foley, M. W., & Hoge, D. R. (2007). *Religion and the new immigrants: How faith communities form our newest citizens.* Oxford: Oxford University Press.

Gisart, B. (2013). Demokratie und politische Partizipation. In Statistisches Bundesamt & Wissenschaftszentrum Berlin für Sozialforschung (Eds.), *Datenreport 2013. Ein Sozialbericht für die Bundesrepublik Deutschland* (pp. 357–362). Bonn: Bundeszentrale für politische Bildung.

Halm, D., & Sauer, M. (2005). *Freiwilliges Engagement von Türkinnen und Türken in Deutschland.* Essen: ZfT.

Halm, D., & Sauer, M. (2012). Angebote und Strukturen der islamischen Organisationen in Deutschland. In D. Halm, M. Sauer, J. Schmidt, & A. Stichs (Eds.), *Islamisches Gemeindeleben in Deutschland.* Nuremberg/Essen: BAMF/ZfTI.

Haug, S., Müssig, S., & Stichs, A. (2009). *Muslimisches Leben in Deutschland.* Nuremberg: BAMF.

Humphrey, M. (1988). Community, mosque and ethnic politics. *ANZ Journal of Sociology, 23*(2), 233–245.

Hunger, U., & Candan, M. (2009). *Politische Partizipation der Migranten in der Bundesrepublik Deutschland und über die deutschen Grenzen hinweg.* Münster: Westfälische Wilhelms-Universität Münster.

Ireland, P. (1994). *The policy challenge of ethnic diversity. Immigrant politics in France and Switzerland.* Cambridge: Harvard University Press.

Jamal, A. (2005). The political participation and engagement of Muslim Americans: Mosque involvement and group consciousness. *American Politics Research, 33*(4), 521–544.

Koopmans, R. (2004). Migrant mobilisation and political opportunities: Variation among German cities and a comparison with the United Kingdom and the Netherlands. *Journal of Ethnic and Migration Studies, 30*(3), 449–470.

McAndrew, S., & Voas, D. (2014). Immigrant generation, religiosity and civic engagement in Britain. *Ethnic and Racial Studies, 37*(1), 99–119.

Monash University. (2009a). *Mapping employment & education among Muslim Australians.* Caulfield East: Monash University.

Monash University. (2009b). *Muslim voices. Hopes & aspirations of Muslim Australians*. Caulfield East: Monash University.

Peucker, M., & Akbarzadeh, S. (2014). *Muslim active citizenship in the West*. London/New York: Routledge.

Posetti, J. (2010). Jihad sheilas or media martys? Muslim women and the Australian media. In H. Rane, J. Ewart, & M. Abdalla (Eds.), *Islam and the Australian news media* (pp. 69–103). Carlton: Melbourne University Press.

Purdam, K. (2000). The political identities of Muslim local councillors in Britain. *Local Government Studies, 26*(1), 47–64.

Putnam, R. D. (2000). *Bowling alone: The collapse and revival of American community*. New York: Simon and Schuster.

Read, J. G. (2015). Gender, religious identity, and civic engagement among Arab Muslims in the United States. *Sociology of Religion, 76*(1), 30–48.

Schiffauer, W. (2010). *Nach dem Islamismus. Eine Ethnographie der Islamischen Gemeinschaft Milli Görüş*. Berlin: Suhrkamp.

Schönwälder, K., Sinanoglu, C., & Volkert, D. (2011). *Vielfalt sucht Rat. Ratsmitglieder mit Migrationshintergrund in deutschen Großstädten*. Berlin: Heinrich-Böll-Stiftung.

Tillie, J. (2004). Social capital of organisations and their members: Explaining the political integration of immigrants in Amsterdam. *Journal of Ethnic and Migration Studies, 30*(3), 529–541.

Underabi, H. (2015). *Mosques of Sydney and New South Wales*. Auburn: ISRA.

Verba, S., Schlozman, K. L., & Brady, H. (1995). *Voice and equality. Civic voluntarism in American politics*. Cambridge: Harvard University Press.

Wise, A., & Ali, J. (2008). *Muslim-Australians and local government. Grassroots strategies to improve relations between Muslims and non-Muslim-Australians*. Sydney: Macquarie University.

Woolcock, M. (2001). The place of social capital in understanding social and economic outcomes. *Isuma: Canadian Journal of Policy Research, 2*(1), 11–17.

7

Goals, Motives and Driving Forces

The question as to why someone becomes actively involved in certain forms of civic or political participation is a highly personal and multifaceted one. Muslims interviewed for this study spoke about two interrelated dimensions. The first was the general goals they pursue through their civic activism. The second are fundamental driving forces that motivate them to become (and remain) engaged and active. This chapter explores the personal dispositions of interviewed Muslims; it does not attempt to investigate the specific aims linked to each individual type of civic activity the interviewed Muslims have been involved in.

General Goals Pursued Through Active Engagement

Notwithstanding the great variety of specific goals, most interviewed Muslims in Australia and Germany demonstrate great ambitions and personal commitment to effecting change in one way or another. The vast majority of them elaborated on how their participation has been tied to their desire to have a transformative impact. The data analysis identified

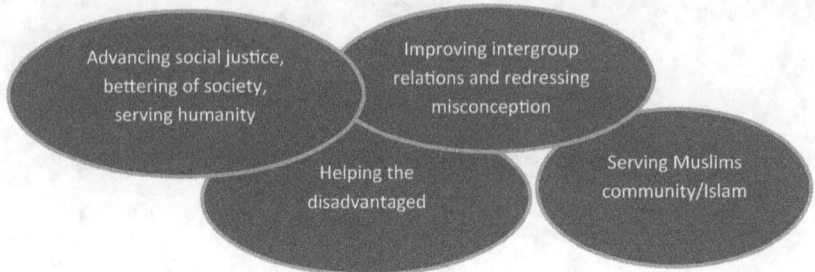

Fig. 7.1 Overlapping types of civic goals as identified in the interview data

four types of goals, ranging from (1) a republican focus on bettering society at large and (2) helping particularly disadvantaged groups (other than Muslims), to (3) improving relationships between Muslims and non-Muslims and (4) a communitarian agenda of advancing the wellbeing of the Muslim community (Fig. 7.1).

There are often no clear boundaries between these four types of goals. Many interview partners pursue different goals simultaneously and some describe their civic goals in ways that elude a rigid analytical classification. In some cases, for example, their active citizenship reflects both a communitarian and a republican agenda (e.g., bettering society by supporting young Muslims, improving intergroup relations to foster social cohesion). Regardless of this complexity, the goals of active Muslims interviewed in Australia and Germany can be described as fundamentally altruistic; pursuing merely (or primarily) personal gains does not seem to play a role in the interviewed Muslims' decision to become involved in civic or political participation.[1]

The examination of the interview data revealed a great variety of goals pursued by interviewed Muslims in both national contexts. Muslim community-only oriented goals are the absolute exception, mentioned as the sole or primary focus only by one interview partner each in the Australian and the German sample. Hence, almost all interviewed Muslims located their active engagement either within an agenda of serv-

---

[1] Only two interview partners, one in the German (DE12) and one in the Australian sample (AUS10), mentioned instrumentalist career-related goals, but in both cases this was only described as a secondary goal.

ing society, helping disadvantaged groups (e.g., poor, youth, migrants in general), or improving intergroup relations and redressing the prevalent misconception of Islam and Muslims. While this applies to both country samples, there are also some marked differences between Muslims interviewed in Australia and those in Germany.

Serving Society

Seeking to contribute to the greater good of society at large and to advance the wellbeing of others regardless of their faith or background is the most commonly expressed goal among the 30 interviewed Muslims. It was stated by many Muslims in the German sample and is the single most important goal of those in the Australian sample. What stands out is that the majority of Muslims whose civic engagement aims primarily at bettering society at large participated within a Muslim community context. This holds true for both sub-samples, but is particularly dominant among Australian Muslims. None of these Muslims articulated any conflicts between their greater good oriented goals and their active citizenship being performed within Muslim community organisations.

Ms Sabbagh (AUS5), founding director of the Muslim community organisation *Benevolence* in Melbourne, elaborated that she wants to 'serve humanity' through her community work and inter-community engagement: 'It is a deep concern for humanity as a whole to be proactive and try to create change. And it is not service to Muslims [only].' She described this goal in religious terms, arguing that she aspires to follow the example of the Prophet whose 'number one concern was not himself, was not the Muslim community, it was humanity'. *Serap* (AUS6), whose active engagement has also unfolded primarily in Muslim organisations (e.g., young Muslim women's group, ICV), similarly referred to God to explain what she seeks to achieve through her community engagement[2]:

---

[2] For *Serap* this overarching goal of being useful to others also extends to her commitment to redressing the skewed media image of Muslims and, in doing so, promoting harmonious coexistence of Muslims and non-Muslims in Australia. This shows that the above outlined rigid classification of goals is not always well suited to capture the multiple rationales of active Muslims interviewed for his study.

Being useful to others is *such* a strong concept in Islam. This [civic engagement] is how I show that, being a useful human being. That's all. I know in our faith our God is pleased when you make another human being happy, whoever that may be.

The Muslim community activist Mr Kamareddine (AUS7) stressed that he tries to 'change the life of others in a good way'. Quoting the Hadith *The best of people are those that bring most benefit to the rest of mankind*, he referred to all people in society, both Muslims and non-Muslims—without mentioning any difficulties in reconciling his communitarian and republican goals:

So I need to make a change, the more [Muslim] youth I bring towards the religion and away from trouble and [towards] doing the right things, the better I am … The more I contribute to the betterment of the society, the better my reward will be. We belief [that God] created us to be good in this life, to do the good.

Mr Ahmed (AUS3) is one of the few Muslims in the Australian sample that described his basic goals as primarily related to making society a better place who is not involved in a Muslim community context. He explained that his personal experiences of war and violence in Africa have shaped his civic agenda of 'making society the best so my kids don't have to suffer what I experienced'. He emphasised that he has a strong commitment to building a peaceful Australian society because 'this society has given me so much—education, employment, a better life—… so I have to give back'.[3] Like Mr Ahmed, the NSW state parliamentarian, Ms Faruqi (AUS13), whose active citizenship has unfolded entirely outside the Muslim community context, pursues the general goal of contributing to the greater good of society. She asserted that she has always sought to foster social justice in Australia and beyond. This agenda has been driven also by her previous experiences with injustice, discrimination and poverty in her country of birth (Pakistan). 'I've always tried to influence

---

[3] This primarily republican goals is complemented by Mr Ahmed's endeavour to live up to his self-declared responsibility (as an educated person, as he explained) 'to speak on behalf of those who can't speak [for themselves]', which is tied to his goal of supporting a disadvantaged group, in Mr Ahmed's case, primarily immigrants and minorities of African background.

change for what I thought was something good, better. Mainly driven by environmental justice and social justice … So I always had this social justice element, and then moved into the environment as well'.

In the German sample, goals related to advancing the society at large also play an important role for several Muslims. However, compared to the Australian sample, it was mentioned by fewer interview partners, it was usually less emphasised, sometimes only implicitly alluded to or described as a secondary goal in combination with others. One of the few Muslims interviewed in Germany who did stress their strong personal commitment to taking responsibility for the whole society was Mr Yerli (DE14), a trade union activist and chairman of a mosque association in the small town of Penzberg (Bavaria). He said: 'For me it has always been like that … if you want to change things, you have to participate … this is one society and everyone, regardless of religion, has to take responsibility'. Mr Yerli's elaborations on his multiple forms of activism underscore that he pursues these republican goals through both his Muslim community work (including cross-community engagement) and his mainstream engagement within the trade union. For example, he described his previous volunteering for Muslim youth as his first step 'into social responsibility', and in his capacity as mosque chairman he explained that the mosque's agenda has always emphasised contributing to and engaging with the greater society. Despite his leadership position within the mosque, he stressed that, while volunteering for a Muslim community organisation is valuable, his civic engagement 'is not about a religious group, but about society'.

The media activist Mr Şenol's (DE6) described it as his key goal to effect change by actively contributing to the public and political discourse and by providing a media platform for others to do so. His decision to give up his online legal commentary blog and to establish a more professional online media platform (MiGAZIN) was driven by his ambition to get his voice out more widely: 'I wanted to reach many more people, wanted to move more, wanted to participate more in the debate'. Although Mr Şenol did not explicitly mention the aim of advancing the greater good of society, his eagerness to add his and others' alternative voices (often of non-professional writers with a minority or migration background) to the public debate reflects such a republican agenda of non-electoral political participation.

Helping the Disadvantaged

Several interviewed Muslims, around one-third in each sub-sample, explained that their active citizenship has also, or primarily, been aimed at helping people, regardless of their religion, who they consider to be disadvantaged. The data analysis suggests some differences between interviewed Muslims in Germany and Australia regarding the specific groups they direct their attention to. While many Muslims in the German sample referred to migrants as the target group of their civic engagement, Muslims in the Australian sample commonly define the target groups of their civic commitment more broadly and not in terms of their minority or migrant status. Given that disadvantaged population groups are obviously part of the wider society, this category of goals often reflects a republican agenda, but it may also encompass communitarian components, depending on the specific group in question.

Mr Merhi (AUS1), a trade union representative from Melbourne, who has volunteered for different civil society organisations, is a particularly illustrative example. His professional activities as well as his civic engagement, which included volunteering as football coach and mentor for disadvantaged youth, have been driven by his eagerness to 'help the disadvantaged' (AUS1). Who exactly his activism is aimed at varies, but a general focus has been on young people. Within his professional environment at the trade union, for example, he tried to improve the, in his views, exploitative working situation of young apprentices in the construction industry. About his time as a volunteer football youth coach, he said: 'I coached teams with homeless kids, with disabled kids, Somali, very poor people. That was very rewarding. To get a young group of kids together who are disadvantaged … I'd pay for their fees so they could play footy'.

His engagement with the Uniting Church, where he volunteered as a mentor for young people, was also aimed at helping disadvantaged youth. He recalled:

> I was a mentor for the … Uniting Church, which surprises a lot of people. [They were] thinking: "You are Muslim, why are you a mentor for the Uniting Church?" And I say: "You know what? That doesn't mean nothing

to me". I do not care if they are Muslims or not, these young kids, who are orphans, who do not have father figures in their lives. If I can contribute a little bit, then I'll do that …. I'd see them twice a week for around four hours each time, go to the movies, see a footy game, just sit and talk somewhere.

Mr Sattar (AUS8), who coordinated a project for at-risk youth in Bankstown (Sydney), run by the Muslim-led organisation Mission of Hope, stressed that his general goal has been to help the disadvantaged youth of his community, which he explicitly defines not in religious but in spatial terms as the Bankstown community:

When you see your own community, your own youth within your own backyard facing so many problems, you think and reflect and you just can't let them fall into a lifestyle of crime, drugs and alcohol, which is inevitably what it leads to…. Asians, Islanders, Arabs, Indigenous Australians … they all suffer from the same issues within the community. They are not going to get a fair chance until they believe in themselves.

Ms Saleh (AUS10), also an active volunteer for Mission of Hope, has been chair of the government-initiated National Australian Youth Forum and now works for amnesty international. She elaborated that her activism—both professional and as a volunteer—is rooted in her 'commitment to social justice' and a combination of religious, social and personal reasons. Generally her aim is 'being compassionate', 'helping the needy', and, more generally, helping people—which she described as the main way for her to practice and live her religion.

In the German sample, the goal of helping certain disadvantaged population groups often manifested itself in Muslims' civic commitment to supporting first or second generation migrants (sometimes in combination with other goals). *Burak* (DE1) has been active in Muslim and mainstream civil society organisations and as elected councillor. While his political ambitions were mainly framed in republican terms, seeking to influence the wellbeing of society, his volunteering work with young people was partially aimed at supporting disadvantaged people, 'especially migrant youth, because I think that they are sometimes lost in this society'. Alluding to his republican motives, he further explained that 'this does not have much to do with [their] religion. I just wanted to make my contribution to society and against injustice … I wanted to give back'. This line of argument illustrates how republican-oriented activism and communitarian participation sometimes overlap.

Mr Aydin's (DE10) multi-faceted activism is predominantly aimed at 'looking after migrants', encouraging them to integrate and participate, and building bridges between migrants and the mainstream population. Although he stressed that he would help anyone who needs help, these basic goals revolving around migrants shape his work as member of the local migration advisory council as well as his active engagement in, among others, a local neighbourhood committee and an ethnic soccer club, where 'he shows migrant youth that they can really do many great things through sports'.

Ms Theißen (AUS3), Muslim community activist and head of the Muslim women's centre BFmF, has also been committed to promoting migrant integration and participation in society. While her civic engagement (both professionally and, previously, as a volunteer) has been located mainly within a Muslim community context, she described her general goals more broadly as 'standing up for people, who face some difficulties in life'. Her focus on empowering refugees, migrants and, later on, Muslim women has been due to personal experiences and links to the refugee, migrant and Muslim communities. Against this backdrop, Ms Theißen has been seeking to support and empower migrant and Muslim women to claim their rights, become active and participate in society.

Ms Dogan's (DE8) activism has been manifold, encompassing, amongst others, political work as elected city councillor and her engagement in a newly established local NGO for Muslim and non-Muslim women. Depending on the specific activity, the target groups of her civic engagement vary. As an elected local politician, for example, she has been particularly committed (while representing the entire electorate) to improving the situation—including the public perception and recognition—of migrants and Muslims. The purpose of the local women's organisations, which she co-founded and represents, has been aimed more broadly at supporting and empowering *all* women in the neighbourhood (notwithstanding some targeted programs specifically for migrant women).

Improving Intergroup Relations and Redressing Misconceptions of Muslims

Many interviewed Muslims enact their citizenship with the aim of fostering positive intergroup relations between Muslims and non-Muslims and mitigating negative misconceptions of Muslims and the Islamic faith in the wider community. What sets this type of civic goals apart from the others is that the notion of acting as *Muslim* may be at the core of their activism, while the engagement is not primarily about advancing the wellbeing of the Muslim community directly. This reflects in some instances a republican agenda of promoting social cohesion and harmony across the wider community, and, in other cases, this engagement is more concerned with improving the public perception and recognition of the Muslim community for communitarian reasons (the latter being more common). These types of civic goals are an important focus of several Muslims in the Australian sample, and it constitutes the dominant agenda among Muslims interviewed in Germany. Especially, their eagerness to promote civic recognition of Muslims stands out as a typical pattern in the German sample. Through their active engagement Muslims in both samples seek to counter anti-Muslim stereotypes and signal to the wider community that Muslims are ordinary members of society.

In Australia, Ms Saleh (AUS10) has pursued multiple goals, including 'helping the needy', through her various forms of active citizenship, both within a Muslim organisation context and beyond. In addition, she has also been active—as an unaffiliated individual—in the government-initiated National Australian Youth Forum, where she was eventually appointed chair. The goal behind her participation in this forum was to show the government that young Muslims are—contrary to widespread misconceptions—interested in partaking and connecting with 'mainstream government infrastructure and institutions'. She thought engaging in this forum 'would be a really good way to make sure the government is listening and seeing there is this Muslim community, young Muslims are doing some great things'.

Ashtar's (AUS14) activism has been primarily aimed at 'mak[ing] sure that I do something that will benefit my community'. Her main goal has been 'to dispel these myths and misconceptions' of the Muslim community and Muslim women in particular. She explained:

> I know it's a cliché, but even if a couple of people change their views, I would feel like I've achieved my aim. My goal at the end of the day is to help people view Muslim women on an equal playing field, to see them as active citizens of this country.

Ashtar's agenda of 'breaking barriers and misconceptions' has driven her volunteer engagement, for example as media officer at a local (predominantly Muslim) women's football team, as well as her professional commitment as project manager within a government-led commission and radio presenter. She considered it most effective to pursue this goal from 'outside the community' through mainstream media work as a journalist; this would enable her to reach a wider audience than community advocacy. Working as a community radio presenter was for her only a strategic step to 'get to a position where I can do more for my community':

> I want to become a broadcast journalist, and I think by being a broadcast journalist, I can do more for the Muslim community... Just by the fact that I wear the hijab and appear on television I can send a very strong message to a lot of people ... And sometimes the best acts of advocacy and active citizenship is just being you... It's much more powerful and resonates with more people when a Muslim woman talks about politics or sports or whatever.

Both *Ashtar* as well as Ms Saleh pursue a 'role model approach' in breaking down misconception and anti-Muslim prejudice. Through their public demonstration of good citizenship and engagement they seek to offer a counter-narrative to the widespread stereotype of Muslims as being disengaged, passive or invisible. An alternative way of redressing anti-Muslims attitudes is to engage directly in intercommunity or interreligious exchange, seeking opportunities to directly rectify these misconceptions. The Melbourne Imam Ms Galil (AUS11) is one of those interview partners in the Australian sample who have actively attempted to counter mutual misunderstanding through interfaith dialogue. He explains his rationale also with a reference to the benefits for everyone in society:

> It is important that neighbours talk to each other and understand one another. That is important to me personally, very important, that we try to remove any misunderstandings; that would lead to a better life—for everyone.

In the German sample, the majority of interviewed Muslims described their active engagement as in some ways aimed at tackling prevalent misconceptions of Muslims or at promoting recognition of Muslims as ordinary members of society. In some cases, this also includes ambitions to foster positive intergroup relations and mutual understanding. Like in the Australian sample, there is evidence for both basic strategies, pursuing this goal either indirectly through a 'good citizen role model' approach or directly through intergroup dialogue.

Alev (DE11) is one of those whose civic engagement has from the beginning revolved around the goal of 'bringing people from different cultural backgrounds together' and, in doing so, reducing misconceptions of Muslims. This was her declared goal when she became member of the local migrant advisory council (*Ausländerbeirat*) and, even more so, when she set up a local organisation for intercultural dialogue between people (mainly women) of all walks of life. She elaborated on the latter:

> This was primarily about bringing people of different cultures together … primarily with [mainstream] society, but also between cultures, because we realised: You can only reduce prejudice when you … spend time with each other… [People] have to get to know each other.

She considered her civic engagement, inspired by the Gülen movement, as quite successful. She mentioned an informal survey she conducted among participants of her intercultural programs, which demonstrated that many of them have overcome their prejudice and now feel more comfortable 'talking to us [Muslims] and discussing certain things with us'.

Leyla (DE13) has been active in, among others, intercultural dialogue work as representative of a Muslim student association in large city in Germany's south. She emphasised the need to promote and engage in intercultural dialogue and that it is mainly up to young Muslims to take on this task. The goal behind her commitment is redressing the negative perception of Muslims. Although she finds the public image and treatment of Muslims frustrating, it pushes her to work even harder to redress misconceptions:

> I feel the urge to prove that this [biased perception] is not how it is … Of course I'm also tired of being stared at stupidly in the subway, but if I don't do anything against it, at least a little bit, it will never change. Who else should do something about it? … I can't expect the old generation of my grandmother to do it … Therefore it is up to us now, and I hope it will get better eventually.

Leyla has tried to dispel misconceptions of Muslims not only through her dialogue activities but also through other forms of engagement, pursing a more indirect 'citizen role model' approach. She volunteered, for example, as an election poll assistant (*Wahlhelfer*) because she wanted to publicly demonstrate that Muslims are part of this society: 'I go and volunteer there as a Muslim citizen, and I'm there the whole Sunday … in order to show that it is absolutely normal that we [Muslims] also want to participate'. *Leyla* even described it as a fundamental goal of all her engagement to simply express her feelings of fully belonging to this society like anybody else.

In a similar vein, Ms Dogan's (DE8) civic and political engagement has been driven by her desire to redress prevalent anti-Muslim prejudice and misconceptions. The biased attitude climate has not paralysed but rather encouraged her to become active in her neighbourhood: 'We have to convince them that we [Muslims] are quite normal and that we also belong to this society'. This motivation extends also to her political engagement as an elected member of the city council. In her maiden speech as a city councillor she declared: 'I sit in the city council not only as Hülya Dogan, but on behalf of all women with a headscarf' (cited in Peucker and Akbarzadeh 2014: 183).

Some of the interview partners in the German sample underscored that not only the mainstream majority needs to overcome their prejudiced views, but also Muslims themselves. Mr Fetić's (DE4) main area of active citizenship has been his political engagement with the local integration advisory council and as an active member of the Muslim working group *Grüne Muslime* within the Greens party in NRW. Quoting survey results on the widespread prejudice towards Muslims, he described it as his basic goals to contribute to redressing the injustice and stigmatisation of Muslims. He tries 'to show that Muslims are part of this society', but he also stressed that Muslims and their communities, too, have to do their part. More specifically, he lamented that many Muslims still do not consider themselves to be part of German society. To tackle this lack of civic belonging within parts of the Muslim community, he seeks to encourage 'Muslims to contribute to society instead of continuing discussing how badly they are treated', to leave their ethno-religious circles and become politically active. Ms Al-Ammarine (DE2) has also sought to influence the mutual (mis)perceptions of both mainstream society and the Muslim community. Her civic and professional engagement, which is primarily located within the Muslim women's organisation BFmF in Cologne, has been aimed at, among others, building bridges between Muslims and the mainstream community. As community and settlement worker she has been passionate about generating trust among (Muslim) migrants vis-à-vis the German authorities and reducing prejudices that exist within these authorities. More generally, Ms Al-Ammarine described herself as a politically active woman, committed to countering the negative public labelling of Islam:

> That is what I am concerned about. And it is not only the media—though they are hugely responsible for this—but Muslims are partially responsible for it themselves, those who do not live their Islam the way it has been meant originally. And the reason for this is that religion and culture and customs often get mixed up. This is a personal concern of mine, and I consider it my duty … to explain to Muslims that [certain] cultural practices have nothing to do with Islam.

Only one interviewed Muslim (in the German sample) whose engagement is directed at reducing anti-Muslim prejudice locate their aims within the context of a religious duty to positively represent Islam vis-à-vis the wider community. Ms Taraji (DE5) *explicitly* mentioned her commitment to *da'wah* (religious duty to talk about and invite others to Islam) as a key goal of her civic engagement, and more specifically the cross-community cooperation and dialogue components of her civic activism.

> That is what our religious demands from us. That we do not retreat, that we open up. It is also this *da'wah* work, that one has to make others more familiar with Islam. Because those who don't know anything about us can't like us. I think that a lot of fears and hatred is due to the fact that they don't know much. And this is where I see an obligation for me and the [Muslim] community to open up and to present oneself…

Admitting the hitherto prevailing passivity of many Muslims, she stated that Muslim community representatives 'need to actively reduce these [anti-Muslim] fears, we cannot just point fingers at the others and say that it's their fault'.

Advancing Muslim Community

The vast majority of interviewed Muslims in both country samples pursued goals that were either related to the bettering of society at large, supporting certain disadvantaged population groups other than Muslims, or tackling the prevalent stereotypical misconception of Muslims. Not surprisingly, however, given the high number of interviewed Muslims whose activism was at least partially located within a Muslim community context, a substantial number of them have also sought to support fellow Muslims in one way or another. An important finding of the analysis is that these communitarian goals were in almost all cases complemented by other aims that were often regarded as more dominant.

That leaves a very small minority of interview partners whose activism has been—predominantly or exclusively—aimed at advancing the wellbeing of the Muslim community. Such a strictly communitarian agenda applies only to one Muslim in the Australian sample, Mr Tabbaa (AUS12), and, with some limitations, to one person in the German sample, Ms Taraji (DE5).

Although Mr Tabbaa's (AUS 12) (current or previous) engagement as a media activist, president of a Muslim student association and executive board member of the Islamic Council of Victoria (ICV) involved cross-community cooperation and communication, these intergroup activities have occurred merely as a by-product of his community-based commitment. 'I have worked *with* other organisations, but to answer the question: … The priority for me is Muslims'. When he became president of the Muslim student association at LaTrobe University (Melbourne), 'we made it a priority to focus on Muslims on campus. Make sure services are adequate and students find help, things like that'. Outreach activities were only secondary. Similarly, his subsequent community work has revolved around questions of how to contribute to the solution of problems the Muslim community faces. He explicitly stressed the communitarian nature of his activism, when he stated: 'I think about it in terms of community'.

No one in the German sample displayed such an exclusive focus on communitarian goals. While many of those who volunteered within Muslim community organisations sought, among other things, to assist and empower Muslims, only Ms Taraji's (DE5) engagement can be regarded as *predominantly* aimed at contributing to the Muslim community. She has been an active volunteer and leader within various traditional Muslim community organisations for many years. The prime reason for her community engagement, which includes, for example, translating Islamic education material for children or supporting Muslim women in family and health-related issues, is to express her gratitude for what Muslim community organisations have done for her:

> It is all about give-and-take. I'm happy to be who I am today, and I have to thank the Community [IGD][4] for that … I realised there is a need to do something for the [Muslim] youth, that you have to offer something to the youth. So it is about giving and taking. Like others [IGD members] invest time for my kids, I invest also time for other people [in the IGD].

---

[4] Ms Taraji assumedly refers to the Islamic Community Germany (IGD), a Muslim organisation, established as one of the first Muslim organisations in Germany soon after World War II. Ms Taraji has been affiliated with the IGD since her childhood. IGD is a rather orthodox Muslim organisations, which is under surveillance by domestic intelligence agency in several German states.

Concluding Remarks: Goals of Muslims' Civic Engagement

The analysis of the various goals that the 30 interviewed Muslims in Australia and Germany pursue with their activism reveals that a republican agenda of contributing to the bettering of society prevail and that non-altruistic aims play no role at all. In some ways this confirms previous findings on the nature of civic engagement among certain (predominantly Muslim) minority groups. In the German context, Halm and Sauer (2005), for example, found that volunteers of Turkish origin (first and second generation immigrants) primarily sought to help others and contribute to the common good. Similarly, in Australia, a study concluded that surveyed Arabic-speaking volunteers have 'freely given their time and effort to others' primarily for reasons such as helping their own community, doing something worthwhile and helping all Australians (AMF and VA 2007b: 65). Al-Momani et al. (2010: 35) also found in their qualitative study among politically active Muslims in Australia evidence for republican, common good oriented goals of 'giving something back' to society and 'improving things for the whole of Australia'. Moreover, several Muslim respondents in the study by Al-Momani et al. mentioned, similar to the present research, the aim of dispelling public stereotypes about Islam and Muslims has been urge them to become involved in political activism.

The goals interviewed Muslims have tried to achieve through their enacted citizenship are not easy to categorise. Interviewed Muslims tend to have multiple and overlapping foci, which makes it often difficult, if not impossible, to place them on a rigid republican-communitarian spectrum. This complexity of goals echoes the previously discussed diversity of locations and types of Muslims' engagement. Tying this back to the theoretical framework, these findings resonate with Mouffe's (1995) notion of fluid, context-specific, and constantly shifting subject positions who activate different layers of their identities in the democratic process in different contexts. Related to this observation, the findings in this section tentatively points to an association between the types of goals pursed and the individuals' sense of belonging. The data analysis revealed that those two interview partners who have pursued an exclusively or predominantly communitarian agenda were also the only two who described their identity in purely religious terms: 'My identity is Islam', Ms Taraji (DE5) said, and Mr Tabbaa (AUS12) elaborated that his Australian (legal) citizenship is a 'statement of facts', and it 'entitles' him to his activism. However, he stressed that 'in terms of what's here [pointing to his heart], first and foremost for me is Muslim, being part of the Muslim community'.

Interviewed Muslims' sense of belonging appears connected to their goals of active citizenship also in other ways. Muslims' self-identification as Australian and German citizens—the civic layer of their identity—tends to be associated with an inclination to pursue a republican agenda, like contributing to the advancement of society at large. In the Australian sample almost all interview partners expressed a very strong sense of being Australian or being an Australian Muslim. Accordingly, the single most common type of goal among active Muslims in the Australia sample revolves around the greater good or helping other citizens regardless of their faith or background. In the German sample, such a strong emphasis on civic identity was less common, and if expressed, it was usually linked to a specific locality, that is, a sense of belonging to their home city instead of Germany only (see Chap. 4). Similar to the Australian situation, among those interviewed Muslims in Germany who displayed a strong sense of belonging to the (local or national) society and polity a republican agenda was the dominant pattern.

The aim of breaking down anti-Muslim misconceptions and stereotypes is the most widespread type of goal in the German sample, while being less common among interviewed Australian Muslims. It is difficult to explain this finding and how it is embedded in a broader societal context, also due to the small sample size and the nature of the interview data. While further research is required, these findings may suggest a more contested sense of multicultural belonging of Muslims in Germany; and they possibly indicate that active Muslims in Germany are still more occupied than their Australian counterparts with the rather reactive struggle for recognition as members and partners in civil society and public life. Interviewed Muslims in Germany still seem to feel the need and the urge to prove that Muslims are ordinary citizens, who deserve respect and equal treatment. Active Muslims interviewed in Australia seem to have largely moved beyond such a defensive agenda and managed to stress their civic participation efforts to achieve broader—republican—goals. More targeted research, with larger samples, is necessary to gain a better understanding of these complex associations between Muslims' sense of belonging and their active citizenship agenda.

Driving Forces and Fundamental Motivation

Most interviewed Muslims spoke not only about the basic goals they pursue through their active engagement but also about fundamental driving forces behind their performed citizenship. While both dimensions are obviously connected, the analysis of these deeper motivational aspects generated additional insights into Muslims' active citizenship. Interview partners' elaborations on their fundamental driving forces have been examined through two intertwined thematic lenses: the *source* and the *nature* of their motivation. The data analysis shows that most interviewed Muslims emphasised either their general personality and character traits or their Islamic faith as the main *source* of motivation; many mentioned both or did not separate religious from other layers of their personality. The specific *nature* of their motivation can be described along a continuum between defensive forms of engagement in response to (perceived) pressure or obligations to more positively driven types of participation linked, for example, to their personal interest and pleasure. Instrumentalist motives (e.g., improving employability) were expressed very rarely, and where they were mentioned they played only a subordinate role.[5]

The analysis revealed that for a majority of Muslims in the German and the Australian sample the Islamic faith plays a key role as a fundamental driving force for their active citizenship. Even some of those Muslims who have pursued republican goals and whose engagement was located in a mainstream context feel profoundly driven by their religion. The

---

[5] The common concepts of extrinsic and intrinsic motivation proved inadequate to capture the complexity of Muslims' motives: While a majority expressed a personal sense of moral, civic or religious duty—a common indicator for extrinsic motivation –, this sense of responsibility often coincided with their deep—intrinsic—commitment and pleasure to participate.

Islamic faith shapes their participation in different ways. This ranges from an (occasionally mentioned) defensive sense of religious duty to prevalent feelings of empowerment by faith and more spiritual reasons. Typically, positive feelings—joy, pleasure and personal satisfactions—were inextricably linked with the view of living up to religious responsibilities. In several cases faith-based motivations were identified in conjunction with general personality traits and a sense of moral responsibility to tackle injustice.

A number of interviewed Muslims explained that it is primarily their personality, often shaped by their upbringing and previous experiences of injustice in their country of origin, that drives their eagerness to participate. They may become active for a certain civic or political cause because they find it personally rewarding, because it is in 'their nature' or because they feel a moral or civic obligation to do so. Here, religious motives were largely absent or secondary. However, several Muslims who referred to their general personality as a core driving force of their activism also made references to religious layers of their identity, stating that their personality has been formed by, among other factors, their religious family background. The separation between faith-driven motivations and other types of driving forces is a rather analytical one. The following elaborations illustrate the often multiple facets of individual motives behind their active citizenship and their prevalent sense of civic, religious or moral obligations, often combined with their personal commitment to participation.

Islamic Faith as Key Driver of Active Citizenship

For the majority of interviewed Muslims their Islamic faith is the main, or at least a very important, motivational force that drives their civic or political engagement; many of them mentioned a sense of religious obligation. The data analysis unveiled a great diversity within this group of religiously motivated Muslims not only in terms of their goals but also with regard to the way in which their faith influences their engagement. Several Muslims, for example, referred to the Islamic belief that God grants reward 'points' according to Muslims' behaviour in this world to determine their fate in the afterlife; but even those who mentioned this religious reward system often differed quite substantially in the way they interpreted it.

Ms Sabbagh (AUS5) is one of those Muslims in the Australian sample whose active engagement have been strongly rooted in their faith and Islamic spirituality. Her civic engagement aimed at 'serving humanity' and 'her deep concern for humanity as a whole, to be proactive and try to create change' has been fundamentally driven by her eagerness to follow the example of the Prophet:

> [For me] the purpose of life is to know God. But how do we know God? Do you know God just through prayer or through wearing a headscarf or through fasting? You know God through His divine attributes … God's attributes … are such as the all merciful, the compassionate, the all loving, the all forgiving.

Ms Sabbagh emphasised her Islamic motivation, explaining that her civic goal to help and serve others is 'the main path for me to connect with the Divine'. In contrast to many other interviewed Muslims, she describes this core motivation without mentioning any form of religious obligation: 'It is definitely my calling. It is definitely my love and inspiration—serving others. Serving other is what I enjoy. It gets me out every day'.

Ms Abdo (AUS9), community activist and head of the Muslim women's organisation UMWA, also explained that her faith—in her words, an inseparable part of her personality—has been a key driving force and an empowering source of resilience for her committed engagement. In her view this does not only apply to herself but reflects the civic power of Islam more broadly: 'We [Muslims] have a faith that will enhance our citizenship, our participation as Australians'. Referring to her personal experiences, she elaborated:

> If I didn't have my faith and my Creator, I don't think I would be able to overcome all the negative things … And there are days when I think I can't get up the next morning, and I'm not going to put myself out there anymore. And then you think and talk to Allah, the Creator, and you think: What is my purpose in this life? I have a purpose which is to make

this world a better place—not only for me and my children, but for the future generation. So if this is my purpose I better get up now, and I know God will send me people along the way who will support me. And that's what keeps me going.

Ms Abdo's sense of being empowered by her faith stands in no contrast to her belief that one needs to be 'doing the best you can' to please God. She described this dutiful facet of her religious motivation in reference to the Islamic point (reward) system:

> I have this debit account. I don't know what's in it. It's like entering into an exam and I think life itself is an exam…You hope you will succeed and you will get 100%, but you're doing the best that you can, not knowing what you are going to get in the end. That's what keeps me going. I don't keep track, because it could be one little action that will elevate my being with my Creator and one big action that has no weight.

Similarly, Mr Sattar (AUS8) mentioned the motivational and empowering effect of his Islamic faith for his civic engagement. The Qur'anic *If you save one life, it is as if you saved all humanity* is 'constantly in the back of my mind', and he reminds himself, especially when he feels exhausted, that 'our Lord has instructed us to help the disadvantaged and give where you can'. For him, pursing this compassionate goal and gaining points in Islamic terms for the afterlife are inextricably linked:

> My religion teaches me to do this and to have this passion, to be compassionate. So that is intrinsically in me, my second nature. And a natural consequence of that is, you know, the points that come with it. For me they are both just synonymous.

Emphasising the importance of his faith, Mr Sattar also maintained that he would not be engaged 'to this extent' if he were not Muslim. Although he had been active in other forms of civic participation before he rediscovered his spiritual connection with Islam in his mid-20s, he stressed that without his Islamic faith he would 'definitely not [be committed and active] on this level'.

Other interview partners in Australia displayed a more pronounced focus on the notion of Islamic duty and accountability in relation to their active citizenship. *Ashtar* (AUS14), media worker and community project officer within a government initiative, for example, emphasised her obligation before God to defend Islam and help other Muslims: 'It is a religious obligation for me ... Not an *official* religious obligation, but certainly an informal one for me, where I feel I'm doing this for my religion'. She maintained that 'without God's guidance I wouldn't do a lot of the things that I'm doing now [in terms of my civic participation and media work]'. Asked about her view on the Islamic points-based reward system, she replied: 'Everything I do is to get into heaven. That's essentially every Muslim's goal, every religious person's goal'. She explained:

> It is definitely to score more points. I want God to see I'm doing this for his benefit and the benefit of our religion. And I'm trying to abide by this as much as I can. And it is always my end goal, will always be, to please God and not anybody else.

Religious reasons are also central for Mr Kamarredine's (AUS7) performance of active citizenship. Referring to Islam as 'a comprehensive way of life', the community activist from Melbourne explained that without his faith he 'would not be doing this; there would be no motive'. His rationale is closely linked to his interpretation of the Islamic reward system:

> As a Muslim I believe that this life is a short life and the real life is the hereafter. And in the hereafter you will be rewarded the way you were acting in this life. So I need to make a change, the more [Muslim] youth I bring towards the religion and away from trouble and doing the right things, the better I am, the more reward I will have. The more I contribute to the betterment of the society, the better my reward will be. We belief [that God] created us to be good in this life, to do the good ... So this is the main reason!

Despite the fundamental importance of his faith, Mr Kamarredine's engagement is not solely a dutiful, extrinsically driven response to Islamic obligations. He described his engagement as positive and personally rewarding: 'working for the reward of my Lord ... changing the lives of others in a good way ... gives you joy and makes you happy'.

Similarly, Mr Tabbaa's (AUS12) community-based engagement is motivated by his faith and a sense of religious responsibility. This also includes the obligation to leverage his God-given skills to advance the wellbeing of the Muslim community. Mr Tabbaa asserted that,

> if you take a position [for example, at the ICV], ... you're accountable before people and before God. There is an accountability process and there is always this fear that maybe you are not fulfilling it. That drives me and pushes me to work a lot.

Despite this 'fear', he described his community work overall in positive terms:

> I really enjoy it and the people and the community and that ... but there is the doubt whether it is enough and sufficient, whether your intentions are clean and all this sort of stuff. It comes in as a doubt, but the engagement itself is very positive. I don't do it as a burden.

Religion also played an important role for Muslims interviewed in Germany. Similar to their Australian counterparts, they described their faith-based motivation in different ways. Several Muslims referred to their fundamental driving forces as a combination of religious motives and their general personality. It is worth noting that some of these religiously motivated Muslims in Germany are actively engaged in mainstream organisation like the trade union or a mainstream political party.

Burak (DE1), an elected councillor (at the time of the interview) and previously active volunteer for Muslim community and mainstream organisations, for example, described the motivation for his multiple engagement at least partially in terms of religious accountability.

> Let me put it this way, my strength [for my active engagement] I probably get somehow from my religion. Because what am I going to do when one day [I die]. I believe in life after death ... like Christians and Jews. When God then says: You saw the problems, what did you do about it? What was your contribution? ... Did it only bother you? Just complaining does not

help society, so what was your contribution? In this situation I have to be able to provide an answer.

Onur (DE16) explicitly linked his activism within the trade union to his religion, highlighting how principles of the labour movement and those of the Islamic faith dovetail: 'The basic reason for my endeavours to improve working and living conditions is, of course, that the Prophet was also committed to working towards justice'. And he specified: 'Justice, inclusiveness, [and] that all people get the same money for the same kind of work... Those are roughly my dynamic motives'.

Mr Yerli's (DE 14) active engagement within the Muslim community (e.g., as youth worker and mosque chairman) and the mainstream context (e.g., trade union) is driven both by his religious faith and his personal commitment to justice and equality. Mr Yerli stressed the importance of his religious belief as the key underlying cause for his activism: 'My faith makes me responsible for doing this, and that I take responsibility and that I do not simply accept the things the way they are. That's the reason for it'. However, he also stressed that this sense of religious obligation alone does not explain his commitment: 'One learns through religion to do good things, but atheists do that too. That lies, I believe, in the nature of human beings'. He asserted that, while religion does shape one's personality, and he also seeks God's approval, he would 'probably' have also become a committed active person if he were no Muslim. This mix of religious and personality-related driving forces is further complemented by his sense of civic duty: 'This is one society and everyone has to take responsibility for it regardless of one's religion. This is what I deliberately want to do and I also want to show other that this is how it is'.

A sense of religious obligation and other more general factors were mentioned by *Esra* (DE7), describing the motivation for her engagement within Muslim and mainstream community groups as well as for the local advisory integration council. Not only does she consider her volunteering to be socially important and a pleasant and, in her words, 'sensible' way to spend her time, she also referred to her religious motivation:

> It is also part of "living my religiosity". For me that's not only praying, but also being active, doing something for other people. That for me is about

religion. It is part of my religion to do something for other people… It is kind of worship to be there for society… [Instead] of reciting the same Qur'an verse three times, I can help another student who has difficulties at school or help a friend. I find that this is equally valuable.

Despite this religious motivation *Esra* does not describe her engagement in terms of obeying religious rules. She elaborated that God does not simply set rigid duties, but prescribes a broader Islamic framework within which Muslims have the individual freedom to act. While she admitted that she is also motivated by the desire to get God's approval and forgiveness, she stressed that the Islamic point-based reward system is less relevant to her.

I stopped thinking that I have collected this many points for Judgement Day…. I try to live beyond this notion of heaven-and-hell. And I don't do things simply because I want to achieve something before God…. But I don't condemn this. I used to do that too for a long time, [thinking] when I do this and that, I will be rewarded this many points. I think that this is a good basis in the beginning, but it can also make one very tense, and then the motivation shifts, because it is not about the actual cause anymore but all about the reward system itself.

Mr Cicek (DE9) stressed his religion as the main driving force for his activism more than most other Muslims interviewed in Germany: 'Well, the motivation why I do all this has of course a religious background, maybe even predominantly'. He compares his Islamic obligations and convictions with humanistic values, which for him are identical; he also points to the duty of utilise his God-given intellectual capacities to pursue a good cause:

I love people, I love my surroundings, I like to become and be engaged in society. I like it to see a smile on someone's face when I have done something good … For me this is something my religion wants. The religion wants that, if I have the intellectual potential, I use this for a good purpose. This can be done in different areas, it may be in business, it may be in politics, arts, anywhere … But it is always about this responsibility. If you have a gift that God gave you, do something with it, also out of gratitude.

Contributing to the bettering of society and serving God is inextricably linked for him—also with regard to being rewarded by God in the afterlife. He is convinced that one has to live this life in a 'good' manner to be rewarded: 'For me it is important to give, but what makes this important is that it is linked to God. This spirituality is very important'.

Ms Taraji's (DE5) predominantly communitarian-oriented civic participation within a Muslim community context is driven by her eagerness to please God. No other interview partner in the German sample emphasised this more explicitly. Through her community work and interreligious dialogue engagement, she wants to 'pay her duty to thank the Creator for being healthy and well, and that my children are well. It is my duty to do this, collecting a few points … I do this in order to stay well in the future'. At the same time, her community commitment is also aimed at being rewarded in the afterlife.

> The driving force for doing all this—to sacrifice one's time, stay away from home sometimes on the weekend, although your children need you—is of course God's benevolence … One collects good deeds, which you need in this life and in the afterlife.

These personal accounts of Muslims in the German and the Australian sample demonstrate that the specifics manifestations of their faith-based driving forces differ greatly. Each one of them described their individual approach of positioning themselves within the framework of the Islamic duty (or expectation) to be a good person who seeks to help others or to contribute to advancing communities or the society at large. Muslims who have expressed such religious driving forces have become engaged in a variety of contexts—from mainstream organisations to Muslim community groups, from civic to political participation—and with a range of goals, including those linked to a republican agenda of serving society.

Personality Traits as Key Driver of Activism

A number of interviewed Muslims emphasised that their active citizenship has been mainly driven by their personal interests, pleasure or personality traits and values (e.g., moral sense of justice). In some of these cases, Islam has not been entirely irrelevant for their motivation, but played only a secondary role. Several interview partners argued that their religious background or upbringing has influenced the way in which their personality developed, and thus Islamic values may indirectly influence their personality-based motivations. It is worth noting that some of the interviewed Muslims who referred predominantly to their personality as the key diver of their civic engagement have been active within a Muslim community context. Most interviewed Australian Muslims with such a personality-driven motivation mentioned negative experiences overseas prior to their immigration to Australia as one of the root causes for their activism.

One of the Australian Muslims who strongly emphasised their personal attitudes and character as the main driving force for their active citizenship was Mr Merhi (AUS1), a trade union activist with extensive volunteering experiences in mainstream organisations. He highlighted several times during the interview that his civic and professional engagement for the youth and disadvantaged is not aimed at gaining external appraisal or public attention: 'I want to make very clear that this is not about me'. Instead, he explained, 'this is just my nature, helping others, you know. If I died tomorrow, I at least made a tiny difference in society'. He described this attitude, which he has had from 'a very young age', as being in contrast to widespread selfishness and materialistic views in society, which, in his view, hamper people's willingness to become more engaged in volunteering and helping others.

Mr Merhi did not express any sense of obligation or pressure—neither civic nor religious. While he did mention God's reward in the afterlife as an additional bonus, he stressed that his civic commitment 'has nothing to do with religion or the Lebanese community':

> With Islam, I know, you do good […] and it will help you in the afterlife. That is very obvious in Islam. I like to help others because it's my nature to help others. I think I like the reward eventually for it, but […] my driving force is to help those less advantaged than me … If there are people here, interstate or overseas who do not have a voice, who are financially struggling or do not have parents … there is just a real need in my heart to help. You can't change the world, you can't help everyone. But if you see people who don't have money for their next feed, you want to help.

Ms El Matrah (AUS2), who works for the Melbourne-based Australian Muslim Women's Centre for Human Rights and has sat on various boards and committees, described her activism as driven by her desire to tackle injustice and as a way to 'find a place' for herself in Australian society. She explained that her personal experiences as an immigrant resulted in her—initially subconscious—interest in 'issues of migration and displacement', as a particular manifestation of her 'social justice conscience'.[6] She underscored this fundamentally identity-driven nature of her civic engagement: 'I had no sense that I wanted to change the world. My conscience was very much trying to find a place for myself in it'. Her professional and volunteering engagement for Muslim women issues has explicitly *not* been aimed at representing Islam, but has been closely tied to her general sense of justice:

> I actually had no real interest in the representation [of Muslims] at all! It was purely social justice ... I saw Muslim women as having a particular vulnerability. And that had some currency for me in the sense that I understood it. I understood Muslim women very well, and it was an easy path for me to go.

Empowering Muslim women has been Ms El Matrah's way of enacting her opposition to what she described as an unjust and unequal society, 'where the strongest and the fittest ... and the privileged have a good quality of life' and can set the rules for all others. Against this system-critical backdrop, she asserted that 'another reason why civic engagement becomes important [is that] the powerful need to stop being the ones who define society and who dictate who belongs and who doesn't'. Standing up against this general power imbalance—which puts Muslim women, like many other groups, in a position of vulnerability and voicelessness—has been Ms El Matrah's main motive behind her multifaceted civic activism.

Similar to Ms El Matrah, some other interview partners whose active citizenship has been located within a Muslim community context did not mention primarily religious motives for their engagement. This applies,

---

[6] Ms El Matrah initially worked with homeless men for a mainstream charity organisation; this professional focus derived in her view from her general interest in issues of displacement.

for example, to Mr Galil (AUS11), imam at a Melbourne mosque. As Muslim community representative, he has been active in various interfaith and cross-cultural initiatives. His prime motivational force, however, has not been directly linked to his faith, but primarily to his personal general interests and the pleasure he gets from engaging with people from diverse backgrounds. His particular interest in interfaith dialogue started in his early childhood back in Egypt and has continued until today. It drives his everyday interactions with other people as well as his volunteer commitment to interfaith dialogue and work for the local multicultural advisory council. In reference to his longstanding involvement in interfaith initiatives, he expressed his personal pleasure:

> I think we are very fortunate to be in Victoria ... to enjoy to a great extent talking to people of different beliefs. We are not going to agree on the beliefs. That's not what life is about, life is about engagement. And that makes my life a lot richer as if we were restricted to just one way of thinking. And I enjoy it.

In addition, Mr Galil considers his engagement a civil obligation, which is tied also to religion. He stressed, however, that this is not Islam-specific: 'Civil duties are part of the religion! It is actually part of every religion, not only Islam'.

Mr Ahmed's (AUS3) engagement as an African community leader and his active political work has unfolded primarily in response to his personal experiences of violence in war-torn Eritrea, where he was born. His personal mission and key motive for all his activism seeking to empower African youth and communities in general is to minimise conflicts, promote cohesion and prevent the outbreak of violence.

> Since I came to this country something has haunted my life ... I saw societies breaking in Eritrea because of war ... And that makes you think you have to do something. You have to ask ... why don't we create leadership that foresees the problems? Why would we wait until they fight and kill each other? For me that is the key point why I lost my home, my everything and became a refugee. Why? That still remains in my head until now. And that is the force that pushes me ... Make society the best so my kids don't have to suffer what I experienced.

Stressing the collective responsibility of society to give young people hope and offer role models, Mr Ahmed considers it a 'moral obligation to work towards the best of our ability to make peace, and that is where participation comes in'. More specifically, he feels personal responsibility to represent those—in his case mainly young people of African origin—who do not have the chance of making their voices heard themselves. While he mentioned that accurately representing his 'beautiful Islam' is a part of his civic participation agenda (e.g., organising an African Iftar), the main reason for his engagement lies within his personality, which is shaped by, among many other factors, one's religion: 'Every person is a product of all his surroundings. His background, education, religion, the people, whatever, the environment … is what makes you what you are'.

Ms Faruqi's (AUS13) civic and political participation, which currently revolves mainly around her work as politician in NSW state parliament, is also motivated by her endeavour to contribute to the bettering of society and to 'be a good person every minute I have here'. More specifically, her active citizenship has been 'mainly driven by environmental justice and social justice … I always had this social justice element, and then moved into the environment'. The origins of her civic and moral agenda lie in her first-hand encounters with injustice, poverty and discrimination against women and the poor in Pakistan, the country where she was born and raised. She explained that, while the societal, religious and cultural context of her upbringing have obviously affected her personality, her activism was more influenced by her university studies, her family, feminism and other non-religious experiences. She made it clear that her commitment to social justice has never reflected an attempt to follow or apply Islamic principles: 'It's me and it's my family who have had those values. They have been developed from the many influences from family, culture, religion and so on'.

The analysis of Muslims' key driving forces in the German sample revealed that many of those who described their general personality traits, personal interest and pleasure as the primary motives for their civic activism have been predominantly active within a *Muslim* community context. Similar to the Australian sample, some of them also made additional references to faith-based aspects.

The university student *Leyla* (DE13), representative of the Muslim university student association, referred to her general personality as the key reasons behind her commitment to redress the negative image of Islam with: 'First of all, generally, regardless of Islam, I simply can't bear injustices. As a human being'. Despite this prioritisation of her non-religious driving force, *Leyla* mentioned faith-based facets of her motivation, stressing that her personal values and her Islamic faith are inextricably interconnected.

> If I weren't Muslim, I don't know if I'd have the same personality. I cannot really separate that. But I think that my personality, my Islam, my convictions make it a duty for me to try to effect positive change.

In addition, *Leyla* mentioned that Muslims are urged by their faith to 'do good'. She explained that her engagement for the accurate representation of Islam has been driven not only by her being personally affected by the public perceptions of Muslims, but also by the Islamic 'call to stand up for the good. That gives me strength and simply motivates me'. *Leyla*'s account illustrates the multiple and interconnected motivational facets of many Muslims' active citizenship, which makes it impossible to ultimately classify her civic driving forces.

Ms Theißen (DE3) underscored that her long-standing civic engagement, which has been mainly located within the Muslim community, has been driven by her humanistic values and the pleasure she gets from helping others. Already prior to her conversion to Islam she had been passionate about educating and helping other people. Asked about her motives behind her active citizenship she stated: 'That is in me, I enjoy that… The biggest joy a human being can have is to do something for other people'. Linked to this intrinsic notion of personal pleasure is Ms Theißen's strong personal moral imperative to help those who are less fortunate and to stand up for social justice:

> For me, what's most important are other human beings—and I simply can't sit and watch when someone suffers. I have to help … I can't bear injustice. When I see something unjust, I have to do something about it. My father was also like that, that's how it was at home.

While she stressed that this general character trait stems from her family upbringing and developed before she converted to Islam, Ms Theißen mentioned a potentially reinforcing effect of her Islamic faith: 'It is possible that if I had not become Muslim, I would have lost this [desire to help others]'.

Ms Dogan (DE8), elected member of the city council of Bonn with a long participation history in Muslim and cross-cultural and interfaith initiatives, also stressed her personality as being the driving force behind her activism—in conjunction with her experiences with anti-Muslim stereotypes and marginalisation, especially since September 11. While her primary motivation lies in her resilient personality, the goal of accurately representing Islam has become an important thematic backdrop of her engagement. Asked about the origin of her motivation for her multiple civic and political engagement and the barriers she had experienced, she elaborated:

> Well, I think that's a character trait of mine. Wherever I experience barriers, I tell myself: Now even more! I am not someone who gives up. When I realise that there is still a need [to do something], when there are barriers, then there seems to be a problem. I then think we have to convince them that we [Muslims] are completely normal and that we also belong to this society. And then these prejudices … I've had really shocking experiences …These are of course also reasons that make me say: we have to get to the core of this! What is going on here with this opposition to Muslims?

Concluding Remarks: Driving Forces and Motives

Examining the goals and fundamental drivers of Muslims' active citizenship sheds light on very personal and often multiple motives, linked to one's biography, personality and a complexly interwoven set of individual motives, values and beliefs. What the findings demonstrate are a generally high level of personal commitment and, in most cases, feelings of joy and pleasure when pursuing their varied civic goals. These positive attitudes can be considered a basic personality trait that serves as a motivational precondition for active citizenship. Related to this, the interviewed Muslims have all been driven by altruistic motives. This is often rooted in the individual's strong commitment to the principle of social justice or a general sense of civic duty. Against this backdrop, it is evident that someone's personality is a fundamental driver of active citizenship.

Beyond this general conclusion, the analysis of the motivational patterns of interviewed Muslims particularly underscore the vital role of the Islamic faith as an empowering driving force for active citizenship. This is a key finding of this research, and it resonates with emerging evidence in Australia on the relationship between active citizenship and Islamic principles.[7] The CALD National Survey of Australian volunteers revealed already in the mid-2000s that many Arabic-speaking respondents mentioned 'spiritual/religious beliefs' as a reason for their volunteering (AMF and VA 2007b: 65). This tentative indicator for Islam as a motivating resource for active citizenship has been confirmed and further specified in recent research in Australia. A study by Harris and Roose (2014) on Muslim youth and their 'civic practices' in Australia, for example, offers insights into these faith-based motives for social and civic engagement. Based on an analysis of interviews with 80 young Muslims, the two researchers found that a majority of them expressed a sense of religious obligation 'to help others or make the community a better place'; they also stated that 'being Muslim made a difference to the extent or kind of social or civic action they were involved in' (2014: 808). They argue that

> [s]eeing their religion as a "way of life" allowed them to position themselves as ethical citizens whose everyday lives were always inflected by moral and political reflection and guidance for action. This could then enhance rather than reduce their capacity for civic engagement (Harris and Roose 2014: 807).

The emerging paradigm shift towards the recognition of Islamic faith as a civic resource has recently been confirmed by another study, carried out in Detroit (USA), Lyon (France) and Melbourne, on Muslim

---

[7] Cesari (2013: 76) comes to a different conclusion in her international study on Muslims' citizenship in the West. She states that 'according to our investigations, it is not possible to assert that religiosity increases Muslims' political participation', nor do her findings suggest that 'Muslims' religiosity has a negative effect'.

religiosity in secular cities. Based on a small-scale survey, focus groups and interviews, the researchers found in their Melbourne-based fieldwork that Muslims 'continue to practice their religion in an integrative manner that encourages active participation and engagement rather than the opposite' (Johns et al. 2015: 17). The empirical findings of the present explorative research on active citizenship not only support Harris and Roose's (2014) and Johns et al.'s (2015) conclusion, but also offer deeper explorative insights into Muslims' personal views on how their Islamic faith empowers or drives their civic and political participation.

The majority of interviewed Muslims in Australia and Germany describe their religion as a major motivation for their active citizenship; this holds true for Muslims engaged in a Muslim community context as well for those active in a mainstream civil society or the political arena. The ways in which these faith-driven active Muslims interpret and apply Islamic principles of 'civic duties' to participate in civil society or the political arena differ broadly. While many interview partners mentioned the Islamic point-based reward system, there are major differences in how this reward system was interpreted. What the majority of interviewed Muslims have in common, however, is that their religious duty of helping others targets *all* people—and not only member of the Muslim community.

A clear line between faith-based and general personality based motivations is often difficult, and sometimes impossible, to draw. In many instances, both dimensions are seen as synonymous, inextricable intertwined or as at least closely connected. Some interviewed Muslims do articulate a clear prevalence of Islamic values in their elaborations on their driving forces—often in combination with a sense of religious obligation that tends to go hand in hand with their personal eagerness to participate and the intrinsic pleasure they gain through it. These findings further underscore the complexity of Muslim active citizenship. They fundamentally warn against simplistic, often unsubstantiated assumptions about the links between the type and location of Muslims' civic or political participation, the goals they pursue, and their motivational driving forces.

Muslims' specific goals and their deeper motives are connected in diverse ways. It may not be surprising that those two interviewed Muslims who pursue predominantly communitarian goals (i.e., seeking to advance the Muslim community) emphasise their fundamentally religious motives behind their civic engagement. However, many of those who described their Islamic faith as the primary driving force pursue a republican agenda, trying to contribute to the betterment of society at large or to support certain disadvantaged groups (other than Muslims). Conversely, many of those Muslims who stress their general personality and dispositions (instead of religious reasons) as their primary source of motivation seek to either help disadvantaged groups, to contribute to a more just and peaceful and cohesive society (in the Australian sample) or to redress anti-Muslim stereotypes (in the German sample). Given the explorative nature and small sample of this study, generalising interpretations of these findings are problematic. What the findings clearly show, however, is that Islamic values and convictions do not have to be a barrier to active citizenship—not for a communitarian agenda and not for those who follow republican goals. To the contrary, Muslims' faith has positive facilitating effects as a source of resilience, key motivation and empowerment for active engagement in a variety of civic and political contexts.

References

Al-Momani, K., Dados, N., Maddox, M., & Wise, A. (2010). *Political participation of Muslims in Australia*. Sydney: Macquarie University.

Australian Multicultural Foundation (AMF), & Volunteering Australia (VA). (2007b). *National survey of Australian volunteers from diverse cultural and linguistic backgrounds*. Melbourne: VA.

Cesari, J. (2013). *Why the West fears Islam. An exploration of Muslims in liberal democracies*. Basingstoke: Palgrave Macmillan.

Halm, D., & Sauer, M. (2005). *Freiwilliges Engagement von Türkinnen und Türken in Deutschland*. Essen: ZfT.

Harris, A., & Roose, J. (2014). DIY citizenship amongst young Muslims: Experiences of the "ordinary". *Journal of Youth Studies, 17*(6), 794–813.

Johns, A., Mansouri, F., & Lobo, M. (2015). Religiosity, citizenship and belonging: The everyday experiences of young Australian Muslims. *Journal for Muslim Minority Affairs, 35*, 171–190.

Mouffe, C. (1995). Democratic politics and the question of identity. In J. Rajchman (Ed.), *The identity in question* (pp. 33–45). London/New York: Routledge.

Peucker, M., & Akbarzadeh, S. (2014). *Muslim active citizenship in the West*. London/New York: Routledge.

8

Empowering and Discouraging Factors

Many interviewed Muslims mentioned a number of factors that have had enabling or encouraging effects on their activism. These elaborations partially overlap with the previously analysed fundamental driving forces behind Muslim active citizenship. Many interview partners, for example, referred to their Islamic faith, their commitment to social justice or their general personality traits of resilience and altruism as empowering factors for their active citizenship. A closer examination of the interview data reveals additional insights into what encourages or enables Muslims to get involved in civic or political participation or intensify their engagement. Moreover, some interview partners also described circumstances or conditions that, in their views, *discourage* or *hamper* Muslims' civic commitment, although these disempowering factors were usually mentioned as barriers experienced not by themselves but by *other* Muslims.

This analysis points to many similarities between interviewed Muslims in Australia and Germany. In both national samples, several Muslims explained that the negative public climate towards Muslims and Islam has not inhibited their active citizenship, but, in many cases, rather motivated them to become more involved in the civic or political landscape. Another commonly raised aspect is that Muslims' positive engagement experiences have motivated them to continue or further expand their civic commitment. Many interviewed Muslims feel they have been successful in pursuing at least some of their civic goals, and they asserted that they have established networks of mutual trust, which have further strengthened their capacity to participate and increased their civic efficacy. In addition to these mutually reinforcing factors of active citizenship, many Muslims in both country samples reflected on the enabling effect of personal resources, such as time, skills and knowledge, and (to a lesser degree) socioeconomic status, on Muslims' civic or political participation.

Public Stigmatisation and (Media) Misrepresentation

The stigmatising and exclusionary public discourse and misrepresentation of Islam and Muslims fundamentally and collectively deny Muslims' substantive citizenship and their recognition as equal members of society and the political community. Accordingly, these exclusionary discourses and experiences have been described by several interview partners in terms of their deterring and paralysing implications for Muslims' civic engagement activism. However, interviewed Muslims emphasised that these discouraging effects did not apply to them personally; rather to the contrary, they either claimed that public stigmatisation, misrepresentation and anti-Muslim experiences has not affected their active citizenship at all, or, as many highlighted, these external factors ultimately encouraged them to become civically or politically engaged. This ambivalence between paralysis and empowerment resonates with previous research. On the one hand, studies have found that the media discourse and exclusionary public image of Muslims are commonly considered barriers for civic and political participation (Gendera et al. 2012: 106; CIRCA 2010; Al-Momani et al. 2010). These discourses create and reinforce a climate of suspicion and stigmatisation that many Muslims perceive as a major source of frustration and a contributor to their personal or their community's sense of marginalisation and exclusion, sometimes fuelling tendencies of civic disengagement (Aly 2007). On the other hand, as some studies have demonstrated, this public misrepresentation of Islam may also have positive implications for the activism of some Muslims and their efforts to actively work towards recognition as full member of society and the 'desired status of equal citizenship' (Yasmeen 2007: 44). Already more than one and a half decades ago, Pnina Werbner (2000: 309) observed in the British context that Muslims' public protest and mobilisation against what they viewed as unfair and unequal treatment of their faith community (e.g., during Rushdie affairs) played a key role in 'the development of a Muslim British civic consciousness and capacity for active citizenship'. More recently, researchers similarly found that the negative public attention in the aftermaths of the 9/11 terror attacks also resulted in a rise of interfaith initiatives and other community outreach activities, which have become central sites of Muslims' active civic engagement also in Australia (Amath 2013: 116–117; Peucker and Akbarzadeh 2014: 162–165) and Germany (Peucker and Akbarzadeh 2014: 186–188). Another effect of the negative portrayal of Islam in the media for Muslims' active citizenship is the proliferation of (Muslim) minority 'community media intervention' (Dreher 2010) and media activism, as several studies have discovered in Australia (Dreher 2010; Amath 2013), Germany and elsewhere (Peucker and Akbarzadeh 2014: 111–120).

The analysis of the interviews with active Muslims in Germany and Australia for this research highlights that the public climate, media misrepresentation and, in some cases, even personal experiences of anti-Muslim racism have further empowered or encouraged their activism in the area of media engagement and various other forms of civic and political participation. It offers deeper insights into what Al-Momami and his colleagues (2010: 35) tentatively conclude in their study on Muslims' political participation in Australia: 'To some, the negative publicity about Muslims after September 11 2001 was a motivating force'. Several Muslims in both national samples stated, for example, that misrepresentation, stereotypes and prejudice are a reflection of ignorance, which needs to be addressed through dialogue and providing more accurate information.

Around one-half of all Australian interview partners expressed such views, highlighting that the negative media discourse and, more generally, the stigmatising public climate or experiences of racism have urged them to become more civically or politically active. Many Muslims in the Australian sample share the view that these motivating effects apply to many (or at least some) other Muslims, although several interview partners also stressed the negative ramifications of this public discourse for some Muslims' reluctance to engage in civic or political participation.

Ashtar (AUS14) is one of those Australian interview partners who underscored that the media bias and personal experiences of racism and exclusion encourage more active citizenship among many Muslims. Drawing from her experiences as a multicultural community project coordinator, *Ashtar* maintained that many young Muslims would not 'disengage because they face racism issues, [although] this is obviously not applicable to everyone, and everybody deals with it in his own personal way'. Altogether, she assumes that the negative public climate and experiences of racism 'is a lot more a motivator than it is a deterrent' for active citizenship of Muslims.

Mr Delall (AUS4) and Mr Kamarredine (AUS7) stated that they feel personally challenged by the negative public climate to become more active, but they both also see the adverse effect on some or many other Muslims. Mr Dellal, executive director of the Australian Multicultural Foundation (Melbourne), who has extensively worked with Muslim communities and especially Muslim youth, asserted that 'some withdraw. That's what they do, they withdraw and keep within their own circles and do whatever. Some participate even more! For me it was like "*bring it on*"! The more [negative labelling of Muslims], the better' . Mr Kamarredine, who has worked with young Muslims from the Newport mosque community in Melbourne's west, elaborated that the public climate towards Muslims has discouraged many Muslims from becoming more active citizens. He even suspects that this deterring effect applies to the majority of Muslims—but not to himself: 'For most people, this has discouraged them. For me, it actually challenges me more! More things need to be done'.

8 Empowering and Discouraging Factors

Ms Abdo (AUS9) and Ms El Matrah (AUS2) both claimed that the public stigmatisation of Muslims has overall encouraged Muslims to become involved in civic engagement. Ms Abdo spoke about this motivating effect of the negative climate in collective terms for the Muslim community in general: 'I honestly think the more [public scapegoating and stereotyping] is taking place, the more we are encouraged to participate'. Ms El Matrah was more critical about the type of civic engagement triggered by this exclusionary public discourse. Expressing her sceptical views on Muslims' strictly communitarian engagement, she stated:

> I think it encourages them to do more, but it means that they misunderstand what the challenge is about. I think it increases the ethno-centric or religious-centric view to activism, which in the long term is bad for them and bad for society.

Mr Sattar (AUS8), youth worker volunteer and board member at Mission of Hope, recalled an incident that supports Ms El Matrah's view. He argued that such negative collective or personal experiences of exclusion can be a 'barrier for citizenship in the wider community', although, in contrast to Ms El Matrah, he did not consider such a communitarian focus to be problematic:

> I remember when I participated in Clean Up Australia … about a year ago with a friend [a Muslim girl]. And we headed out to Cronulla… And the comments we got was like "Clean up your own country! This is Clean Up Australia Day—and you are not Australian". So it is definitely a barrier. She is too hurt to get into wider community citizenship [again], she does local community work now, where she feels safe.

Mr Sattar's account about the possible exclusionary effect of anti-Muslim discriminatory experiences resonates with what the above mentioned study by AMF and VA (2007a: 2) found about some Muslims' reluctance to do voluntary work in non-Muslim organisations: 'Muslim youth participants identified the fear of being isolated, harassed or discriminated against as a major barrier' to enacting their citizenship in a mainstream context.

Interviewed Muslims in Australia explained the motivating effects of this stigmatising societal climate for their personal commitment in different ways. Some alluded that the prevalent suspicion and stereotypes in the wider community require them to actively counter these public images by acting as good Australian citizens and leading by example. Mr Sattar (AUS8), youth worker volunteer at the Mission of Hope, described this attitude and role modelling strategy:

> We feel like we have to be the role models and the example of what an Australian Muslim is—just a normal Australian who has a faith … But we also know we have to work ten times as hard as any other group in the country to show that we don't have an agenda … We just want to help.

Others argued explicitly along religious lines. Ms Sabbagh (AUS5), for example, referred to the 'prophetic model' and her endeavour to follow the example of the Prophet. Her personal experiences of anti-Muslim racism and aggression have made her civic engagement 'more compassionate', because the Prophet also 'responded to ignorance with compassion and mercy. And this is the only way we are going to move forward'.

In the German sample, the view that the negative public climate, experiences of exclusion and the media misrepresentation encourage Muslims' active citizenship was also articulated. About one quarter of the interviewed Muslims in Germany expressed this view. *Leyla* (DE13), representative of a Muslim university student association and active in, among others, interfaith dialogue, stated that the skewed media image and personal experiences of exclusion have encouraged her to become more active. She described her active response to rectify the negative public climate as both a civic and religious obligation. Instead of withdrawing, she said,

> it is rather a "now-even-more" attitude. This urge to prove that it is not like that … If I don't do anything about it, at least a little bit, nothing will ever change. Who should we be waiting for? Who else should do something about it?

Mr Cicek's (DE9) active citizenship is *directly* linked to the public discourse on Muslims. His decision to become active was triggered by a particular media debate in 2010 on the allegedly failed integration of Muslims. Mr Cicek felt urged by this divisive and stigmatising media debate, which, in his view, targeted him personally as a Muslim, to contribute to the public discussion by setting up his own online blog. This independent media activism marked the beginning of Mr Cicek's active and multifaceted civic career.

Several interview partners in the German sample shared their views on the effects of the societal climate on other Muslims' proneness to enact their citizenship. Two of them, *Leyla* (DE13) and *Esra* (DE7), disagreed with the claim that the negative public climate discourages Muslims from becoming civically active. *Esra* stated that the engagement of young Muslims is generally underestimated and that, in her view, 'those who are discriminated against in one way or another tend to be particularly active'. Other interview partners were less optimistic in their assessment. Mr Fetić (DE4), for example, who feels personally empowered by the negative public imaginary to become more active, expressed some sympathy for those Muslims who feel demotivated by the public climate and consequently choose not to become actively engaged. 'I don't approve of this, but I can understand it sometimes', he said. Similarly, Mr Yerli (DE14), trade union activist and chairman of a mosque association in Penzberg (Bavaria), stated that, given the mammoth task of countering the media bias and public misconceptions, some Muslims have decided to not get involved in any civic engagement. He added that 'they are a minority in our own local community here, but these people do exist. And there are of course other [local Muslim] communities, where they are the majority'.

Two other interviewed Muslims, *Burak* (DE1) and Ms Aydin (DE10), drew a more indirect link between the societal climate and public misconception of Muslims, on the one hand, and their general inclination to civic engagement, on the other hand. Both alluded that the public climate in Germany fails to give Muslims a sense of civic recognition (Mr Aydin) and sense of belonging (*Burak*), which they consider a precondition or key driver of active citizenship.

Spiral of Empowerment: Positive Experiences and Expanded Networks

Muslims in both national samples commonly mentioned two empowering factors directly linked to their pervious experiences of active engagement. These factors did not initiate their active citizenship, but have served as a civic catalyst for future engagement. First, many interviewed Muslims explained that their achievements and experiences of success (civic efficacy) in the course of their civic or political participation have encouraged them to continue or expand the intensity and scope of their activism. Secondly, many mentioned that their civic activism has resulted in increasing cross-community ('bridging') networks (Putnam 2000), which has made their subsequent engagement more effective and successful. These observations underscore the dynamics of active citizenship biographies, pointing to the mutually reinforcing effect of participation and the empowering sense of civic efficacy, which Verba et al. (1995: 344) describe in their Civic Voluntarism Model: '[B]eing more active may increase engagement as participants become more interested, informed, and efficacious'. Initial engagement tends to—if experienced by the individual as successful, effective and meaningful—lead to more activism, or in Mr Merhi's words (AUS1): 'The more I do the more I believe I can help'.

All interviewed Muslims consider their active engagement an overall positive experience, and most of them articulate a more or less optimistic view regarding their achievements. Some of them explicitly highlighted the empowering and encouraging effect of their sense of civic efficacy and their expanded social networks for their subsequent civic or political engagement. While these views have been found among Muslims in both national samples, they were articulated more commonly by Muslims in Australia than by their German counterparts. Given the small sample size, this is not necessarily a reflection of the possibly greater civic efficacy and higher level of bridging social capital among Australian Muslims. It does, however, resonate with other findings of this study that show that Muslims in the Australian sample more often regard their engagement as successful than interviewed Muslims in Germany and that cross-community networks have more commonly led Australian Muslims from civic engagement into positions of political decision-making.

A majority of interviewed Australian Muslims stated that their activism has borne fruit, and some of them either alluded or explicitly stressed that this sense of efficacy has motivated them to continue or expand their engagement. Several interview partners in the Australian sample also explained that their increased—usually cross-community—social networks have assisted them in their endeavours of active citizenship. In some cases, both empowering factors appear closely connected. Mr Delall (AUS4), a former teacher, vocal advocate for diversity and multiculturalism, and member of various boards and committees, for example, emphasised that the success of his activism—facilitated also by the supportive social and political environment in Australia—has been a constant motivator for his continuously evolving engagement:

> I think what has changed for me is that seeing the direct benefits and the direct outcomes of the work that I do, how it plays out in people's lives. That has been a very positive experience for me in the sense that you can do it … What has changed me is that, if you have an environment like Australia that values diversity—the majority [does]—than things can happen. I think if you've got the political, social and community will, things can happen. That's probably for me the greatest experience and motivation to move forward.

Mr Dellal's accounts also demonstrate how civic engagement can continuously grow and lead to manifold social networks with political stakeholders and, as a consequence, pave the way into increasingly powerful positions: 'I sit on boards and committees … So I can make a difference but it [also] allows me to bring people into those situations to make a difference as well. So, I suppose, through my position I can open doors'.

Ms Sabbagh (AUS5) expressed her preference for local community activism, pointing to the immediate effectiveness of this work: 'I'm a grassroots worker. I create change for the people, there's been change happening. But I like to connect to people and create change from the grassroots, going up'. Ms Sabbagh also mentioned the importance of cross-community networks for getting new projects off the ground. She explained that she benefited enormously from her positive 'connections with my local community, local council' and other local community organisations like the Migrant Information Centre, when launching her fashion show *My Dress, my Image, my Choice*, aimed at redressing ignorance and stigmatisation related to the hijab.

Ms El Matrah (AUS2) is one of the very few interviewed Muslims in Australia who explained that experiences of poor progress and success have discouraged her from certain forms of participation.[1] She critically elaborated on the sense of exhaustion that arises from the low level of achievement within her political activism. She explained how she has come to fundamentally question her political involvement in government-led initiatives and as a member of committees and boards, more broadly. As a consequence, she had made the decision to withdraw from these platforms of political decision-making: 'I won't go on boards anymore! Very little changes, unless you speak to the bureaucracy the way bureaucracy likes. But that is a very distinct culture that is very disconnected from how things are on the ground'.

Ms Faruqi (AUS13), an environmental activist and state politician, mentioned the enabling and empowering effects of social networks for her political and civic engagement. Similar to some other Muslims in the Australian sample, Ms Faruqi alluded to the issues of having gained a public profile and recognition as a committed active citizen. She maintained: 'Meeting so many people, inner city to country ... It's been incredible. And those networks, I think, again have helped me influence change as well, because once people know you and respect you that changes things a lot'. In a similar vein, Ms Abdo (AUS9) illustrated how cross-community relationships of trust, established in the course of her longstanding engagement as representative of the Muslim women's organisation UMWA, have facilitated her effective activism. Personal and organisational links with governments and mainstream organisations have led to successful cooperation and initiatives (e.g., Voices of

---

[1] Ms El Matrah also reported highly satisfying experiences of civic achievements: 'And other times, something works out, it is completely wonderful and unexpected. And there are some really personal moments, you feel like it couldn't have been done, had I not done the work that I'm doing'. She explained, however, that for her these moments of success do not directly motivate her to continue with her civic engagement.

Peace, Sydney Alliance), which have, in turn, contributed to continuously strengthening these relationships and increased the effectiveness of their political lobbying. Ms Abdo explained how UMWA has moved into a position where the state government now approaches *them* to request their input into policymaking.

Some Muslims in the German sample similarly described how their sense of achievement and civic efficacy has motivated them to continue or expand their active engagement. However, this featured less prominently among Muslims in Germany; and many of those who did express such positive experiences additionally mentioned negative experiences and institutional barriers that have also discouraged their active citizenship, especially in the area of political participation. *Esra* (DE7), for example, highlighted her positive experiences as a volunteer at the local socialist youth group. Similar to several Australian interview partners, she stressed the effectiveness of local grassroots work: 'I have had very positive experiences there because I realised that one can do very good work on the local level, in the neighbourhood'. This sense of achievement is contrasted by *Esra*'s negative experiences within the context of her political engagement as a member of the local integration council. When she was asked to run for a seat in this advisory council, she was initially enthusiastic about the prospects of having a say in the city's political decision-making. This hope was soon disappointed as she realised that the integration council has merely consultative status and cannot make any binding decisions. She learned that, as a member of this advisory council, she could attend the city council's committees but that she did not have a voice in these committees. She described her frustration about this as follows:

> You are not even 20 years old and you are totally interested in politics and think: that's great [to be member of the advisory council], and then the [elected councillors] sit in their corners [during the council committee meeting], and you want to vote, too. And then you are told that you are not eligible for voting here. And that was the point where I thought: Well, why do I sit here then?... It doesn't make a difference whether I am here or not. The people here do not care at all.

Esra's positive experiences with civic engagement and discouraging experiences with her formalised political activism are mirrored by Mr Aydin's (DE10) elaborations. He emphasised that his committed involvement with various civil society initiatives, be it within the Turkish-Muslim parent group or other cross-community forms of civic engagement, has been characterised and motivated by his sense of achievements. Asked about the reason for his civic participation commitment, he explained:

> It was interesting, and I realised that I can also contribute to bring about change, that one can contribute his ideas, even when you're a migrant or of Turkish descent. That didn't matter, [these civil society groups] were happy about any new ideas.

In contrast to these positive experiences, Mr Aydin has been frustrated by the lack of efficacy during his short-lived political ambitions within a political party. He joined the leading conservative party Christian-Social Union (CSU), because he hoped this would give him a platform to change the public attitude on the local level towards migrants and more specifically towards those of Turkish background. However, he soon realised that this was not possible, and, as a consequence, he renounced his party membership, which ended his party political ambitions.

Mr Şenol's (AUS6) engagement as a media activist has continuously expanded mainly because he felt motivated and empowered by his own success. While studying law at university, he set up the online blog *JURABLOG*, which constitutes his first attempt to contribute to the political debate on issues of migrant inclusion and citizenship. The positive reception of his blog 'motivated me, of course, to continue', as he explained. When he realised that JURABLOG had reached its capacity, he abandoned it and set up the much more professional online magazine MiGAZIN with a similar (although broader) thematic focus on diversity, inclusion and racism. The popularity and success of this online platform, which Mr Şenol considered an effective vehicle for him and many other contributors to add their voices to the public and political debate, came as a surprise to him. This sense of achievement motivated him to continue his political media activism: 'We did not anticipate that this would be so well received. The number of online visitors grew daily, and then you feel sort of responsible to keep this alive'.

While almost all 30 interview partners across both samples stated that their cross-community social networks have expanded as a result of their active engagement (see Chap. 9), only very few interviewed Muslims in the German sample described this growing social capital as a catalyst for their subsequent engagement activities; and those few who did mention it, did so only briefly and less prominently than in the Australian sample. Mr Yerli (D14), for example, confirmed that through his engagement in various Muslim and mainstream organisations he has developed social networks that subsequently paved the way into other forms of civic activism. *Asim* (D15), whose engagement has revolved around his active role within the Muslim youth organisation MJD, considered these cross-community contacts very important. He stated:

> I would like to continue volunteering, where you deal directly with other people, but you need these contacts. They are very important, and it is, of course, nice to know that certain politicians support you and say: "I know them. I know what they are doing".

These country-specific findings on the effects of social capital for deepened and more efficient engagement resonate with the empirical insights of this study into Muslims' recruitment to civic and political participation. While active Muslims in both national samples commonly stressed the expanded social network as a result of their activism, this social capital has been utilised more effectively by Muslims in the Australian sample. The common trajectory and recruitment pattern of Australian Muslims from community-based activism to more influential forms of political participation (e.g., in committees and boards) is an indicative example.

Active Citizenship Resources: Time, Education and Socioeconomic Status

Interviewed Muslims elaborated in different ways on the facilitating effects of education and socioeconomic factors on their own and other Muslims' active citizenship—or, conversely, the disempowerment associated with a lack of these resources. Moreover, many pointed out that their time availability has affected the intensity of their activism. These resource-oriented accounts support key tenets of the Civic Voluntarism Model by Verba and his colleagues (1995: 270–271), stressing that citizens' personal resources are crucial determinants of their participation. They argue that citizens who lack time, money and civic skills are less likely to engage in any form of political activism. Representative surveys in Australia (ABS 2011a) and Germany (BMFSFJ 2010; Halm and Sauer 2005) have found evidence that socioeconomic and education-related resources facilitate both political and civic participation—the latter most prominently enacted as volunteers in civil society organisations. This general association seems to apply also to *Muslims'* civic and political participation, as recent studies have highlighted. Al-Momami and colleagues (2010: 27), for example, conclude that 'political participation was still, by and large, the domain of the privileged. Like other communities ... the politically active tend to be drawn from higher educated and more prosperous socio-economic groups'. The CIRCA (2010: 6) study on civic and social participation of Muslim men in Australia also found that many young Muslims seem to lack 'civic participation skills' , and identified '[l]anguage and literacy issues, and lower levels of educational attainment among some segments' and the 'socioeconomic disadvantage' as some of the key barriers for their participation. In addition, studies have highlighted that time, or the lack thereof due to other commitments, is seen by many as an important barrier of civic engagement—and Muslims are no exception here (Gendera et al. 2012: 106, CIRCA 2010: 36; AMF and VA 2007a).

Time

Many Muslims interviewed for this study mentioned time as an influential factor for their activism. Most of them expressed the view that available time resources do not determine whether they become active or not, but rather affect the *intensity* of their engagement. Some of these elaborations also referred to the link between time resources and one's financial situation. Related to that, a few interviewed Muslims mentioned differences between men and women with regards to their capacity to participate in—usually unpaid—forms of civic and political participation. Overall, the analysis suggests that interviewed Muslims negotiate the time they spend on their civic engagement activities against the backdrop of their family commitments and the need to pursue gainful employment (or in some cases, tertiary education). This resonates with the CIRCA study findings (2010: 36) that many Muslims 'identified a lack of time or resources to commit to activities outside of their work, study and family obligations'. The present research suggests that interviewed Muslims in Germany and Australia tend to reduce—but do not abandon—their engagement, when both family and work commitments become more dominant and time consuming.

In the Australian sample, Ms Faruqi (AUS13) explained that she decided to expand her political engagement within the political party The Greens NSW and run as an election candidate—parallel to her job commitment—when her family obligations became less time-consuming: 'It was a good time for me. I had more time because the children were older, my daughter was in Year 8 and my son was at uni'. Ms Faruqi seems to have balanced the intensity of her activism against her other main obligations, career and child-raising commitments. Ms Saabagh (AUS5) also emphasised the impact of time on her active engagement. She stated that she has always been able to spend a lot of time on her community work because she has never had to earn a living for the family. In her view, this traditional family model, which obliges only the husband to be the 'breadwinner', also applies to many other one-income families and partially explaining the supposedly higher level of community activism among (Muslim) women:

> Generally speaking, in the community, women are more active in community work ….I would say there is a reason for that: it is not compulsory for women to be the breadwinner. So I had the luxury to make that choice. But my husband doesn't have that luxury. He is active but he has to provide for the family. So his activism has to come second… I can say my activism comes first … I guess that's what it is: Men have to earn an income.

The active citizenship accounts of several Muslims in Germany also highlight that time resources affect the intensity of their engagement.

Some of them explained how family commitments (e.g., caring for sick family members, DE10) and/or professional considerations (DE6, DE7) have limited their capacity to participate. Ms Taraji (DE5), for example, mentioned that she had more time for her multiple activities within the Muslim community while her children were young and she worked only part-time as a medical doctor. 'But because I have been self-employed for three years now and have worked full-time since, time is getting scarce of course'. In Ms Taraji's case, having to care for her young children coincided with a significant reduction in her workload as a doctor, which enabled her to expand her civic engagement, while full-time employment (in combination with reduced family obligations) limited the intensity of her community work.

Ms Theißen (DE3) mentioned, similarly to Ms Sabbagh (AUS5), that she did not have to pursue paid employment because her husband earned enough to support her. This gave her time to expand her civic activism career: 'I had no obligations. I studied at university … I volunteered running swimming lessons for Muslims, and I studied Islam—and I made new contacts. This was a reorientation phase, and I just looked around where I could contribute'.

Socioeconomic Resources

Some of the interview accounts indicate that not facing financial pressure increases the chances to engage more intensely in civic or political participation. Related to this, a few Muslims in both samples described the generally disempowering implications of a low socioeconomic status for Muslims' civic engagement. Mr Tabbaa (AUS12) took a particular strong stance on this issue, maintaining that 'a stable life in terms of income' is a prerequisite for any community engagement. He was the only interviewed Muslim who refers to his own personal experiences in this thematic context:

> I had this for a long time—struggle between community work and feeding the family. It is very much impossible. You can't do it. And if I hadn't been doing my PhD with a decent income, there would be no way I would be

doing any of this work. For me, in my experiences, there is a very direct link: If the socioeconomic [resources] are not there, you are pretty much erased.

Other interview partners in the Australian sample mentioned socioeconomic disadvantages as a general barrier or disempowering factor for active citizenship. Ms El Matrah (AUS2), for example, asserted that 'there are standard barriers that Muslims have always faced, and that is that there are significant economic barriers. They are substantial'.

In the German sample, only two interview partners made some references to socioeconomic factors as potentially disempowering, though expressing different views. *Burak* (DE1) stated that 'people who struggle every day with their income and other problems hardly have time and also not the motivation to volunteer'. In contrast, *Asim* (DE15), active member of a Muslim youth group, explained that even those without a job usually do not face extreme hardship and therefore could still volunteer. He said:

> Just to give you an extreme example: If someone in Pakistan just manages to feed his family, he would not find time to become engaged in social issues. Here in Germany, even if you don't have a job, you usually make ends meet, even if it's not great at the time… Your life is not threatened, and you can still do something. That is great in Germany: you have these opportunities.

Overall, the data analysis suggests that most interviewed Muslims do not seem to consider personal socioeconomic resources to be as central for civic and political participation as general explanatory models of participation, like the Civic Voluntarism Model, indicate (Verba et al. 1995; also Peterson 1990). The aforementioned CIRCA study on participation of Muslim men in Australia (CIRCA 2010: 45) maintain that there is a more indirect link, arguing that it is not the socioeconomic status itself, but Muslims' feelings of 'economic exclusion' that hamper their sense of social acceptance and belonging, which 'in turn impacts on their capacity and willingness to participate both within their individual community and the wider society'. Some evidence supporting this indirect link was found in this research, when Mr Ahmed (AUS3) mentioned the 'crisis of unemployment' and labour market discrimination against Muslims that 'pushes them into a corner'—with a disempowering effect on their engagement.

Skills and Education

The CIRCA report suggests a close relationship between socioeconomic resources and education-related factors, concluding that those Muslims 'who are socioeconomically advantaged are more likely to ... have the requisite awareness, knowledge and skills for how to participate' (2010: 45). This points to another key finding of this present study on active citizenship, which has been well documented in previous research and is widely accepted: Certain skill sets, including language proficiency, and education have been regarded as a major empowering factor for active citizenship. While this general view is shared by a majority of Muslims in both national samples, a more detailed examination revealed great variations within these common education-related arguments. In general, the responses fall into two categories of empowering factors, focusing either on formal education, educational degrees and attainments, or on individuals' personal skills, knowledge (e.g., range of volunteering possibilities) and competence.

The relationship between both, and the way in which they interact in influencing someone's inclination to participate, has been a subject of academic debates for many years. There is little disagreement, however, that civic engagement and political activism is more common among those with a higher level of education. The fact that the vast majority of the 30 Muslims, interviewed for this study, turned out to have a tertiary degree or be enrolled in tertiary education supports this basic assumption. For Verba and his colleagues (1995: 271) 'civic skills', defined as someone's 'organizational and communications capacity', are key determinants for political participation; these skills are described as being acquired in a life-long process that involves mainly four institutions: family, formal education, workplace and volunteering in civil society organisations. In contrast, Rosenstone and Hansen (1993: 136) place a greater emphasis on formal education within education institutions that 'imparts knowledge and skills most essential to a citizen's task'.

Approximately half of the 14 interviewed Australian Muslims mentioned skills or education-related factors as empowering or enabling for civic activism. Mr Tabbaa (AUS12), a PhD student and media and community activist from Melbourne, is one of those who rigorously emphasised the importance of education for civic engagement. Asked whether his education and communication skills (being 'articulate') help with his activism, he answered: 'Not [only] helps, [it] decides! Absolutely decides'! More specifically, he critically asserted that many positions within Muslim community organisations (e.g., board member) are 'for the elite Muslims' and thus not accessible for those with a lower level of education.

This resonates with Mr Sattar's (AUS10) observations of his fellow volunteers at the Sydney-based Muslim organisation Mission of Hope, where he volunteers in a project for at-risk youth and also sits on the board. He explained that this active involvement with Mission of Hope has given him the

> opportunity of having a voice for those who don't have that voice or this platform to express their concerns. Maybe they cannot even articulate their concerns. So I'm privileged enough to be on a level where I can do that for them.

Being a university student himself, Mr Sattar reflected on the educational background of his fellow Muslim volunteers at Mission of Hope: 'The whole team [of 35 male Muslims in this particular project] have some kind of tertiary education or are engaged in tertiary education'. He added, however, that this might be different among active Muslim women: 'Looking at female volunteers at Mission of Hope and elsewhere, I realise that some of them have tertiary education and others have not'.

Ms Faruqi (AUS13) spoke about the effects of having a higher education degree, although she emphasised that actual knowledge and skills are more important. After assuring that her communication skills have both facilitate her civic and political engagement and further improved as a result of her activism, she mentioned the impact her PhD title has had on others. She illustrated this with her experiences during her political campaigning, which involved visiting homes and introducing herself and the party program within the electorate: 'When we went door knocking … it was suggested that the person that accompanied me should introduce me as doctor… And that can sometimes immediately change people's [perception] about you. People do think suddenly you are more credible;'. But Ms Faruqi also stressed that her actual skills and expertise have been more central than the formal degree: 'I think that more important than the degree and titles are your work and life experiences. For example, you can talk about [public] transport using your experience … that improves your credibility—not just that you have a PhD'.

Ashtar (AUS14) also saw a link between Muslims' educational level and their engagement, asserting that 'a lot of the active ones are the ones who are educated'. She further elaborated on the limiting influence of 'not having an education' for their activism as many young people are not aware of the various opportunities of enacting and expressing their citizenship. In *Ashtar*'s view, this makes them less likely to become outspoken citizens, although they may become active *within* the Muslim community:

> Young people not having an education, not understanding how the world works, are passionate about an issue but don't know how to approach it. The understanding or the facilities or the structure of how to approach these issues … I know so many young people who are so smart and so passionate about things, … but they would never speak in public because they don't have the skills. The most that they may probably do is volunteering … for the [Muslim] community, because they feel that's all they can give, and that is not true! They can give so much more.

Language skills were mentioned only by a few Muslims in Australia. Mr Kamareddine (AUS7), who is actively involved in various community and cross-community initiatives, for example, highlighted that his bilingual proficiency in Arabic and English has been a key factor for his activism: 'But it is very important that there are not many people who speak very well Arabic … and English! To have the knowledge and that's why I have been [active] in different places'. Mr Galil (AUS11), an imam and active member of several interfaith and multicultural initiatives, agreed that English language skills are crucial for certain forms of (cross-community) engagement. However, he stressed that those without English proficiency can still be committed community members and active citizens: 'Among those people who are lacking in the area of communication and language, they are still leaders within their own [community], which is good'. *Serap* (AUS6) emphasised the enabling effects of having good English language skills. She called upon everyone to learn English in order to be able to participate in social life: 'How are you going to knock on your neighbours' door and say: "Would you like a plate of fruit"? or "I heard your baby crying, do you need something? Is there something wrong?"'. However, *Serap* rejected the view that, beyond speaking the language, a particular level of education or skills would be necessary for active engagement. She explains this by pointing to the many different—also informal—ways in which one can participate in society and help others in an everyday context: 'Active citizenship is a very individual thing … civic [engagement] can go down to keeping an eye up on your neighbour'. She stressed that, 'to use a Christian term, being a Good Samaritan' does not require people to be well educated.

Serap's opinion that civic skills and education are secondary for being an active citizen was also expressed by a few other Muslim interview partners in Australia. For Ms Abdo (AUS9), for example, it all boils down to people's sense of 'self-worth' and individual resilience. Drawing from her longstanding experiences as a Muslim community leader in Sydney, she said:

> I'm just thinking about some young people in the community who have come to me and said that they wish they could do this but they can't. Because they just don't think that they are good enough. So their self-worth again—not as a result … of a university degree! There are so many with a university degree and every materialistic wealth in the world who still don't have this self-worth. It is … also that some have the resilience and others don't.

This resonates also with Ms Sabbagh's (AUS5) perceptions. More specifically, she posited that the fundamental precondition for engagement is the person's general openness and passion to engagement and serving others. Asked whether one needs a broad level of education to engage, she replied: 'I don't think you do! I think you need a heart that is open to it'.

Many of the Muslims interviewed in Germany also made references to the effect of education-related factors on civic and political engagement. In contrast to the Australian sample, not a single interview partner explicitly questioned the relevance of education, knowledge or skills. Muslims in the German sample predominantly emphasised their German language skills and bilingualism or their intercultural competence as facilitators of engagement.

Two interviewed Muslims in Germany—both young, female university students—consider education as being crucial for Muslims' proneness to engage. One of them is *Leyla* (DE13), who stated that education is a factor that enables people to participate and voice their views. She associated education with an increased level of knowledge about society, greater communication skills as well as a higher degree of recognition by others:

> I think it is important that you know society well enough to stand your ground. Because young people who may not have a good education often lack the capacity to express themselves well, or they don't know where they can contribute, or maybe others don't take them seriously.

Miran (DE12), active member of the German-Turkish youth subgroup *Ve biz* within the Social Democratic Party, maintained that the prevalent 'lack of education' is the key reason why so many young people of Turkish decent refrain from civic or political engagement. She explains that, in her view, those with a low level of (formal) education are often not aware of the various opportunities to participate and of the importance of volunteering for their future.

> In a nutshell: it's a lack of education. Because if you don't have proper formal education, you do not even get in touch with these things ... Through education you learn, for example, how important it is to volunteer and to get in contact with other people—also for later in life. You find out about this only through education. And most [young people of Turkish origin]

end up in the [lower secondary school tier] *Hauptschule*[2] where this might not be a big topic.

To support her argument, *Miran* stated that all of her 15 colleagues at *Ve biz* were either currently studying at university or were about to do so. Similar observations were made by at least two other interviewed Muslims in Germany. *Asim* (DE15), active volunteer and board member of the Muslim youth group MJD, explained that MJD volunteers predominantly have a medium to higher level of education. And Mr Şenol (DE6), who runs the online news magazine MiGAZIN, where people without any media training can write contributions to the public debate, also stressed that the majority of those who submit their contributions to the magazine 'aren't just some school drop-outs, but are either studying, intending to study or have completed their university degree'.

Having intercultural or bicultural competence—in conjunction with multilingual proficiency—has been mentioned by several interview partners as a particularly important skill set that has facilitated their civic and political engagement. *Miran* (DE12) elaborated on these skills, which enable her to effectively mediate conflicts and strengthen her capacity to adopt and understand different perspectives. Similarly, *Onur* (DE16) mentioned his 'intercultural competence' and his multilingual proficiency, and Ms Al-Ammarine (DE2) described it as a privilege to 'be at home in both languages and cultures—German and Arabic', stressing in particular her German proficiency as vital when engaging with the wider community:

> I'm very grateful for that, not all people with a migration background have these opportunities [of being literate in both cultures and languages]. And I have realised it makes a big difference in terms of acceptance. Someone who doesn't speak German that well may, unfortunately, be treated in an unjust way or not taken seriously. Someone who is articulate experiences more ... respect.

---

[2] *Hauptschule* refers to the lowest tier in the German secondary school system. Graduates from this type of high school are not directly entitled to enter tertiary education at university.

Ms Taraji (DE5) emphasised German language skills as a key enabler of cross-community engagement, mentioning that many of her fellow community members at the Islamic Community (IGD) struggle with this. Asked about barriers that hamper the engagement of other Muslims, she answered:

> First and foremost, it's the language, which of course plays a major role. As I grew up here bilingually, it has never been a problem for me to interact with the wider society. I think the language is a big hurdle, because I know many from the *Islamische Gemeinde* [IGD] who struggle with their poor German ... to get in contact [with the wider community].

One education-related facet stands out in the German interview sample in comparison with the elaborations of Australian Muslims: Muslims' general awareness of current political debates as a facilitator of engagement. Mr Aydin (DE10), for example, explained that his job as a printing machinist at the local newspaper *Donau Kurier* has given him access to information about the latest political developments. This resulted in his increased awareness of the current debates on migration and integration, and his knowledge has empowered him to become more active.

> Since I work at the *Donau Kurier*... I have read a lot about the problems of migrants, and you feel like you are urged to do something for migrants. Because migrants read German newspapers rather rarely ... Therefore I try to do something about these problems so that they can be countered.

Mr Şenol (DE6) and Mr Cicek (DE9) added another dimension to the argument that a higher level of political awareness and knowledge about the current political and public debates empowers engagement. Both explained how their initial decision to actively contribute to the public discourse resulted from becoming aware of certain political decisions and public debates. Mr Cicek considers a basic level of awareness and interest in politics (something he 'lacked as a teenager', as he stated) to be a precondition for his engagement, which started in response to the public debate in 2010 on the allegedly failed integration of Muslims in Germany. Similarly, Mr Şenol asserted that media activism (both his own and of many others) is often triggered by personal anger and frustration about current political decisions and debates. He concluded that this anger only develops among those who 'ready the newspaper on a daily basis and follow the news', who happen to be those 'who are well integrated and who participate already'.

Concluding Remarks: Empowering and Discouraging Factors

This analysis of Muslims' civic and political participation confirms the well-documented findings of previous research that individual resources and (human and cultural) capital constitute important facilitators for civic and political participation. This is underscored by the fact that most interview partners themselves are highly educated, articulate, proficient in the respective language (English or German), and in a financially stable situation. Moreover, those interviewed Muslims who referred to the education background of their fellow Muslim volunteers and activists described them also as generally highly educated.

The interview analysis provides deeper insights especially into the facilitating or empowering effects of time, socioeconomic and education-related factors on Muslims' performance of active citizenship. From a cross-national comparative perspective, similarities between the views of Muslims in Australia and Germany dominate, especially with regard to the significance of time and socioeconomic resources (the latter receiving generally less attention than the former). While many Muslims in both country samples agree that education-related resources—and not necessarily formal education attainments—affect Muslims' inclination to perform certain types of civic activism, different facets of education have been emphasised in the two sub-samples.

Muslims interviewed in Germany particularly highlighted their German or bilingual proficiency and intercultural competence as a vital prerequisite for their engagement, whereas Muslims in the Australian sample more commonly referred to their communication skills and 'being articulate'—beyond mere language skills. A possible explanation for that might be that Australian Muslims take high English proficiency for granted, while this seems to be less the case among interviewed Muslims in Germany. Moreover, a few interview partners in Australia—but none in Germany—explicitly questioned the fundamental importance of education for the performance of active citizenship, highlighting instead personal convictions and resilience as being more decisive than someone's education.

Beyond the empowering impact of resources, the interview analysis sheds light on other enablers or facilitators of Muslims' engagement in Australian and Germany. Some of them apply specifically to *Muslims*, while other mechanisms seem to be broader in nature. One of the most prominently discussed factors that have encouraged interview partners to become (more) active in one way or another is, the negative public climate and media misrepresentation of Muslims and Islam, partially in combination with personal experiences of exclusion and everyday anti-Muslim racism. These issues have been regularly raised in both country samples, but were even more widespread among Australian Muslims. This result is not entirely surprising. In 2010, for example, Al-Momami and colleagues (2010: 35) concluded that some of the Muslims in their interview sample feel motivated by 'the negative publicity about Muslims after September 11 2001'. However, the prevalence of the view that collective or individual experiences of exclusion encourage participation is a significant finding of the present study. It is noteworthy that many interviewed Muslims stressed that this encouraging effect does not apply to all Muslims; many fellow Muslims would feel further alienated and marginalised by the exclusionary discourse and experiences of racism and thus refrain from becoming active citizens.

Against the backdrop of this ambivalent picture, a crucial question arises: What sets the interviewed active Muslim citizens apart from those Muslims who allegedly feel disempowered and pushed away from the area of active citizenship by the negative public discourse and experiences of exclusion? While the interview data do not provide sufficiently robust evidence to ultimately answer this question, they do offer some indicators that, together with previous research findings, suggest some tentative insights.

First, almost all interviewed Muslims in both countries expressed a strong sense of civic belonging, often combined with a profound religious identity. The stigmatising public discourse does not seem to be seen as something that calls into question their firm civic identity as member of the Australian or German society. Several interview partners in both national samples alluded to the interrelation between someone's sense of belonging and their willingness to participate. Ms Sabbagh's words (AUS5) illustrate that very well: 'When [people] belong, when they feel they are getting something back, then they are contributing, they feel a sense of belonging. Everyone wants to feel belonging'. This general notion is supported by the CIRCA study on social and civic participation of Muslim men in Australia, which also found a 'link between a strong sense of belonging and self-esteem and propensity to social and civic involvement' (2010: 74). Similarly, Al-Momami and his colleagues (2010: 100) emphasised the importance of Muslims' 'strong sense of identity and belonging within the wider community' for their eagerness to become politically active citizens and, more specifically, their 'increased confidence about speaking on Australian politics and social issues'.

This sense of civic belonging is complemented by interviewed Muslims' general optimism, resilience and, in many cases, their ability to rationalise and de-personalise the public discourse, for example, by interpreting it as a reflection of ignorance and of lacking knowledge about Islam among members of the society at large. Several interview partners have argued along these lines and pointed out that, as a consequence, they see an even greater necessity to engage and dispel these misconceptions. This confirms Al-Momami et al.'s (2010: 35) general observation that politically active Muslims in Australia 'tended to describe themselves as highly self-motivated, and not easily discouraged'. Several Muslim interview partners in Al-Momami et al.'s (2010: 35) study stated that they regard negative experiences and 'opposition' rather as 'a stimulus to try even harder'. If Muslims lack this personal strength and self-confidence, the public misrepresentation of Muslims and experiences of exclusion appears more likely to fuel a sense of marginalisation and helplessness that can contribute to disengagement and civic and social withdrawal.

The data analysis also suggests that, especially in the German sample, Muslims who demand more civic recognition and less stereotyping by the wider community as a *precondition* of engagement appear more likely to accept their second-class citizenship status as excluded group and thus tend to refrain from active participation.

Second, what seems to further empower many civically active Muslims to withstand the temptation of disengagement in the face of the public exclusionary discourse and experiences of anti-Muslim sentiments is their civic or faith-based values and convictions. Interviewed Muslims commonly articulated that their strong sense of social justice or, in many cases, their Islamic faith urged them to become active. Remaining passive, not seeking to contribute to the wellbeing of others, and not standing up against what they consider to be injustice did not appear to be a viable option for them—regardless of the general public climate and personal experiences of exclusion, misrepresentation and stigmatisation. This powerful commitment is often rooted in people's personal values, norms and, in many cases, interpretations of the Islamic principle and duty to 'do good', help others and contribute to the wellbeing of society more broadly.

Finally, the interview data analysis pinpoints a third factor that may help explain why some Muslims feel disempowered by the negative public discourse and experiences of anti-Muslim exclusion and refrain from active participation, while others become civically or political active despite similar experiences—or even feel motivated by these anti-Muslim sentiments and discourses to enhance their active citizenship. Being equipped with the human, social and cultural capital—in particular relevant knowledge, language proficiency and civic skills as well as multiple social networks of trust—enables Muslims, similar to others, to translate this eagerness into concrete civic or political action. These resources and capital-related factors do not only facilitate Muslims' active citizenship, but also tend to increase their civic efficacy and make their engagement a more positive experience, which subsequently feeds into the self-reinforcing circle, empowering them to sustain or expand their civic commitment and activism.

References

Al-Momani, K., Dados, N., Maddox, M., & Wise, A. (2010). *Political participation of Muslims in Australia*. Sydney: Macquarie University.

Aly, A. (2007). Australian Muslim responses to the discourse on terrorism in the Australian popular media. *Australian Journal of Social Issues, 42*(1), 27–40.

Amath, N. (2013). The impact of 9/11 on Australian Muslim civil society organisations. *Communication, Politics & Culture, 46*, 116–135.

Australian Bureau of Statistics (ABS). (2011a). *Voluntary work Australia*. Canberra: Commonwealth of Australia. Online document viewed 21 April 2015 http://www.ausstats.abs.gov.au/Ausstats/subscriber.nsf/0/404350EEC6509985CA2579580013177A/$File/44410_2010.pdf

Australian Multicultural Foundation (AMF), & Volunteering Australia (VA). (2007a). *Muslim youth and volunteering. Research bulletin* (June 2007). Melbourne: VA.

Bundesministerin für Familie, Senioren, Frauen und Jugend (BMFSFJ). (2010). *Hauptbericht des Freiwilligensurveys 2009. Zivilgesellschaft, soziales Kapital und freiwilliges Engagement in Deutschland 1999 – 2004 – 2009*. Berlin: BMFSFJ.

Cultural and Indigenous Research Centre Australia (CIRCA). (2010). *Civic and social participation of Australian Muslim men*. Leichhardt: CIRCA.

Dreher, T. (2010). Community media intervention. In H. Rane, J. Ewart, & M. Abdalla (Eds.), *Islam and the Australian news media* (pp. 185–205). Carlton: Melbourne University Press.

Gendera, S., Pe-Pua, R., & Katz, I. (2012). Social cohesion and social capital: The experiences of Australian Muslim families in two communities. In F. Mansouri & V. Marotta (Eds.), *Muslims in the West and the challenges of belonging* (pp. 89–113). Carlton: Melbourne University Press.

Halm, D., & Sauer, M. (2005). *Freiwilliges Engagement von Türkinnen und Türken in Deutschland*. Essen: ZfT.

Peucker, M., & Akbarzadeh, S. (2014). *Muslim active citizenship in the West*. London/New York: Routledge.

Peterson, S. A. (1990). *Political behaviour: Patterns in everyday life*. Newbury Park: Sage.

Putnam, R. D. (2000). *Bowling alone: The collapse and revival of American community*. New York: Simon and Schuster.

Rosenstone, S. J., & Hansen, J. M. (1993). *Mobilization, participation, and democracy in America*. New York: Macmillan Publishing Company.

Verba, S., Schlozman, K. L., & Brady, H. (1995). *Voice and equality. Civic voluntarism in American politics*. Cambridge: Harvard University Press.

Werbner, P. (2000). Divided loyalties, empowered citizenship? Muslims in Britain. *Citizenship Studies, 4*(3), 307–324.

Yasmeen, S. (2007). Muslim women as citizens in Australia. Diverse notions and practices. *Australian Journal of Social Issues, 42*(1), 41–54.

9

Personal Implications of Civic Activism

Civic and political participation has multiple positive implications for active Muslims personally. Every interview partner elaborated on how their engagement has changed them. The most commonly mentioned areas of change related to acquiring new skills and knowledge as well as expanded social networks. Some also described deeper forms of personality and identity transformation as a result of their active citizenship. These areas of personal growth and changes have consistently been recorded by previous studies as general effects of volunteering. Volunteering Australia, drawing from an large survey among volunteers in across Australia, concludes, for example, that volunteering can, among others, 'offer people skills, social contacts, support a greater sense of self worth and challenge the stereotypes we have about different social groups' (2010: 12). While the personal accounts of interviewed Muslims in Australia and Germany on the personal implications of their activism show strong similarities, some country-specific differences have been identified.

Expanded Social Networks

Almost all interviewed Muslims in Australia and Germany confirmed that their social networks have expanded significantly as a result of their active engagement. The data analysis illustrates that this increase in social contacts has occurred in various ways and contexts. The network enhancing implications can be described along three interconnected dimensions.

- *Types and organisational location of expanded networks*: This dimension refers to the question of who are the new contacts. It encompasses both intercommunity networks with other Muslim individuals and organisations and connections with mainstream institutions and their representatives. Deploying Putnam's concept of social capital, these networks may be described—in somewhat simplistic terms—as either (inter-community) 'bridging' or as (intra-community) 'bonding' networks (2000: 22).
- *Quality of networks*: This dimension focusses on the depth of new networks, which include, for example, formal organisational contacts to certain institutions or personal relationships of mutual respect and trust. Some interview partners also mentioned that they have found friends through their activism. This quality dimension of trust and reciprocity is a crucial facet of social capital.
- *Effects and dynamics of expanded networks*: This dimension describes the interview partners' views on how these networks have further facilitated their subsequent engagement and increased their (sense of) civic efficacy (see Chap. 8).

Many Muslims in both samples explained that they have developed new sustainable relationships with representatives of a range of mainstream institutions, including governments, authorities, police, church groups, non-religious NGOs and—in Australia—the media. This is hardly surprising given the prevalent cross-community nature of Muslims' engagement activities in both samples. A number of interview partners also asserted that their civic engagement has led—partly *in addition* to their increased mainstream networks—to more expansive contacts within the Muslim community. While country-specific findings are the exception here, Muslims in Australia more often stressed the high quality of their contacts with mainstream stakeholders, often describing them with words like mutual trust and respect. This quality dimension was clearly less dominant in the German sample.

Ms Sabbagh (AUS5) is a typical example in the Australian sample. The Melbourne community worker highlighted how her engagement with the Muslim youth group YMA (which she had co-founded) resulted in the establishment of multiple networks of mutual trust with mainstream institutions. These cross-community contacts have proven helpful for her subsequent activism, for example, when she launched her fashion show *My Dress, my Image, my Choice*, bringing together women of all walks of life to redress misconceptions of the hijab. The connections Ms Sabbagh had established during her time at YMA with mainstream institutions, like local councils, schools, and local and federal police, continued to facilitate her cooperation with these institutions after she had left YMA. She recalled one particular incident illustrating the quality and personal importance of these networks:

> The day of 9/11 I had two phone calls at 7am. The first one was from my local police station saying: "Saara, it is going to be a tough time for you, but we want you to know we are here for you". The second phone call was from the local church saying the same thing … "tough time for your community, but we are here for you". These two phone calls—I still recall them today, because they were so important. You can't build that relationship over night for the local police and local church calling you and supporting you.

Mr Galil (AUS11), an imam from West Heidelberg (Melbourne) who is active in several interfaith and multicultural initiatives, mentioned a similar experience. He confirmed that his social networks and friendships have expanded massively as a result of his multiple (mostly cross-community) civic engagement. He emphasised that 'the word "trust" is very important here. Trust has developed between myself and a number of people'. He further elaborated on this quality dimension and its practical implications after 9/11:

> I have been privileged to know so many good people from every faith I can think of. And some of them are [now] very close friends. … And I will

never forget this phone call a couple of days after 9/11 in 2001 … the caller from [the Jewish organisation] Leo Baeck said: "Listen, Riad! We have been in your shoes before! We know exactly how you feel. So what can we do?" And I said: "I don't know". And he said: "So, we [at Leo Baeck] got together last night and decided that you and your mop from West Heidelberg will come to us here. And we will also invite people from the three Churches … and you talk about Ramada, the Christians will talk about Christmas and we are going to talk about Hanukkah"… And we turned up … and that was a beautiful day! And we felt really more secure! That we are not alone in this world! That was a very incredible feeling after the 9/11 situation.

Mutual trust between Muslim and non-Muslim organisations was also emphasised by Ms Abdo (AUS9) from the Muslim women's organisation UMWA in Sydney's west. Her accounts demonstrate how, through persistent community work in the neighbourhood and engagement with various local stakeholders, she managed to establish multiple networks of trust, for example with other civil society (community) groups who joined forces within the NGO network Sydney Alliance. She also mentioned how UMWA has been able to utilise its existing networks to respond to critical incidents, for example, the debate around police identity checks of face-covering Muslim women (in the early 2010s) or the series of gang rapes in Western Sydney (in the late 1990s and early 2000s). Regarding the latter crisis, Ms Abdo explained that they could respond more effectively because 'we had already the trust amongst us as agents of change, as people who work at the forefront … council, police, sexual assault units, health community organisations'.

Mr Merhi (AUS1), whose civic engagement has been located entirely in the mainstream non-governmental sphere (e.g., trade unions, church group, football club), also underscored the 'massive' expansion of his social networks and contacts with, for example, the media and organisations in the voluntary sector, as a result of his activism. He is convinced that these relationships can be readily harnessed if needed—also for his future civic engagement plans to work with indigenous people and help orphans in Syria. He stated:

If there were any issues I want to follow up, I'm lucky to have contacts to the Herald Sun, The Age, [the talkback radio station] 3AW … I'm fairly well known in the media [and the voluntary sector]. … Has it improved my contacts? Yes. Has it improved my circle of friends? Yes. I'm very well connected, to be honest. If I ever need them…

Other Muslims interviewed in Australia also elaborated on these dynamics of how their social networks have developed in the course of their civic careers and subsequently strengthened their engagement. Ms Faruqi (AUS14), for example, an environmental activist and politician from NSW, developed sustained relationships over time and 'those networks, I think, again have helped me influence change as well. Because once people know you and respect you, that changes things a lot'. Mr Sattar (AUS8) stressed social connections within and beyond the Muslim community. During his training for a volunteering role at the Muslim organisation Mission of Hope he 'met these amazing bunch of guys, who I became really good friends with … some really good friendships developed from there'. In addition, he mentioned the great opportunities to develop 'professional networks' during his involvement with Mission of Hope, where he has cooperated with, among others, the police, government departments, teachers, doctors, lawyers and others:

> On a professional networking level, the opportunities and the contacts and the relationships I've developed professionally is unbeatable! … It's nothing that working at a bank for six years could give you. It has really given me connections which I have been able to utilise then.

Ashtar's (AUS14) accounts reflect a rather unusual way of how civic engagement can have network-expanding implications. Her role as project coordinator for a government initiative in NSW first introduced her to the Muslim community. *Ashtar* stated that she 'didn't get community exposure until I started my role in government' and she 'didn't know anybody in the Muslim community'. Since then her social contacts have expanded enormously especially (but not exclusively) within the Muslim community: 'My contact lists are huge now …, the people I know and I am known around the community'.

Muslims in the German sample also stressed the network enhancing effects of their active engagement, both within and outside Muslim communities. References to quality factors like mutual trust and respect, or concrete examples of how these networks have been utilised in practice, however, have been less prominent. Mr Aydin (DE10), who emphasised that his social networks have skyrocketed as a result of his civic engagement, was one of the very few interview partners in the German sample who did refer to relationships of trust with mainstream organisations and authorities, but he also asserted that he had to actively struggle for this recognition in the beginning:

> Of course, in order to [develop positive relationships with authorities], one has to have discipline, in order to win the trust of those people and also of the authorities and associations. You have to give in order to be recognised.

His contacts with local authorities initially evolved as a result of his active volunteering within a local Turkish-Muslim parent association. Within this context, he '*had to* deal with authorities' (DE10) involved in school-related decision-making processes, and he managed to develop positive relationships with them. Mr Aydin claimed he has now 'access' to many local authorities and that through his commitment he has gained a reputation as local activist, which has led to his recruitment into other cross-community initiatives. His elaborations suggest, however, that it was not his social networks themselves that paved the way into more cross-community engagement, but rather his public profile. He further explained that building positive relationships with local authorities is the result of committed work; in his view, civic recognition cannot be taken for granted, but needs to be earned.

While Mr Aydin was the only one in the German sample who explicitly referred to the issue of trust vis-à-vis mainstream stakeholders, some others alluded to the quality and utility of their expanded networks. Ms Al-Ammarine (DE2) and Ms Theißen (DE3), both community workers at the Muslim women's organisation BFmF in Cologne, emphasised how they have benefitted from the growing networks and contacts between BFmF and various mainstream institutions, such as local authorities and police, employment agencies, women's support groups as well as Muslim community organisations. Both described these networks as institutional rather than personal connections and stated that it is part of BFmF's work to establish such contacts. Ms Al-Ammarine explained that her engagement with BFmF has resulted in the expansion of her professional networks. These networks have also 'contributed to the development of my personality, [finding] my place in society', she asserted. Moreover, she explained that she has become close friends with some of her colleagues at BFmF, which 'has enriched my life'. Ms Theißen also stressed the increasing institutional contacts with mainstream and Muslim organisations, elaborating that she, in her capacity as the director of BFmF, can utilise these networks for her community work:

> If we need something, and these people [like the head of the local police or of the employment agency] had been here at the BFmF, then it is, of course, easier to write a letter to the head of the employment agency, for example, and describe an instance where someone was discriminated against.

Similarly, *Asim* (DE15) emphasised his expanded contacts and positive relationships—with fellow Muslims across Germany as well as with non-Muslim religious groups, experienced social work volunteers, politicians and other public figures—as a result of his engagement within the Muslim youth group MJD. He explained that especially contacts with political decision-makers and other public opinion leaders are important: 'You need these contacts; they are very important, and it is, of course, nice to have politicians behind you who say: "I know them [at MJD], I know what they are doing"'.

Most other Muslims in the German sample mentioned such network-enhancing effects of their civic engagement only briefly and without much emphasis. Ms Fetić (DE4), leading member of a local integration advisory council and of the working group Green Muslims within the Greens Party, for example, stated that he has not only developed connections within the political party landscape, but also established positive contacts to many Muslim community organisation and mosques beyond the Bosnian Muslim community, which he had been affiliated with for many years. *Leyla* (D13), representative of a Muslim university student organisation, also stated that her contacts with Muslim and non-Muslim individuals and organisations have increased, which has resulted in improved access to information about 'job opportunities or scholarships or things like that'. She further asserted that having at least some social connections is necessary to initiate one's civic engagement in general. 'I've always wanted to do something along those lines [since I started university], but I had to get these connections first'. While several Muslims in the German sample stressed their growing social contacts within (amongst others) the Muslim community, Ms Taraji (DE5) also briefly elaborated on how these intra-community networks can be readily utilised. She explained that she can more easily help other community members who have problems, for example with their marriage: 'I know, for example, the imam in Munich or Frankfurt, who I can quickly contact and ask to help us with this question. It definitely helps to know these people and that they trust you'.

These findings sit well within theoretical accounts on social capital, which emphasise the effects of community engagement and volunteering for the development of social networks of 'reciprocity and trustworthiness' (Putnam 2000: 19). Muslims in both national samples consistently reported deepening social connectedness with a range of mainstream organisations and in some instances also other Muslim groups. These emerging relationships appear, however, more sustainable among Australian Muslims, who commonly characterised them as being based on mutual trust. In line with the prevalent social capital discourse, such networks of trust have a positive effect, both on the societal level and the individual level, enhancing social cohesion and interpersonal cooperation.

New Skills and Knowledge

Interviewed Muslims commonly highlighted that they have acquired a range of new skills and knowledge through their civic or political participation. Various types of capabilities have been mentioned, most prominently, organisational, communication and management skills, interpersonal and intercultural skills and knowledge, for example, about Islam and the diverse Muslim community. A few interview partners emphasised that these skills are transferable to other situations within and outside the sphere of active citizenship. Muslims in the Australian and the Germany sample do not differ significantly in their personal accounts of gaining new skills and knowledge. Similar to social networks, which feature as both a result and a facilitating factor of activism, the acquisition of skills also reflects the dynamics of active citizenship. Many of these new or enhanced capabilities, gained as a result of civic engagement, are typically also regarded as determinants of active engagement. Verba and colleagues, for example, describe civic skills, defined as 'organizational and communications capacity' (1995: 271), as a key resource for political participation—and they expand and grow as people become more active. This 'virtuous circle' has been confirmed by several studies (Walsh and Black 2015: 22).

In the Australian sample, several Muslims explained how they have improved their communication skills through personal engagement with a range of interlocutors. Muslim community activist Mr Tabbaa (AUS12) elaborated how his role as president of the Muslim student association at LaTrobe University and as ICV board member 'introduced [him] to new communities, new conversations, to new types of education and so on, which was very helpful'. He learned to respect different views from within the community: 'These are some of the things I learned and I guess dealing more frankly with people and openly'. In addition, he has overcome his previously rather antagonistic mentality of 'them or us' within the Muslim community, which he now sees as diverse, but belonging to 'the same' family. Asked if his experiences have also improved his communication with mainstream organisations, Mr Tabbaa explained how he has acquired interpersonal skills of adjusting his communication style to specific groups:

> I learned a lot of that from LaTrobe in my role as president, which was again very beneficial. Going to the ICV, I had to re-learn a different type of language, dealing with multicultural groups, multifaith groups … Yes, I had to learn different languages for different groups.

Similar learning experiences of interpersonal open-mindedness and improved communication skills were described by Ms Faruqi (AUS13), whose civic biography has been located outside the Muslim community context in the area of environmental activism. During her civic and, subsequently, also political engagement in Australia she has become more flexible and open to different views, goals and approaches to pursue these goals. She realised that having grown up in a culturally and religiously more homogeneous society (Pakistan), her 'views on the world were quite narrow'. She further elaborated that she has always had strong views, 'but [now] I express them in a different way. You can express strong opinions but also be open to listening to others' strong opinions. I have really learned that'.

Some interview partners in the Australian sample also referred to other capacity-building effects of their engagement. Ms El Matrah (AUS2) mentioned organisational and management skills she acquired during many years as a community worker at the Muslim Women's Centre for Human Rights. Moreover, she alluded to having become better at writing opinion pieces for newspapers. Similar learning experiences were described by *Serap* (AUS6), a PR officer at a young Muslim women's group in Melbourne, referring to the training she received from professional journalists also in public speaking: 'I've been trained, trained for free, like in PR work, I've met great journalist who have trained me how to do this work, how to talk'. Mr Sattar (AUS8), volunteer youth worker and board member at Mission of Hope, also mentioned intensive training he undertook in preparation for his volunteering for the Hayat House Street Outreach, provided by a range of experts, including psychologists and police detectives.

The majority of Muslims interviewed in Germany also maintained that they have gained new skills and expanded their horizon as a result of their civic and political participation. While some stated only vaguely that they have 'learned a lot', others elaborated in greater detail on these learning experiences. Many of these accounts seem predominantly related to acquiring new practical capabilities. *Asim* (DE15), for example, spoke at length about these implications of his volunteering within the Muslim youth group MJD. He emphasised that over the years he has had many opportunities to lead discussions and give talks, which has taught him to become a confident public speaker—something he used to have problems with before he started volunteering. He has also developed an interest in German politics, which he considered necessary given that he now regularly liaises with politicians. *Asim* is the only interview partner in both samples who mentioned that he has obtained an additional formal qualification, in his case an officially recognised volunteering youth worker certificate. During an intensive training course he learned various aspects of running youth group (e.g., psychological and legal issues), which helped him to act more effectively in his MJD youth work activities. He highlighted that this formal qualification demonstrates his professionalism as a volunteer youth worker. Mr Şenol (DE6) stressed that he has obtained new skills and competencies as a media activist—all through 'learning by doing'. This includes information technology skills, like web design and programming, as well as, even more importantly, journalism skills. He said that neither himself nor any of his colleagues at his online news platform MiGAZIN had been trained as journalists. 'We had to teach ourselves in an autodidactic way', he asserted and further emphasised: 'Although I've never had such training, I would see myself today as someone who can keep up with a genuine, trained journalist… . Personally, my horizon has expanded a lot'.

Other Muslims in the German sample briefly mentioned new skills they developed through their engagement. *Burak* (DE1) asserted that he has personally benefitted from his civic and political involvement, gaining enhanced interpersonal and communication skills. In a similar vein, *Onur* (DE16) explained that his communication and analytical skills have improved through his engagement within the trade union: 'I don't see things black and white anymore. I can analyse issues … I definitely learned that through my work here'. *Alev* (DE11), a community worker active mainly in intercultural dialogue, stated that she has gained intercultural competence over the years, and the two university students *Leyla* (DE13) and *Miran* (DE12) both highlighted that they have learned new management and organisation skills. *Miran* explained: 'I have learned a lot … like my own competencies, for example time management, and that I've become much better at organising. You grow from event to event'. *Leyla* similarly stressed her enhanced organisational skills and that she has constantly grown as a person and learned new practical skills.

Personality and Identity

For some interviewed Muslims, their active citizenship experiences have led to deeper personal transformation that go beyond the acquisition of new skills and knowledge, and the expansion of social networks. While some rather generally explained that the feel they have 'grown as a person', others elaborated more specifically on their identity changes or how they have become more open-minded and accepting of differences; the latter overlaps with the development of (intercultural) competence.

Mr Ahmed (AUS3) and Mr Galil (AUS11), for example, both explained how their interpersonal engagement with different people from all walks of life and various community groups has 'enriched' themselves and their lives. Mr Ahmed stated: 'If you broaden [your engagement], you always enrich yourself...there are more people to talk to and interact with, and that creates richness in you'. Ms Sabbagh (AUS5) articulated a holistic transformation that includes multiple forms of learning and personal growing as result of her community-based and cross-community activism, alluding also to her experiences with anti-Muslim hostility:

> When you put up with their harshness, their arrogance and their words against you, it disciplines you! When I prepare classes, I'm learning. So I believe... I'm the greatest recipient! I'm involved as a human being. I can't ask for more than that. This is something you don't get at university... And if someone tells me that I have been wrong in this and that, I take that as an opportunity to grow. So how have I benefitted? I have just grown immensely as a human being. And I'm always on guard not to cut anybody off, not to hurt anybody.

Several Muslims in the Australian sample described how their engagement and personal interaction with a range of people and communities have made them more open to the multicultural reality of everyday life. Ms Faruqi (AUS13) asserted that 'meeting so many people, inner city to country, has opened up my mind. And I'm so grateful for that'. Mr Kamareddine (AUS7), Muslim community worker with cross-cultural engagement, stressed that he has benefitted personally from direct personal encounters. He explained:

> Speaking with other communities and other groups I can tell them who we [Muslims] really are. And I benefitted also a lot from them. The first time I spoke to a Jewish person was in Australia, he's a police officer in Pakenham... The relationship between Jews and Muslims is not good worldwide. But no matter... this person was a good person, very friendly.

9 Personal Implications of Civic Activism

Ms El Matrah (AUS2) elaborated how her life has enormously transformed through her community work for the Muslim Women's Centre for Human Rights. She linked this transformation also to the expanded networks she developed:

> There are times when I think of this girl [herself] from the slums of Lebanon who [now] speaks to ministers, who has been overseas to do women's human rights work. If we had stayed in Lebanon, it's unlikely me and my sister would have even survived. There is this sense that… not so much that migration transformed us, although that is probably true… but this job has meant a transformation of my life and what it might have become.

Mr Sattar's (AUS) identity transformation, driven by his civic engagement with Mission of Hope, has a strong religious dimension. He stressed that his active involvement helped him overcome a deep identity crisis that began to unfold when he moved as a teenager from the wealthy, Anglo-Saxon dominated suburb of Mossman in Sydney's north to the highly diverse and socioeconomically disadvantaged suburb of Bankstown with a large Muslim community. 'I didn't know where I fit. Like always on the outside', he described his sense of (non)-belonging. After he had turned his back to his religious 'roots' and the Muslim community ('I was quite racist towards my own community'), he re-discovered his 'spiritual connection [with his Islamic faith] again'. Rather coincidentally, he started volunteering for the Muslim organisation Mission of Hope, where he became friends with many other Muslims. This has had fundamental implications for his identity struggle: 'I struggled with it for a long time. But working with Mission of Hope has given me this peace with my identity', he highlighted. He elaborated in depth how his views of what it means to be Australian—and an Australian Muslim—has changed through his personal experiences within his engagement with Mission of Hope:

> On a personal level [my engagement] has broadened my understanding and perspective of what it means to be an Australian. When I was in my teens and early twenties, my idea of being Australian was to run down to the pub…, because that is the culture that is perpetuated, that's the archetype you have to fit in to… [My engagement] has opened my eyes to—no!

that is *not* the archetype I need to fit in to—and I can be Australian in my own way and be just as Australian as anyone else.

Links between social interactions, expanded networks and identity shifts have also been expressed by some other interview partners in the Australian sample. Similar to Mr Sattar's account, their deeper involvement with the Muslim community as a result of their civic engagement has led to a reinforced religious identity as Muslims. Ms Saleh (AUS10), for example, explained how she has 'met the majority of these wonderful active Muslims … and even the not active ones' through her volunteering for Mission of Hope. She underscored the implications for her religious identity:

> That is how I came into the community, because I did not know anyone in the Sydney or Melbourne Muslim community before I started all this! That really helped me figure out where I want to go with my religion and who I am.

In a similar vein, *Ashtar* (AUS14), elaborated that her role as a community engagement project coordinator for a governmental initiative introduced her to the local Muslim community and that this community exposure has strengthened her Islamic faith:

> The more I got involved in the Muslim community, there more religious I became, and I think it's because of the people that I began to hang around with, my social environment. Initially, I had more non-Muslim friends than Muslim friends, but then I realised that there is a great community.

Such faith enhancing effects of active participation were not mentioned in the German sample, and only a few interviewed Muslims articulated deeper identity of personality transformation experiences. Ms Taraji (DE5), for example, explained that her multiple Muslim community-based engagement has given her life meaning and she has 'become more confident'. Mr Fetić (DE4) alluded that he has become more open-minded to other views and groups since he has moved beyond his previously rather narrow social circles within the Bosnian Muslim community and has become more active within the mainstream political landscape (e.g., The Greens). Ms Al-Ammarine (DE2) asserted that her volunteering and professional engagement at the Muslim women's organisation BFmF in Cologne has had a major impact not only on her professional profile, but also more broadly on the development of her personality and her identity. She highlighted the multiple institutional networks as being particularly influential: 'It certainly contributed to the development of my personality, [finding] my place in society, also because we [at the BFmF] are well connected with authorities, the police, women's shelter houses, mosque communities, with other social welfare institutions… That has left many positive marks'.

Concluding Remarks: Personal Implications

All Muslims confirmed that their active citizenship has had multiple positive effects for them personally. Most interview partners mentioned their expanded social networks and newly acquired skills and competencies. This applies broadly to Muslims in Australia as well as Germany—with only minor differences between both sub-samples. These cross-national convergences suggest that the positive effects of civic engagement are not mediated by certain country-specific conditions but seem to be predominantly linked directly to the concrete participatory activities these Muslims have been involved in.

The qualitative insights confirm previous theoretical accounts and empirical findings that consistently highlight that civic participation and volunteering offer opportunities for citizens, regardless of their religious or ethnic background, to acquire new skills and knowledge. Verba et al. (1995: 369) argue along these lines in their Civic Voluntarism Model, describing how non-governmental organisations serve as a 'training ground' for organisational and communication skills. As these civic skills facilitate effective participation, active involvement in these organisational settings promotes citizens' capacity to enact their citizenship. In referring more specifically to individuals' volunteering within an organisational context, Newton (1999: 11) highlights that 'organisations… socialise them into a democratic culture and teach them the subtleties of trust and cooperation'. Volunteers commonly need—and apply—communication, organisational and conflict resolution skills, and at the same time further develop these soft skills (Foner and Alba 2008: 364–365; Cesari 2013: 73; Jakubowicz et al. 2012: 49). These positive implications of civic participation are generally well recognised in empirical research. The German researcher Susanne Huth points out that volunteering usually involves a series of informal learning processes, offering 'numerous opportunities to acquire knowledge and various skills and utilise them in practice' (2012: 2; own translation). Empirical evidence supports this claim: A large-scale representative study on civic volunteering in Germany, for example, found that almost one-half of all surveyed volunteers stated they have gained new skills to a high or very high extent, and only one in 10 respondents did not learn any skills through their civic engagement (BMFSFJ 2010: 226). The same study concluded that the new skills acquired through volunteering also have a positive impact on the personality development and social competence, in particular, of young people (BMFSFJ 2010: 225). Similarly, in the Australian context, the Volunteering Australia (VA) (2010: 47) survey found that two thirds of surveyed volunteers stated they have benefitted from training opportunities provided within their volunteering.

The second commonly highlighted positive effect of active citizenship was Muslims' growing social networks, which also confirms previous and more general findings on the implications and opportunities of volunteering. According to the representative VA (2010: 47) study, almost eight in 10 surveyed volunteers have had the opportunity to meet new people and develop new networks as a result of their civic engagement. The present study on Muslims' active citizenship indicate more specifically that many participants have successfully established new, valuable communication channels with a range of mainstream civil society organisations, policymakers and, in some instances, within Muslim communities. These new relationships range from institutional contacts to close personal friendships. The networks are, like civic skills, not only a result of citizens' engagement, but they also facilitate further—and possibly more efficient—participation. Especially, Muslims in the Australian sample have emphasised the importance and effective utilisation of social networks as an empowering factor for their expanded engagement. The depth and quality of these social contacts appear crucial. It was mainly Australian Muslims who elaborated on the high level of mutual trust and cross-community recognition when describing these new social relationships.

These findings sit well within general theoretical accounts of social capital, as conceptualised and investigated by various scholars like Bourdieu (1986), Coleman (1988) or Putnam (2000), who have all argued that social capital is not primarily about the size of social networks but about 'the norms of reciprocity and trustworthiness that arise from them' (Putnam 2000: 19). It is this network *quality* that makes contacts valuable for individuals and their active citizenship as well as, collectively, for strengthening social cohesion. Arguing along these lines, Portes concludes that 'social capital stands for the ability of actors to secure benefits by virtue of membership in social networks or other social structures' (1998: 6). Active Muslims interviewed in Australia made this quality dimension more explicit than their German counterparts, and they also described their social networks more commonly as empowering or facilitating resources for their engagement. This resonates with the finding about the more systematic recruitment into new (and often more political and influential) sites of active citizenship among Muslims in the Australian sample. One possible interpretation of this is the arguably higher level of institutional recognition of Muslim communities as civil society stakeholders and of Muslim voices in the public and political debate—at least in comparison to the situation in Germany. This will be discussed further in the conclusion.

The majority of Muslims in both samples referred primarily to cross-community networks, and some interview partners also mentioned an expansion of community-internal contacts as a result of their engagement. In Putnam's (2000: 22) terminology, the former cross-community contacts can be described as 'bridging', bringing together different communities and groups of people, and the latter as 'bonding', strengthening community-based networks. According to social capital theorists, such as Putnam (2000) and Xavier de Souza Briggs (2003), these two types of networks differ in terms of their functionality and benefits. While bonding social capital is regarded as more suited to enhance community-based identities and community-internal solidarity, bridging capital help build social cohesion by reinforcing a cross-community sense of belonging. The empirical findings of this study, however, challenge the sharp distinction between both in everyday practice of interviewed Muslims in Australia and Germany. This is mainly attributed to the fact that those Muslim community groups that interview partners were involved in have all been (more or less) well connected with various mainstream organisations and institutions. Therefore, enhanced community-internal engagement and bonding networks have ultimately resulted in individual Muslims having also more cross-community dialogue and thus expanding social contacts with non-Muslim groups and individuals—in other words: bridging as a result of bonding social capital. This supports the argument that bonding social capital is not necessarily an indicator for minorities' social or civic segregation but can 'promote migrants' political [or civic, M.P.] participation because it constitutes an additional resource for otherwise marginalised groups' (Achbari 2015: 2295).

This aligns with Newton's observation that the level of social connectedness of any given organisation needs to be taken into account. He argued that well-connected organisations tend to 'link citizens with the political system and its institutions, aggregate and articulate interests and provide the range and variety of competing and cooperating groups which constitute the pluralistic polity' (1999: 11). In a similar vein, Paxton found that 'connected associations had a strong *positive* influence on democracy, while isolated associations had a strong *negative* impact on democracy' (2002: 272; emphasis in original). None of the Muslim organisations that interview partners in Australia and Germany were involved with were socially isolated—they all offered volunteering Muslims the opportunity to expand their cross-community networks and contribute to a socially more connected cohesive and diverse society.

Some Muslims interviewed for this study also mentioned personality or identity transformation as a result of their engagement. These changes range from becoming more open-minded and accepting of diversity to developing a deeper connection with their faith or 'finding their place in society'. It was often precisely the cross-community nature of their activism (commonly located within a Muslim community context) that facilitated these transformation processes of broadening worldviews, tolerance and openness by intensifying Muslims' positive interaction and engagement with many non-Muslim groups. Only a small group of interviewed Muslims mentioned identity shifts as a result of their engagement, and those who did described these transformations as a very positive experience that has strengthened their sense of belonging and self. Those who elaborated on their deepened religious identity as a result of their active involvement with Muslim communities (which was found only in Australia) have also articulated a very strong civic identity as Australians that stands in no contrast to their strengthened faith-based layer of identity. It has rather empowered them to become even more active citizens. This has, on the one hand, an Islam-specific dimension as their faith serves as a powerful driving force and source of encouragement and resilience for many active Muslims (Chap. 7). On the other hand, feeling comfortable with one's own identity might be a factor that makes Muslims more open and inclined to enact their citizenship.[1] The CIRCA report on social and civic participation of Muslim men in Australia tentatively argues that 'being comfortable with one's ethnicity' is one of the factors that make Muslim men more 'able to enter the mainstream' (2010: 44). This claimed link between a stable sense of self and participation, also found in this study, calls for more empirical attention in future research.

References

Achbari, W. (2015). Bridging and bonding ethnic ties in voluntary organisations: A multilevel "schools of democracy" model. *Journal of Ethnic and Migration Studies, 41*(14), 2291–2313.

---

[1] Ms Abdo (AUS9), for example, strongly agreed that 'accepting your own identity in depth' makes you a stronger person and citizen. Similarly, Ms Taraji (DE5) stated that one needs to find peace within oneself and come to terms with who you are before you can engage in cross-community activities: 'You can only reach out after you have stabilised yourself. As long as you are still searching, you are not ready'.

Bourdieu, P. (1986). The forms of capital. In J. Richardson (Ed.), *Handbook of theory and research for the sociology of education* (pp. 241–258). New York: Greenwood.

Coleman, J. C. (1988). Social capital in the creation of human capital. *American Journal of Sociology, 94,* S95–S120.

Briggs, de Souza X. (2003). *Bridging networks, social capital, and racial segregation in America* (John F. Kennedy School of Government Harvard University Faculty Research Working Papers Series). Cambridge: Harvard University.

Bundesministerin für Familie, Senioren, Frauen und Jugend (BMFSFJ). (2010). *Hauptbericht des Freiwilligensurveys 2009. Zivilgesellschaft, soziales Kapital und freiwilliges Engagement in Deutschland 1999 – 2004 – 2009.* Berlin: BMFSFJ.

Cesari, J. (2013). *Why the West fears Islam. An exploration of Muslims in liberal democracies.* Basingstoke: Palgrave Macmillan.

Cultural and Indigenous Research Centre Australia (CIRCA). (2010). *Civic and social participation of Australian Muslim men.* Leichhardt: CIRCA.

Foner, N., & Alba, R. (2008). Immigrant religion in the U.S. and Western Europe: Bridge or barrier to inclusion? *International Migration Review, 42*(2), 360–392.

Huth, S. (2012). *Freiwilliges und bürgerschaftliches Engagement von Menschen mit Migrationshintergrund – Barrieren und Türöffner.* Bonn: Friedrich-Ebert Stiftung.

Jakubowicz, A., Collins, J., & Chafic, W. (2012). Young Australian Muslims: Social ecology and cultural capital. In F. Mansouri & V. Marotta (Eds.), *Muslims in the West and the challenges of belonging* (pp. 34–59). Carlton: Melbourne University Press.

Newton, K. (1999). Social capital and democracy in modern Europe. In J. van Deth, M. Maraffi, K. Newton, & P. Whitely (Eds.), *Social capital and European democracy* (pp. 3–24). London: Routledge.

Paxton, P. (2002). Social capital and democracy: An interdependent relationship. *American Sociological Review, 67*(2), 254–277.

Portes, A. (1998). Social capital: Its origins and applications in modern sociology. *Annual Review of Sociology, 24,* 1–24.

Putnam, R. D. (2000). *Bowling alone: The collapse and revival of American community.* New York: Simon and Schuster.

Verba, S., Schlozman, K. L., & Brady, H. (1995). *Voice and equality. Civic voluntarism in American politics.* Cambridge: Harvard University Press.

Volunteering Australia. (2010). *National Survey of Volunteering Issues 2010.* Melbourne: VA. Online document viewed 3 December 2015 http://www.volunteeringaustralia.org/wp-content/files_mf/1377045662VANSVI2010.pdf

Walsh, L., & Black, R. (2015). *Youth volunteering in Australia: An evidence review.* Braddon: ARACY.

10

Conclusion

Drawing from an explorative analysis of 30 in-depth interviews with self-declared Muslims who have been involved in various forms of civic or political participation, this study offers new insights into the diverse ways in which Muslims enact their citizenship. Most of the key findings apply, with some variations, to Muslims in Australia and Germany. In some thematic areas, however, the study found significant country-specific differences between the ways in which Muslims' active citizenship has unfolded over time. As the above analysis noted several times, on closer inspection, these divergences appear to be influenced, at least partially, by country-specific opportunity structures (Ireland 1994).

Political Opportunity Structures Make a Difference

While it is beyond the scope of this explorative study to ultimately explain what shapes Muslims' active citizenship in general, the data analysis tentatively pinpoints some factors on the structural and policy level that may affect the divergent emergence of Muslims' participation in Australia and Germany. Examined against the backdrop of the outlined collective resources of Muslim communities and the political framework (Chap. 5), several interconnected factors have been identified.

Availability and Accessibility of Institutional Platforms for Political Participation

The institutional opportunities for Muslims (and other minority groups) to contribute to the political discourse appear more limited in Germany than in Australia. Many active Muslims in Australia have been involved in a range of committees, advisory boards and councils within the political landscape, on the local, state and national level, and have represented their communities in political debates and decision-making processes. Their experiences with these non-electoral forms of political participation have been predominantly positive; in many cases it has been described as effective and successful in influencing policymaking. The availability of such committees and advisory bodies and their accessibility for ethnic and ethno-religious minority members reflect the political recognition of the pluralistic nature of Australian civic society, encompassing diverse communities—including Muslims—which all deserve opportunities to contribute to the public and political discourse.

In contrast, in the German sample, Muslims' political participation is limited to only one type of institution outside the political party structures, the local advisory integration/migration councils, which have been criticised by some as tokenistic and ineffective. The fact that no other, and arguably more powerful, committee work was recorded tentatively points to the prevalent lack (or lacking accessibility) of institutions of political influence for Muslim community groups. This may be, directly or indirectly, attributed to, among others, the lack of formal recognition of Muslim communities as a religious corporation under public law according to German constitutional law.

Active membership in political parties has been relatively common among Muslims in Germany—however, often with very limited success, which led many to eventually abandon their (party) political ambitions.

Those who consider their party-internal engagement to be successful either explain this with the exceptional support from local political leaders or have chosen alternative platforms for their political commitment, like establishing their own political party or becoming active within mainstream party sub-structures specifically set up for members of ethno-religious minority background.

Overall the civic commitment within political parties and electoral participation of Muslims in Germany and Australia (and elsewhere) remains severely underexplored in contemporary social and political science. The same holds true for minorities' engagement in committees and boards and other non-electoral forms of political participation beyond party structures. While some ground work has been done (see, for example, Bird et al. 2011b), more research is needed to gain better insights into these increasingly important facets of Muslim citizenship and their political incorporation.

Collective Recognition of Muslim Communities and Institutional Cross-Community Networks

The findings about the shifting locations of Muslims' engagement, recruitment patterns and the implications of their activism consistently point to more, and closer, institutional networks between Muslim community organisations and mainstream civil society and political institutions in Australia. This study suggests that Muslims in Australia have more commonly moved from civic to political participation as a direct consequence of their engagement in Muslim community work, compared to their German counterparts. They are commonly recruited through institutional channels (instead of coincidentally through acquaintances), and Muslims in Australia more often highlight how they have developed sustainable cross-community networks of trust as a result of their engagement—which continues to make their participation more effective.

All these findings indicate that communication channels and cooperation between Muslim organisations (and their representatives) and mainstream institutions, especially in the political sphere, are more advanced in Australia. These supportive political opportunity structures seem to be, at least partially, linked of Australia's long-standing (although at times faltering) policies of multiculturalism, which have historically given support and recognition for minority community groups as stakeholders in a pluralistic civil society (Peucker and Akbarzadeh 2014: 148). Such a proactive policy framework, even though it has become less pronounced in recent years in Australia, generally 'plays an important role in building immigrant [and other ethno-religious minority, M.P.] communities' organisational capacity' (Bloemraad 2005: 867) and in establishing institutional relationships between Muslims and mainstream institutions. These bridging institutional relationships linking social capital in Woolcock's (2001) terminology may weaken in turbulent political times and periods of retreating government support, but they do not cease to exist and can be reactivated to offer Muslims platforms for cross-community communication and collaboration, which facilitate their active citizenship.

This contrasts with the situation in Germany. Although the communication and collaboration channels between policymakers and Muslim community groups have expanded over the past decade or so, these relationships are still less robust and sustainable than in the Australian context. Muslims in the German sample only occasionally mentioned networks of trust with representative of mainstream institutions, especially in the political landscape, and the recruitment into new areas of political participation through cross-institutional networks has been weaker. This seems to be attributed, partially, to less favourable political opportunity structures. On a general level, German integration policies have largely refrained from systematically provide 'funding, technical assistance and normative encouragement' (Bloemraad 2005: 867) to immigrant and minority communities; self-representation of these community groups in the political sphere has been rigorously discouraged for decades (Peucker and Akbarzadeh 2014: 169, 181–182), with some changes occurring only recently. Muslim organisations—as ethno-religious communities—have been particularly affected by these collectively marginalising political structures and administrative practices. Moreover, as a religious group, Muslims have been denied formal recognition according to the German constitution, which excludes them from the right to be officially represented in certain mainstream committees (e.g., public broadcasting) and disadvantages their collective civic standing. As a result, collaboration channels and relationships between Muslims and mainstream institutions have had fewer opportunities to develop and to grow into sustainable networks.

Citizenship Regime: Access to Political Rights

Active citizenship may not rely on Muslims' legal status and full political rights. Nevertheless, a country's citizenship regime does have direct implications for Muslims' (and other minorities') civic and political participation. Obviously, holding full citizenship rights enables or, in Australia, even obliges citizens to vote in general elections. Moreover, only legal citizens have the right to run as candidates in elections and hold a political mandate in the local council, state or federal parliaments.

Among Australian Muslims in this study, access to legal citizenship status seems to be a non-issue. Having full political rights has hardly been mentioned by interviewed Muslims, all of whom are citizens of Australia. Those few who did refer to their legal citizenship either praised the easy access to citizenship rights or mentioned the generally enabling implications of this legal status for their activism.

An entirely different picture emerged in the accounts of Muslims in Germany. Notwithstanding the modernisation of Germany's citizenship regime in the year 2000, existing legal provisions and administrative practices continue to hamper minorities' access to full political rights—and Muslims appear to be particularly affected by this. A key principle of Germany's citizenship regime is to avoid dual citizenship wherever possible. In effect, this legal provision serves as a deterrent particularly for first and second generation immigrants of Turkish nationality to apply for German citizenship. This was highlighted by several Muslims, confirming that many Turks would be eager to become German citizens if they were not legally forced to renounce their Turkish citizenship. One interview partner highlighted that he would apply for citizenship if he could keep his Turkish passport and that he would then become much more politically active in the city council.

In addition, the Germany's citizenship regime has established particularly high naturalisation hurdles for Muslims, who are or have been affiliated with, or holding a position in, certain Muslim community organisations. It has been administrative practice until today to deny citizenship to those who are or have been active within any Muslim group monitored by the domestic Intelligence Agency, the Federal Office for the Protection of the Constitution—even if these organisations are not legally banned.[1] Some interviewed Muslims in this study have been active within such Muslim organisations (e.g., Milli Görüş, Islamic Community Germany/IGD, Muslim Youth Germany/MJD). One of them had applied for citizenship but his application was rejected due to his previously active role at a local Milli Görüş-affiliated mosque. He was currently re-applying and explained that, if successful, he would like to expand his political commitment and run for a seat in the local council. Although the negative effects of this securitisation of citizenship regime in Germany cannot be quantified, this legal provision and its administrative implementation may play a potentially important role in inhibiting Muslims' active citizenship, given the prevalence of Muslim community organisations as facilitator of civic participation and the large number of Milli Görüş members potentially affected (approximately 31,000).

Overall, comparing these dimensions of political opportunity structures in both national settings, Australia's policies and administrative practices, shaped by four decades of multiculturalism and an inclusive citizenship regime, appears to be more supportive of Muslims' activism. These preliminary findings on the—potentially very influential—effects of structural and political context factors on the emergence of Muslims' civic and political participation call for closer empirical attention in future research.

---

[1] This 'guilty by association' provision in Germany's citizenship law mixes up two different logics of administrative practice: While the intelligence agency operates on the basis of suspicion and monitors organisations who are regarded as potentially acting against the constitutional order of Germany, the administrative decision about one's naturalisation application needs to consider each individual case (I would like to thank Professor Heiner Bielefeldt, UN Special Rapporteur on Freedom of Religion and Belief, for pointing out this line of argument during a meeting in June 2011).

Summary of Key Findings

On a very general level—and this applies to both national settings—this research highlights the enormous complexities and dynamics of Muslims' active engagement in civil society and the political arena. This complexity has multiple intertwined dimensions. It refers to the various locations and ways in which individual Muslims become active. Related to that, it applies to the shifts and transitions from one to another form of activism, often driven by external recruitment, and to the variety of motives and goals pursued. Furthermore, this complexity becomes evident when examining how civic skills, personal commitment, and social networks serve not only as empowering facilitators of active citizenship, but also expand as an effect of their participation—with positive implications for Muslims' sense of civic efficacy and ultimately their tendency to become even more committed.

While this research confirms some findings of previous studies related to Muslims' active citizenship, it also offers new evidence that challenge widespread myths about Muslims' place in liberal democratic societies. The following summary of key findings illustrates this, indicating also gaps that future research needs to address.

Diverse Locations and Prevalence of Muslim Community Context

Organisations, often Muslim community groups, play a major role for Muslims in Australia and Germany as a site of active citizenship. In some cases, independent and unaffiliated forms of (political) participation (e.g., media activism) occur *in addition* to such organisation-based activities. The research confirms previous study findings in both countries that have illustrated, on the one hand, the diversity of organisations Muslims are actively involved in, and on the other hand, the importance of Muslim community groups and institutions as platforms for their civic participation (Halm and Sauer 2005; Monash University 2009b).

An innovative contribution of this study is the analysis of Muslims' participation trajectories. This longitudinal perspective on civic biographies has proven vital for gaining a better understanding of how Muslims' active citizenship has developed over time and the transition between different stages. Similar to very few previous studies (Schönwälder et al. 2011; Al-Momami et al. 2010), this research found evidence for commonly occurring shifts from civic to more political participation. More specifically, the study sheds new light on how Muslim community organisations often serve as gateways for other (often mainstream-based) civic engagement. An illustrative example for these dynamics is the pattern of several interviewed Muslims who begin their civic careers as community activist, developing a public profile and reputation over time, which would subsequently lead to their invitation to become active on political committees, advisory boards or other institutions in the political arena.

More generally, this confirms previous research findings on the 'spill-over' effects that volunteering in religious settings often has on citizens' proneness and capacity to become engaged in other non-religious areas of civic and political participation (Verba et al. 1995; Read 2015; Roßteutscher 2009: 38; ABS 2004: 183). These findings, though not representative for all Muslims in Australia and Germany, raise doubts about the often undifferentiated concerns about Muslim (or other minority) community organisations allegedly being 'isolated islands, located at a dangerous distance from the mainland', as Herman and Jacobs (2015: 117) describe a widespread misperception.

Increasing Focus on Mainstream and Cross-Community Activities

Herman and Jacobs (2015: 117) critically note that minority community activists are often falsely perceived as getting '"trapped" in their own world, cut off from the rest of society'. Supporting Herman and Jacobs' critique, this research also questions allegations of self-segregation by community activism. All 30 Muslims in this sample, including those who performed their active citizenship within the Muslim community, have been—and have often increasingly become—involved in either mainstream-based or cross-community initiatives and cooperation activities. This applies even to those who pursue purely communitarian goals and whose activism was located exclusively within the Muslim community context. The findings do not only challenge the broad-brush perception of disconnected and 'trapped' participation; they also underscore the prevalent shifts in Muslims' civic biographies towards increasingly mainstream-oriented or cross-community activities. These shifts have occurred either as a result of deliberate personal decisions to strengthen these intercommunity and mainstream facets of engagement or as a consequence of institutional changes within the respective Muslim community group (e.g., expanded interfaith dialogue activities). Ultimately, Muslims' active civic involvement, be it within mainstream or Muslim groups, tends to build sustainable bridges of intergroup trust and cooperation and to break down walls of mutual misunderstandings and ignorance.

Prevalence of Republican Goals

All 30 interviewed Muslims are committed to pursuing altruistic goals, which can be analytically categorised in four interconnected and overlapping areas:

- Republican agenda of serving humanity and bettering society
- Helping disadvantaged population groups (other than Muslims)
- Redressing widespread negative misconception of Muslims and Islam
- Communitarian goals of serving the Muslim community.

While the sampling rationale of this study was aimed at reflecting a broad diversity of Muslims active citizenship, enacted within a Muslim community context as well as within mainstream civil society or the political arena, the majority of interviewed Muslims have been civically (or politically) active because they sought to contribute to the wider community, the society at large or—more generally—promoting social justice. Similarly to previous studies (Al-Momani et al. 2010; AMF and VA 2007b; Halm and Sauer 2005), this research underscores the prevalence of republican, commongood oriented goals, including the aim of helping disadvantaged groups other than Muslims (e.g., youth, women, immigrants). Countering the negative public misconception of Muslims has been mentioned especially by Muslim in Germany. Only a very small minority have pursued exclusively or primarily communitarian goals of advancing the status and recognition of the Muslim community.

While this four-fold typology analytically captures the manifold civic aims of all 30 participants, it does not reflect the complexity of Muslims' multiple civic goals. The intention to dispel negative public attitudes towards Muslims, for example, has been described by some as a tool to foster more harmonious intergroup relations and contribute to a more cohesive society—which reflects a republican agenda. In general, many Muslims discussed how they pursue different goals through their engagement. They seem to activate different layers of their civic or religious identity and follow shifting personal ambitions, as Mouffe's (1995) theoretical elaborations on fluid, context-specific and constantly shifting subject positions suggest.

Driving Forces: Prevalence of Religious Motives

Muslims have—like any other citizens—very personal reasons and motives that fundamentally drive them to become civically or politically active. What they seem to have in common, however, is a high level of commitment and feelings of pleasure in being actively involved in their chosen forms of participation. Such a positive altruistic mindset appears to be a basic precondition of active citizenship for the interviewed Muslims. These motivational attitudes and views are either seen as being an integral element of their personality or as being driven by their Islamic faith; often *both* these sources of motivation are closely intertwined or described as being synonymous.

Very few studies in Australia (Harris and Roose 2014; Johns et al. 2015) have recently found evidence that Islamic principles and beliefs are motivating factors for some Muslims to participate and contribute to the wellbeing of others in various ways. This research not only confirms these findings, but suggests that faith-based driving forces are often of paramount importance for active Muslim citizens. This holds true, not surprisingly, for many of those who are involved in Muslim community work, but it also applies to some of those who are active in mainstream contexts. This conclusion offers a counter-narrative to the allegedly hampering effects of Muslims' religious convictions on their citizenship. Moreover, it demonstrates that, Islamic norms and beliefs are not only compatible with the principles of liberal democracies (March 2009), but can even empower some Muslims' participation in civil society and the political arena.

Moreover, the research sheds light on the different ways in which Muslims interpret and experience their faith as a key driver for their citizenship. This makes an innovative contribution to the academic discussions on the interplay between Islam and civic engagement. Some Muslims feel empowered by their faith or, more specifically, by the good example, set by their Prophet, and they mentioned how their faith strengthens their personal resilience, for instance, in dealing with personal and collective experiences of exclusion. For many, the main reason for their active citizenship is directly linked to the Islamic belief that God obliges and rewards Muslims for serving others and seeking to make positive changes in this world. According to this religious reward system, Muslims' behaviour in this world determines their fate in the afterlife. This religious conviction is interpreted differently, ranging from an (sometimes rather defensive) sense of accountability to a more spiritual striving for 'connecting with the Divine' by following the Prophet's example of serving humanity.

Empowering Factors: Exclusionary Experiences and Resources

The widespread public misconception and media misrepresentation as well as personal experiences of exclusion are of concern for many Muslims interviewed for this study. However, these experiences do not have a hampering but often a rather empowering effect on their active citizenship. This confirms the tentative conclusion of other studies (Al-Momami et al. 2010; Peucker and Akbarzadeh 2014). Nonetheless, active Muslims in Australia and Germany agree that this empowering effect does not apply to everyone, arguing that many or some within the Muslim community feel discouraged and disempowered by this stigmatising discourse and experiences of exclusion and thus refrain from active participation.

More research is necessary to identify what sets these two groups of Muslims apart—those who feel empowered and those who feel paralysed. This study[2] tentatively suggests that a combination of personality traits (e.g., self-confidence, optimism, resilience), strong civic values (e.g., commitment to social justice) and religious convictions (e.g., sense of faith-based duty) plays an important role, together with the availability of individual resources that enhance the proneness to civic and political participation.

The Civic Voluntarism Model by Verba et al. (1995) describes resources—time, money and skills—as key determinants of political participation. Similarly, large-scale surveys have found that civic participation (volunteering) is significantly more widespread among those with higher level of education and socioeconomic status (ABS 2011; BMFSFJ 2010). Confirming these general findings, this research offers deeper explorative insights into the effect of these personal resources. Time resources, for example, seem to affect the intensity of active Muslims' engagement, but do not ultimately determine whether they became active or not. Even during phases in life when time was scarce and they needed to prioritise—balancing family, work and education-related commitments –, they continued their engagement, though on a lower intensity level. Socioeconomic resources appear less central, except for the inhibiting effect that particularly dire financial situations may have.

The empowering effect of educational resources was stressed by many, although different arguments and viewpoints were put forward. While a few considered formal educational attainments to have an impact on their activism, others elaborated on the facilitating effects of civic skills (e.g., communication and organisation skills). Language skills and bicultural competencies have also been mentioned, especially by Muslims in Germany. Despite this emphasis on education-related factors, several Muslims in Australia argued that active citizenship requires a certain mindset rather

---

[2] While the interview sample did not include any disengaged Muslims who do *not* participate, many interviewed Muslims shared their views about various factors that hamper other Muslims' readiness to become more active.

than specific skills or qualifications. These findings call for more in-depth research into the effects of educational resources for civic and political participation, taking into account the manifold opportunities to participate in community groups, mainstream civil society or the political landscape.

What this study demonstrates, thanks to the biographic lens it deploys, is the empowering dynamics of civic skills and social networks, which often facilitate participation but also expand as a result of their engagement. Advanced civic skills and social capital tends to make participation more effective, and this sense of civic efficacy further motivates them to increase their commitment as active citizens. This conclusion underscores the importance of longitudinal analyses of how Muslims' civic biographies unfold and shift over time.

All these findings are selective, and they do not claim to be representative of Muslims' performance of citizenship in Australia and Germany in general. With its focus on those who are actively engaged in community work, civil society or in formal and informal political participation, the study ignored the disenfranchised pockets of Muslim communities, where active citizenship is likely to be less prevalent or, where it occurs, may be of a different nature. Despite this caveat, these evidence-based insights have the power to paint a picture of Muslims' activism in the West that stands in stark contrast to widespread undifferentiated perceptions and allegations of Muslims' social and political integration deficits and the incompatibility of Islam with liberal, democratic values. Viewing Muslims not as objects of securitisation, domestication or exclusionary 'othering' but as active members of civil society and the political community reveals the often overlooked dimension of Muslims as 'ordinary' citizens often extraordinary levels of resilience, civic commitment and compassion. It is currently impossible to quantify this active segment within Muslim communities in both national contexts, but there are indicators that the scope of Muslims' civic engagement is currently underestimated as their intra-community and commonly informal volunteering remains hidden from the eyes of the wider public. To recognise, harness and foster these civic potentials is a major task for the future—and it requires the efforts of all those dedicated to promoting and strengthening a socially cohesive diverse society and ensuring the stability and legitimacy of liberal democracies.

References

Al-Momani, K., Dados, N., Maddox, M., & Wise, A. (2010). *Political participation of Muslims in Australia.* Sydney: Macquarie University.

Australian Bureau of Statistics (ABS). (2004). *Australian social trends* (Catalogue No. 4102.0). Canberra: Commonwealth of Australia. Online document viewed 25 April 2015 http://www.ausstats.abs.gov.au/ausstats/subscriber.nsf/0/174FDA6313BDC7DECA256EB40003596E/$File/41020_2004.pdf

Australian Bureau of Statistics (ABS). (2011). *Voluntary work Australia. 2010 (No. 4441.0) Canberra: Commonwealth of Australia.* Online document viewed on 25 April 2016 http://www.ausstats.abs.gov.au/Ausstats/subscriber.nsf/0/404350EEC6509985CA2579580013177A/$File/44410_2010.pdf

Australian Multicultural Foundation (AMF), & Volunteering Australia (VA). (2007b). *National survey of Australian volunteers from diverse cultural and linguistic backgrounds.* Melbourne: VA.

Bloemraad, I. (2005). The limits of de Tocqueville: How government facilitates organisational capacity in newcomer communities. *Journal of Ethnic and Migration Studies, 31*(5), 865–887.

Bird, K., Saalfeld, T., & Wüst, A. M. (Eds.) (2011). *The political representation of immigrants and minorities. Voters, parties and parliaments in liberal democracies.* London: Routledge.

Bundesministerin für Familie, Senioren, Frauen und Jugend (BMFSFJ). (2010). *Hauptbericht des Freiwilligensurveys 2009. Zivilgesellschaft, soziales Kapital und freiwilliges Engagement in Deutschland 1999 – 2004 – 2009.* Berlin: BMFSFJ.

Halm, D., & Sauer, M. (2005). *Freiwilliges Engagement von Türkinnen und Türken in Deutschland.* Essen: ZfT.

Harris, A., & Roose, J. (2014). DIY citizenship amongst young Muslims: Experiences of the "ordinary". *Journal of Youth Studies, 17*(6), 794–813.

Herman, B., & Jacobs, D. (2015). Ethnic social capital and political participation of immigrants. In L. Ryan, U. Erel, & A. D'Angelo (Eds.), *Migrant capital: Networks, identities and strategies* (pp. 117–132). Basingstoke: Palgrave Macmillan.

Ireland, P. (1994). *The policy challenge of ethnic diversity. Immigrant politics in France and Switzerland.* Cambridge: Harvard University Press.

Johns, A., Mansouri, F., & Lobo, M. (2015). Religiosity, citizenship and belonging: The everyday experiences of young Australian Muslims. *Journal for Muslim Minority Affairs, 35*, 171–190.

March, A. F. (2009). *Islam and liberal citizenship. The search for an overlapping consensus*. Oxford: Oxford University Press.
Monash University. (2009b). *Muslim voices. Hopes & aspirations of Muslim Australians*. Caulfield East: Monash University.
Mouffe, C. (1995). Democratic politics and the question of identity. In J. Rajchman (Ed.), *The identity in question* (pp. 33–45). London/New York: Routledge.
Peucker, M., & Akbarzadeh, S. (2014). *Muslim active citizenship in the West*. London/New York: Routledge.
Read, J. G. (2015). Gender, religious identity, and civic engagement among Arab Muslims in the United States. *Sociology of Religion, 76*(1), 30–48.
Roßteutscher, S. (2009). *Religion, Zivilgesellschaft, Demokratie. Eine international vergleichende Studie zur Natur religiöser Märkte und der demokratischen Rolle religiöser Zivilgesellschaften*. Baden-Baden: Nomos Verlagsgesellschaft.
Schönwälder, K., Sinanoglu, C., & Volkert, D. (2011). *Vielfalt sucht Rat. Ratsmitglieder mit Migrationshintergrund in deutschen Großstädten*. Berlin: Heinrich-Böll-Stiftung.
Verba, S., Schlozman, K. L., & Brady, H. (1995). *Voice and equality. Civic voluntarism in American politics*. Cambridge: Harvard University Press.
Woolcock, M. (2001). The place of social capital in understanding social and economic outcomes. *Isuma: Canadian Journal of Policy Research, 2*(1), 11–17.
Wüst, A. M. (2011). Migrants as parliamentary actors in Germany. In K. Bird, T. Saalfeld, & A. M. Wüst (Eds.), *The political representation of immigrants and minorities. Voters, parties and parliaments in liberal democracies* (pp. 250–265). London: Routledge.

Index

Abbott, T., 117, 132
Abitur, 57
aboriginal, aborigines, 148, 176
activity focus, 160, 169–71, 174–6, 178
   intercommunity, 169, 170
   intra-community, 169, 171
   mainstream, 169
advisory board, 156, 162, 163, 258, 264
advisory councils, 125, 150, 151, 154, 156, 164, 166–8, 177, 184, 196, 208, 211, 213, 229, 247, 273. *See also migrationsrat, integrationsrat*
advocacy, 25, 129, 163, 164, 190, 210
African community, 52, 150, 153, 160, 164, 189, 190, 229
African Think Tank, 164, 190
afterlife, 220, 221, 226, 227, 267
agency, 14, 17, 21, 23, 26, 27, 29–31, 34, 37, 45, 46, 87, 96, 116, 118–20, 125, 127, 128, 130, 132, 135, 136, 138, 159, 215, 273, 292
Akbarzadeh, S., 3, 55, 59, 66, 78, 82, 84, 91, 96, 98, 119, 120, 127, 130, 131, 133, 136, 152, 156, 158, 168, 179, 194, 212, 239, 290, 297
Alevi, 56, 126, 134, 186
Allah. *See* God
Al-Momani, K., 90–2, 157, 161, 216, 238, 295
Aly, A., 82, 83, 157, 239
Amath, N., 131, 179, 239
Amnesty International, 52, 57, 148, 207

© The Author(s) 2016
M. Peucker, *Muslim Citizenship in Liberal Democracies,*
DOI 10.1007/978-3-319-31403-7

Arabic, 64, 93, 100, 152, 172, 182, 187, 193, 216, 233, 256, 259
At Home in Europe, 80
attitude, 84–6, 125, 212, 227, 242, 248
Ausländerbeiräte, 125, 211. *See also* advisory councils
Australian Bureau for Statistics (ABS), 60–2, 67, 99, 250, 294, 298
Australian Citizenship Act, 117
Australian Federation of Islamic Councils (AFIC), 128, 129, 182, 183
Australian Labor Party (ALP), 163, 189
Australian Multicultural Foundation (AMF), 99, 100, 187, 216, 233, 241, 250, 295
Australian Muslim Women's Centre for Human Rights, 152, 163, 228
authorities, 87, 120, 127, 131, 132, 135, 213, 268, 272, 281

B

Bankstown, 147, 151, 207, 279
Begegnungs-und Fortbildungszentrum muslimischer Frauen (BFmF), 174, 193, 208, 213, 272, 273, 281
Bellamy, R., 10, 14, 23–5
belonging, 2, 13, 16, 19, 20, 24, 59, 77, 79–81, 83, 88, 89, 101, 105, 116, 118, 122, 124, 157, 212, 213, 216–18, 243, 253, 263, 275, 279, 284, 285. *See also* identity

Benevolence, 145, 172, 203, 226
Berlin, 50, 80, 165, 192
Betriebsrat, 146, 150, 185. *See also* work council
bicultural, 259, 268
Bündnis für Innovation und Gerechtigkeit (BIG), 146, 153, 158, 166, 167
bilingual, 256, 261
Bird, K., 32, 50, 90, 117, 289
Bleich, E., 82
Bloemraad, I., 17, 33, 34, 90, 290
blog/blogging, 23, 153, 155, 165, 190–2, 205, 243, 248
Bonn, 149, 154, 158, 166, 167, 232
Bouma, G., 82, 119, 120, 128, 129, 131
boycott, 23, 92, 93
Brettfeld, K., 65, 79–81, 87
Bundestag, 95, 96
Bürgerinitiativen, 161

C

candidate, 52, 90, 150, 154, 163, 167, 183, 187, 197, 251, 291
census, 55, 60, 61, 66–8, 70, 73, 75, 98, 99
Central Council of Muslims in Germany (ZMD), 135–7, 173
church–state pattern, 115, 127. *See also* church–state relation
church–state relation, 32, 115, 116, 119, 121, 126
citizenship
  acts of, 13, 24, 89
  communitarian, 16, 17
  components of, 10, 14

conceptualisation of, 13
do-it-yourself, 24
liberal, 9–37
pluralistic models of, 19
regime, 32, 115, 117, 121, 122, 124, 158, 159, 291–2
republican, 15, 16, 20
civic biography, 162, 180, 181, 191, 275. *See also* civic trajectory
civic career, 144, 146, 155, 160–80, 186, 187, 189, 190, 192, 243. *See also* civic trajectory
civic duty, 224, 233. *See* civic obligation
civic efficacy, 153, 238, 244, 247, 264, 268, 293, 299
civic obligation, 219
civic skills, 15, 27–9, 32, 33, 75, 77, 105, 106, 250, 254, 257, 264, 275, 281, 282, 293, 298, 299. *See also* communication skills
civic trajectory, 163, 192. *See also* civic biography; civic career
Civic Voluntarism Model, 26–33, 37, 59, 93, 167, 244, 250, 253, 281, 298
claim-making, 13, 16, 23, 25, 32–4, 88, 119, 127
Clean Up Australia, 241
cohesion, 4, 14, 79, 84, 91, 92, 94, 99, 132, 202, 209, 229, 274, 283, 284
Cologne, 174, 193, 213, 272, 281
committee, 126, 150–2, 156, 162, 163, 168, 170, 171, 181, 188, 194, 195, 208, 228, 245–7, 249, 288–90, 294

common good, 16–18, 102, 216. *See also* greater good
communication skills, 255, 258, 261, 275, 277, 281. *See also* civic skills
communitarian, 4, 15–20, 46, 56, 143, 142, 202, 204, 206, 208, 209, 214–17, 226, 234, 235, 241, 295, 296
community
  activist, 1, 52, 150, 153, 181, 186, 192, 194, 204, 208, 220, 222, 255, 275, 294
  ethnic, 17, 35
  leader, 128, 135, 153, 157, 162, 176, 189, 190, 229, 257
  Muslim organisations, 45, 46, 54, 100, 103, 104, 120, 121, 124, 125, 127, 129, 131–8, 145–7, 152, 155, 159, 167, 170, 174, 176, 177, 188, 203, 209, 215, 241, 255, 270, 271, 273, 279, 284, 289, 290, 292
  political, 10, 11, 15–20, 81, 97, 105, 121, 123, 238, 299
compassionate, 207, 220, 221, 242
constitution, 126, 137, 290, 292
consultation, 152
cooperation, 36, 125, 126, 129, 131, 132, 134–8, 169, 177, 181, 188, 191, 214, 215, 246, 269, 274, 282, 289, 292, 294
Coordination Council of Muslims in Germany (KRM), 137
corporation under public law. *See Körperschaft öffentlichen Rechts*

council, 21, 52, 54, 129, 134–7, 146–8, 150, 151, 153, 154, 158, 159, 162–4, 166, 167, 171–3, 176, 177, 183–7, 197, 212, 213, 215, 224, 229, 232, 246, 247, 270, 273, 291, 292
councillor, 53, 146, 149, 161, 163, 183, 196, 207, 208, 212, 223
country of birth, 60, 61, 204
creator. *See* God
crime, 207
cross-community, 54, 67, 100, 130–2, 135, 138, 148, 150, 160, 169–8, 181, 184, 186–8, 194–6, 205, 214, 215, 244–6, 248, 249, 256, 257, 260, 268, 269, 272, 278, 283–5, 289–91, 294, 295
Cultural and Indigenous Research Centre Australia (CIRCA), 99, 238, 250, 251, 253, 254, 263, 285

D

Dagger, R., 15, 16
Darebin, 86
da'wah, 214
decision-making, 22, 27, 89, 90, 124, 125, 151, 154, 156, 162, 167, 168, 195–7, 245–7, 272, 288
Delanty, G., 15, 17
democracy
 deliberative, 15
 elitist, 14, 18
 participatory, 14, 18, 21
 radical, 17–20
demographics, 5, 45, 50, 51, 55, 59–106, 123

demonstration, 92–4, 96, 210
Deutsches Statistisches Bundesamt (DESTATIS), 64, 65, 69, 71, 72, 74, 76
dialogue
 cross-community, 131, 171, 284
 interfaith, 56, 136, 169, 170, 210, 229, 242, 295
discrimination, 34, 81, 85–9, 134, 171, 204, 230, 254. *See also* exclusion; Islamophobia
dissatisfaction, 91
dissent, dissenting, 2, 13, 25
divine. *See* God
Diyanet, 133. *See also* Turkish-Islamic Union for Religious Affairs (DİTİB)
domestication, 4, 138, 299
Dreher, T., 156, 157, 239
driver, 19, 20, 68, 171, 172, 219–33, 243, 297. *See also* driving forces, motives
driving force, 3, 5, 46, 201–35, 237, 285, 296–7. *See also* driver
dual citizenship, 5, 117, 122, 124, 158, 159, 291. *See also* multiple citizenship
Dunn, K., 78, 79, 87, 90, 92, 100

E

education(al), 31, 54, 56–7, 66–77, 87, 93, 103–5, 126, 137, 146, 150, 154, 174, 204, 215, 230, 249–64, 275, 298
 attainments, 66, 103, 261, 298
 formal, 254, 255, 258, 261
 qualifications, 56, 72
 substantive, 66

egalitarian, 2, 4, 82, 116
empowerment, 131, 146, 157, 162, 219, 235, 238, 244–9
environment, 3, 23, 46, 105, 149, 205, 206, 230, 245, 246, 271, 275, 280
equality, 11, 12, 22, 27, 29, 31, 34, 117, 118, 120, 224
Eritrea, 52, 54, 229
Etzioni, A., 16
exclusion, 4, 48, 81–9, 105, 240–2, 253, 262–4, 297, 298

Facebook, 153, 176, 192
faith, 1, 3, 6, 43, 56, 60, 77, 84, 100, 105, 119, 120, 126, 127, 130, 131, 168, 171, 173, 176, 203, 204, 209, 217–26, 229–35, 237, 239, 242, 264, 269, 279, 280, 285, 296–8. *See also* religiosity
fears, 83, 191, 214, 223, 241
financial situation, 66, 68, 75, 250, 298
Fleischmann, F., 29, 34, 167
Foner, N., 36, 282
football, 149, 206, 210, 270
foreigners' council, 125. *See also* advisory councils
Fraueninitiative für Bildung und Erziehung, 146
Freiwilligensurvey, 102
Frindte, W., 81–3

Gallup, 85
gateway, 164, 167, 178, 195, 294
German Islam Conference (DIK), 125, 136
Gillard, J., 117
goals, 3, 5, 15, 16, 20, 45, 46, 50, 102, 143, 146, 148, 160, 193, 201–35, 238, 276, 293, 295–6. *See also* motives
God, 203, 204, 219–7, 297
government
 federal, 91, 106, 119, 135
 local, 91, 136, 181, 195 (*see also* council)
 state, 126, 127, 135, 136, 151, 175, 247
grassroots, 128, 129, 145, 149, 161, 168, 183, 245, 247
greater good, 46, 149, 203–5, 217. *See also* common good
Green Party, 155, 177
Greens. *See also* Green Party
 Australia, 149, 150, 251
 Germany, 273
Grüne Muslime, 53, 155, 157, 164, 177, 213
Gülen, 49, 56, 146, 165, 211. *See also* Hizmet

Hadith, 204
Halm, D., 33, 82, 102–5, 136, 145, 155, 178, 179, 188, 194, 216, 250, 293, 295
Harris, A., 24, 89, 233, 234, 296
Haug, S., 62–5, 69, 70, 73, 74, 77, 80, 96, 155, 157
Hauptschule, 103, 259
Hayat House Outreach, 176
headscarf, 212, 220. *See also* hijab

heaven, 222, 225. *See also* afterlife
hereafter, 222. *See also* afterlife
hijab, 172, 210, 246, 269. *See also* headscarf
Hizmet, 56. *See also* Gülen
Howard, J., 16, 117
humanity, 203, 220, 221, 295, 297
Humphrey, M., 4, 119, 125, 128, 129, 131, 138, 168
Hunger, U., 124, 125, 154

identity. *See also* belonging
   civic, 16, 20, 105, 118, 124, 217, 263, 285
   collective, 17, 19, 31, 116
   ethno-religious, 118
   multiple, 19, 123, 124
   religious, 78, 79, 118, 263, 280, 285, 296
   volatile, 19, 20
ignorance, 125, 130, 239, 242, 246, 263, 295
immigrants. *See* migrants, migration
income, 68, 75, 76, 251–3
indigenous. *See* aboriginal, aborigines
injustice, 204, 208, 213, 219, 228, 230, 231, 264
institutional channelling theory, 26, 30–3, 37, 115, 195
Integrationsblogger, 165, 191
Integrationsrat, 166, 167, 177, 184. *See also* advisory councils
intelligence agency, 138, 159, 215, 292. *See also Verfassungsschutz*
intercultural competence, 258, 259, 261, 277, 278

intercultural skill, 274. *See also* intercultural competence
intra-community, 49, 129, 134, 160, 169–71, 173–5, 178, 194, 268, 274, 299
invitation, 162, 167, 179, 181, 182, 184–9, 192, 195, 294. *See also* recruitment
inward-looking, 36, 130, 179
Iraq, 52, 54, 63, 64, 71, 72, 74, 76, 130
Ireland, P., 26, 31–3, 37, 115, 195, 196, 287
Isin, E., 9–13, 16, 19, 24, 25, 89
Islamic Council of Victoria (ICV), 52, 129, 130, 153, 164, 172, 183, 203, 215, 275
Islamic Society, 147, 151, 162, 172, 183
Islamic Society Newport, 162. *See also* Newport Mosque
Islamic student association, 182. *See also* Muslim (university) student association
Islamische Gemeinde Deutschland (IGD), 159, 173, 215, 260, 292
Islamische Gemeinschaft Millî Görüş (IGMG), 133, 135, 159. *See also* Milli Görüş
Islamophobia, 4, 82. *See also* discrimination; exclusion
Issues Deliberation Australia (IDA), 83, 85

Jakubowicz, A., 78, 87, 118–20, 130, 131, 282
Jamal, A., 29, 33, 106, 127, 167

Jewish-Christian-Muslim Association (JCMA), 171
journalist, 155, 157, 210, 276, 277
Judgement Day, 225
Junge Islamkonferenz, 165, 192
Jungsozialisten (JUSO), 165, 192
JurBlog, 190, 191

Kabir, N., 81, 83
Klausen, J., 81
Knox Council Multicultural Advisory Committee, 171
Knox Interfaith Network, 162, 171
Koopmans, R., 32, 65, 80, 197
Körperschaft öffentlichen Rechts, 126, 168
Kymlicka, W., 12, 14, 17, 18

label/labelling, 27, 28, 47, 213, 240. *See also* prejudice
labour market, 31, 66, 68, 73–5, 88, 254
language skills, 67, 70, 75, 256–8, 260, 261, 298. *See also* proficiency
LaTrobe University, 172, 183, 215, 275
leader. *See* community, leader
lebanese, 51, 52, 55, 61, 129, 176, 227
Lebanon, 52, 57, 60, 63, 68, 71, 72, 74, 76, 79, 279
legal status, 13–15, 32, 59, 65, 105, 291
legitimacy, 2, 4, 299
Leitkultur, 123
liberalism, 1, 15, 123
life after death, 223
Lord, 221, 223
loyalty, 2

mainstream civil society, 36, 134, 144, 148, 149, 181, 207, 234, 282, 289, 295, 299
Mansouri, F., 24, 86
March, A., 3, 297
marginalisation, 2, 82, 88, 105, 232, 238, 263
Markus, A., 79, 84, 91, 92, 94, 99, 116
Marshall, T., 11, 12
McAndrew, S., 34, 167
media, 23, 45, 46, 50, 52, 53, 81–6, 88, 93, 131, 137, 138, 144, 150, 152, 153, 155–7, 164, 184, 190–2, 203, 205, 210, 213, 215, 222, 238–43, 248, 255, 259, 260, 262, 268, 270, 271, 277, 293, 297
media activism, 46, 144, 152, 156, 157, 191, 239, 243, 248, 260, 293
Melbourne, 51, 60, 78, 83, 86, 91, 92, 129, 147, 148, 150, 152, 153, 162–4, 170, 181–3, 190, 203, 206, 210, 215, 222, 228, 229, 233, 234, 240, 255, 269, 276, 280
membership, 4, 9–13, 19, 34, 35, 37, 81, 88, 89, 102, 127, 152, 154, 155, 157–9, 163, 165, 248, 283, 288
mentoring, 131
Micro-Census, 70, 73, 75

Middle East, 62–4, 69, 72–5
MiGAZIN, 190, 191, 205, 248, 259, 277
migrants, migration, 54, 62–4, 69, 73, 76, 87, 94–7, 102, 103, 119, 123–5, 149, 153–6, 161, 163, 164, 166, 167, 177, 184, 191, 205–8, 211, 228, 246, 248, 259, 260, 279, 288
migrationsrat, 154, 166. *See also* advisory councils
Milli Görüş, 133, 134, 159, 292. *See also* IGMG
misconception, 203, 210, 214, 243, 295–7
misrepresentation, 5, 46, 82, 191, 238–43, 262–4, 297
Mission of Hope, 52, 147, 148, 176, 177, 207, 241, 242, 255, 271, 276, 279, 280
mobilisation, 2, 13, 18, 20, 29–36, 88, 106, 132–4, 168, 178, 185, 187, 188, 239
Modood, T., 31, 34, 116
Monash University, 78, 79, 83, 84, 86, 87, 92–4, 100, 101, 145, 155, 178, 293
moral obligation, 219, 230
mosque, 29, 33, 34, 36, 45, 46, 49, 54, 103, 104, 106, 119, 125, 128, 129, 131–7, 145–7, 150, 159, 162, 164, 166–8, 170, 172, 174, 177, 182, 184–6, 193, 205, 224, 229, 240, 243, 273, 281, 292
motives, 5, 28, 43, 44, 50, 130, 201–35, 293, 296–7. *See also* driving forces, drivers
Mouffe, C., 17, 19–21, 25, 216, 296

multiculturalism, 117, 175, 245, 290, 292
multiple citizenship, 19, 117, 122. *See also* dual citizenship
Muslim community context, 34, 144–7, 149, 160, 161, 165, 167, 169, 170, 173, 175, 178, 180, 194, 195, 203, 204, 208, 214, 226–8, 230, 234, 275, 285, 293–5
Muslimische Jugend in Deutschland (MJD), 174, 186, 249, 259, 273, 276, 277, 292
Muslim Life in Germany (MLG), 62–5, 69, 77, 80, 157
Muslim (university) student association, 49, 54, 164, 212, 215, 231, 242, 275. *See also* Islamic student association
Müssig, S., 69, 73, 94–7
My Dress, My Image, My Choice, 171, 246, 269

N

National Australian Youth Forum, 207, 209
national security, 85
naturalisation, 60, 65, 66, 117, 121–4, 158, 291, 292
neighbourhood, 23–5, 60, 63, 79, 80, 86, 89, 97, 100, 118, 134, 149, 150, 208, 212, 247, 270
networks, 5, 32, 34, 35, 45, 53, 54, 100, 118, 130–2, 134–7, 149, 162, 165, 166, 171, 174, 177, 178, 184, 186–9, 192–4, 238, 244–9, 264, 267–75, 277, 279–84, 289–91, 293, 299. *See also* social capital

Newport Mosque, 147, 182, 183, 240
New South Wales (NWS), 52, 60, 83, 91, 149-50, 152, 204, 230, 251, 271
Newton, K., 36, 281, 284
9/11. *See* September 11
North Rhine-Westphalia (NRW), 50, 155, 166, 177, 213

obligation, 117, 214, 218–20, 222–5, 227, 229, 230, 233, 234, 242, 251, 252
occupational background, 56–7
O'Loughlin, B., 2, 25
online, 23, 152, 153, 155, 164, 165, 190–2, 205, 243, 248, 259, 277
open-minded, open-mindedness, 275, 278, 280, 284
Open Society Institute (OSI), 80
opportunity structures, 6, 26, 30–2, 44, 45, 49, 115, 120, 121, 127, 155, 159, 168, 195–7, 287–92
optimism, 263, 298
outreach, 131, 132, 136, 147, 160, 172, 176, 179, 215, 239
overseas born, 55, 60, 68, 79, 94, 117. *See also* country of birth

Pakistan, 52, 54, 60, 63, 64, 204, 230, 253, 276
parliament. *See also* Bundestag
  members of (MP), 46, 52
  state, 92, 149, 230
party membership, 154, 157–9, 248

pathway, 161, 165, 168, 171, 196
Paxton, P., 37, 284
Penzberg, 150, 185, 205, 243
performance, 3, 13, 14, 16, 20, 23, 24, 70, 115, 157, 222, 261, 262, 299
personal disposition, 193, 201. *See also* personality
personality, 218–20, 223, 224, 226–34, 237, 267, 273, 277–82, 284, 296, 298
petition, 23, 46, 92, 93, 96
Peucker, M., 3, 55, 59, 60, 66, 77, 82, 84, 91, 95, 98, 116, 119, 120, 127, 130, 131, 133, 136, 152, 156, 158, 168, 179, 194, 212, 239, 290, 297
Pew, 85
pleasure, 218, 219, 226, 229–32, 234, 296
police, 87, 125, 131, 132, 136, 152, 171, 172, 177, 181, 268–73, 276, 278, 281
policy framework, 4, 5, 31, 48, 115–17, 120, 290
policymakers, 1, 4, 10, 118, 122, 123, 125, 132, 137, 151, 152, 165, 282, 290
policymaking, 96, 106, 247, 288. *See also* policymakers
political arena, 10, 12, 22, 37, 50, 67, 90, 94, 105, 124, 127, 168, 181, 234, 293–5, 297. *See also* political sphere
political participation
  definition of, 21–5
  electoral, 159
  non-electoral, 94, 97, 205
  unconventional forms of, 23, 90

political parties/party, 28, 50, 53, 92, 96, 146, 150, 154, 157, 158, 166, 167, 187, 189, 196, 197, 223, 248, 251, 273, 288, 289. *See also* party membership
political sphere, 1, 25, 94, 153, 163, 168, 177, 289, 290
Poynting, S, 4, 83, 87
Prejudice, 34, 84, 130, 210–13, 232, 239. *See also* label/labelling; racism; stereotypes
proficiency, 62, 67, 70, 75, 91, 94, 103, 254, 256, 257, 259, 261, 264
Prophet, 145, 203, 220, 224, 242, 297
public discourse, 66, 81–3, 126, 132, 150, 194, 196, 238, 240, 241, 243, 260, 262–4
public ethos, 16
public profile, 162, 163, 166, 181, 184, 190, 195, 246, 272, 294
public standing, 128, 138
Putnam, R., 2, 12, 33, 36, 98, 132, 194, 244, 268, 274, 283

Q

Qur'an, 174, 221, 225

R

racism, 82, 84, 86–9, 118, 156, 191, 239, 240, 242, 248, 262. *See also* Islamophobia
Ramadan, T., 3
Rat der Muslime, 149, 186
Read, J., 29, 34, 106, 127, 167, 191, 294
recent arrivals, 64, 65

recognition, 2, 4, 13, 18, 20, 24, 31, 33, 34, 46, 48, 59, 81–9, 105, 115–30, 132, 135–7, 151, 154–6, 166, 168, 184, 193, 194, 208, 209, 211, 217, 233, 238, 239, 243, 246, 258, 264, 272, 283, 288–91, 296
recruitment, 27, 74, 179–97, 249, 282, 283, 289, 290, 293. *See also* invitation
redistribution, 11, 13
refugee, 153, 158, 163, 208, 229
religiosity, 55–6, 77, 103, 224, 233, 234. *See also* faith
religious obligation/duty, 214, 218–20, 222, 224, 233, 234, 242
representation, 18, 32, 50, 82, 83, 90, 91, 95, 106, 118, 124, 137, 154, 183, 184, 228, 231, 290
republican, 4, 15, 16, 18–21, 46, 143, 146, 202, 204–9, 216–18, 226, 235, 295–6
resilience, 220, 235, 237, 257, 262, 263, 285, 297–9
resources, 26–30, 32, 34, 35, 59–106, 115, 129, 238, 249–64, 283, 288, 297–9
respect, 21, 27, 34, 83, 217, 246, 259, 268, 269, 271, 275
reward system (Islamic), 222
rights
    equal, 10–14, 20, 31
    human, 21, 25, 82, 123, 148, 151, 152, 163, 176, 195, 228, 276, 279
    legal, 10–13, 81, 89
    political, 11, 30, 31, 65, 77, 94, 105, 115–17, 121, 159, 291–2

social, 11
role model, 210–12, 230, 242
Roose, J., 24, 89, 233, 234, 296

S

Sarrazin, T., 191
Sauer, M., 65, 87, 102, 103, 104, 105, 136, 145, 155, 178, 179, 188, 194, 216, 250, 293, 295
SBS. *See* Special Broadcasting Service (SBS)
Scanlon, 79, 84, 91, 92, 94, 99
Schiffauer, W., 123, 133, 137, 138, 159
Schönwälder, K., 63, 95, 124, 161, 294
school
   attainments, 93
   degree, 57, 69–71, 193
   Islamic, 130, 147, 182
second-class citizen, 2, 12, 86, 264
secularism (secular), 4, 119, 120, 126, 234
securitisation, 4, 5, 125, 132, 292, 299
segregation, 49, 63, 284, 294. *See also* spatial concentration
self-confidence, 263, 298. *See also* self-worth
self-esteem, 263. *See also* self-worth
self-worth, 257. *See also* self-confidence; self-esteem
September 11, 130, 152, 156, 269, 270
settlement, 60, 65, 68, 94, 104, 118, 119, 121, 125, 131, 134, 162, 174, 213
Shia, 56

social capital
   bonding, 194, 284
   bridging, 132, 244
   collective, 33–7, 130, 134, 138, 187, 189, 194
   linking, 188, 194, 290
social cohesion, 4, 6, 14, 79, 84, 91, 92, 94, 99, 132, 202, 209, 274, 283, 284. *See also* cohesion
Social Democratic Party (SPD), 155, 157, 186, 192, 196
ve biz, 155, 186
socialist youth group, 177, 247
social justice, 204, 205, 207, 228, 230, 231, 233, 237, 264, 295, 298
social movements, 13, 14, 20, 30, 35
socioeconomic resources, 32, 252–4, 261, 298. *See also* income; resources; socioeconomic status
socioeconomic status, 66–77, 238–64, 298
spatial concentration, 60. *See also* segregation
SPD. *See* Social Democratic Party (SPD)
Special Broadcasting Service (SBS), 52, 148
spiritual/spirituality, 56, 176, 220, 221, 226, 233, 279, 297
sport, 100, 102–4, 148, 151, 208, 210. *See also* football
stereotypes, 6, 157, 171, 209, 210, 216, 217, 232, 235, 239, 242, 267. *See also* prejudice
stigmatisation, 48, 105, 213, 238–43, 246, 264
Studendenparliament, 192

Sufism, 56
Sunni, 56, 133–5
suspicion, 83, 123, 125, 137, 159, 238, 242, 292
Sydney Alliance, 148, 247, 270

terrorism, 5, 85, 86, 106, 132, 137
Thomas Theorem, 44
Tillie, J., 26, 35, 127, 132, 187, 189, 194
tokenistic, 154, 156, 168, 192, 196, 288
tolerance, 119, 285
trade union, 32, 46, 50, 52, 54, 57, 143, 146, 149, 150, 161, 185, 186, 205, 206, 223, 224, 227, 243, 270, 277
training ground, 29, 281
transition, 5, 144, 167, 179–97, 293, 294
trust, 2, 35, 36, 82, 213, 238, 246, 264, 268–72, 274, 282, 283, 289, 290, 295
Turkey, 52, 54, 56, 60, 62–4, 72–4, 95, 133, 134, 154
Turkish, 52–6, 61–5, 69–77, 80, 87, 88, 95, 96, 101–4, 122, 133–5, 146, 155, 157, 158, 164–6, 184, 186, 188, 190, 193, 196, 216, 248, 258, 272, 291
Turkish-Islamic Union for Religious Affairs (DİTİB), 133–6
Turner, B., 9, 11–13

Underabi, H., 179
unemployment, 67, 68, 73, 74, 254
United Muslim Women's Association (UMWA), 148, 151, 152, 162, 220, 246, 247, 270
Uniting Church, 149, 206
university degree, 56, 57, 66, 68, 70, 77, 93, 103, 257, 259
University of Münster, 84, 85
urban, 60, 62, 63, 119, 126

van Deth, 23, 30
Verba, S., 22, 26–30, 33, 34, 59, 77, 93, 167, 185, 188, 244, 250, 253, 254, 275, 281, 294, 298
Verfassungsschutz, 159
victimhood, 5, 157
Victoria, 52, 60, 91, 129, 153, 163, 164, 172, 183, 190, 215, 229
violence, 85, 86, 151, 204, 229
Volunteering Australia (VA), 99, 100, 187, 216, 233, 241, 250, 267, 282, 295
Volunteering Survey, 102, 103. *See also Freiwilligensurvey*
voting, 65, 90, 91, 94, 160, 247

wahlhelfer, 149, 212
welfare agency, 32, 124. *See also* welfare system

welfare system, 119, 124, 131
Werbner, P., 239
Western Sydney, 84, 90, 147, 151, 270
White Australia, 116
withdraw, 240, 246
women, 13, 19, 30, 50, 51, 72, 85, 92, 135, 146, 150–2, 162, 163, 172–4, 182, 184, 186, 193, 208, 210–12, 215, 228, 230, 250, 251, 255, 269, 270, 295
work council, 184, 185. *See also* Betriebsrat
Wüst, A., 50, 90, 95, 289

Yasmeen, S., 77, 89, 239
Young, I., 17, 18
Young Muslims of Australia (YMA), 171, 172, 181, 269
youth
  at-risk, 147, 176, 207, 255
  work, 147, 159, 162, 182, 224, 241, 242, 276, 277

Zahnräder, 165, 177, 178, 192

GPSR Compliance

The European Union's (EU) General Product Safety Regulation (GPSR) is a set of rules that requires consumer products to be safe and our obligations to ensure this.

If you have any concerns about our products, you can contact us on

ProductSafety@springernature.com

In case Publisher is established outside the EU, the EU authorized representative is:

Springer Nature Customer Service Center GmbH
Europaplatz 3
69115 Heidelberg, Germany

www.ingramcontent.com/pod-product-compliance
Lightning Source LLC
Chambersburg PA
CBHW071507230426
43749CB00028B/726